the vineyard kitchen

the vineyard kitchen

Menus Inspired by the Seasons

maria helm sinskey

HarperCollins*Publishers*

HarperCollins books may be purchased for educational, business, or sales promotional use.
For information, please write: Special Markets Department, HarperCollins Publishers Inc.,
10 East 53rd Street, New York, NY 10022.

FIRST EDITION

Designed by Joel Avirom and Jason Snyder
Photographs by Robert Sinskey

Printed on acid-free paper

Library of Congress Cataloging-in-Publication Data

Sinskey, Maria Helm
   The vineyard kitchen : menus inspired by the seasons / Maria Helm Sinskey.—1st ed.
      p. cm.
   Includes bibliographical references and index.
   ISBN 0-06-001396-6
   1. Cookery, American—California style. I. Title.

TX715.2.C34S56 2003
641.59794—dc21   2003040699

03 04 05 06 07 ❖/RRD 10 9 8 7 6 5 4 3 2 1

This book is dedicated to

my great-grandmother

Nana DiGregorio,

my grandmothers,

Antoinette and Gertrude,

and my mother, Barbara,

all of whom, over the years,

lovingly prepared meals and

fed us without complaint.

acknowledgments

Many thanks and much gratitude go to all who made this book a reality:

My friend Pam Hunter, who encouraged me to write this book and who introduced me to my wonderful and extraordinary agent Fred Hill; to my husband and photographer Rob Sinskey, whose talent and patience far exceed mine, and who endured tasting every recipe in the book multiple times.

The organic farmers Jim Durst of Durst Farms, Michael Manfre of Frank Capurro & Son, Nancy Skall of Middleton Farms, and Bradley Cantor of Canyon Acres, who took time out of their frenetically busy schedules to meet with Rob and me and gave permission to photograph their beautiful farms.

The cheese producers who allowed us to gawk while they spun milk into gold. Cindy, Diane, and Liam Callahan of Bellwether Farms; Barbara and Rex Backus of Goat's Leap; and Peggy Smith and Sue Conley of Cowgirl Creamery.

My dearest friends Donia Bijan, a chef of extraordinary talent who has inspired my cooking from the day we met, and Amanda Gamble, who tested recipes and offered encouragement every step of the way. Sue, Pam, Jenni, and those too numerous to mention who tested recipes without complaint and begged for more.

The cheerful butchers of the Vallergas Redwood Meat Department—David, George, and Randy—who helped me translate names of chef cuts into consumer cuts of meat and let me know what was easily available to everyone; and Mark and Ed, also of Vallergas, who saw me every single day for a year and a half and always had something new to say.

Jim Galle of Grimaud Farms, who always heeded my call for information, foie gras, ducks, and guinea hens; and Viking and All-Clad for their support over the years.

All of my immediate and extended family, especially my daughters, Ella and Lexi, who would have rather eaten the dough raw, but patiently waited until it was cooked.

And last but not least, a great big thank-you goes to my editor, the brilliant and kind Susan Friedland, who distilled my massive ramblings into a cohesive book, and to Califia Suntree and everyone else at HarperCollins who helped bring this book to fruition.

contents

foreword

Deep inside, all of us feel a need for food that nourishes both body and soul, but for many of us this awareness may lie dormant for years until we come face-to-face with what we've been missing. It may be a Nutmeg Custard that reminds us of a rainy evening, a sour Cherry and Almond Clafoutis that bursts with the colors and flavors of summer, a sumptuous Chocolate Soufflé Cake that fills our mouths with a creamy sweetness of childhood, or a crispy onion tart that snaps as we bite into its savory crust. When you turn the pages of Maria's book, you will find these experiences waiting for you—and more. This is the food that many of us have been looking for. Food that represents those simple, satisfying delights that warm the heart and linger in memory.

Food and our respect for the pleasures that it can give us can inform our entire lives. In recent years, with the abundance of processed foods filling our pantries, the art of home cooking has waned, wedged between the needs and time pressures of a busy life and the idea that foods we zip out of plastic or empty out of boxes and cans will somehow make our lives better and more efficient. What is forgotten in all this is that cooking, a craft born out of necessity, is crucial to our emotional well-being, creativity, and social interaction. It remains one of the ways that we can still connect with who we are and what is important in our lives. If we take the time to become aware of this, then we can let ourselves be educated by the foods that we prepare.

Maria is telling us if we treat our food with respect and pay attention, we can cultivate that knowing part of ourselves that understands the perfection in the ripeness of a peach, or in freshly churned butter, or in the briny freshness of a glistening bream. She tells us that we can begin to sense when flavors are as they should be, when the succulent squash is cooked just right, or when a steak is finished, its edges crisp and its flavor sparked by crushed black pepper and thyme.

She understands the value of memory and family and the importance of fresh foods lovingly prepared. I have always had an appreciation for clean unaltered flavors. The basis for the enchantment of any dish is the essence of what already exists in a product. As chefs we strive for this in the kitchen, and it always brings me joy when I find a book such as this one that helps guide people to achieve this.

Maria also understands the relationship of the quality of the food we bring to our recipes to the quality of the end product. She understands the importance of paying attention to the seasons and she believes, as I do, in the importance of knowing one's purveyors, and of establishing and maintaining those relationships. At the same time she reminds us that quality food products do not have to be the most expensive. With meats, for example, Maria shows us that we don't always need, or even want, the most expensive cuts of meat. Braising is a prudent alchemy for tougher cuts of meat. Moist braises, including those using beef or lamb shanks, as well as Coq au Vin, will keep for days when stored properly and their flavors will only improve. In this way, Maria's style of cooking works just as well for a single person as it does for an entire family or social gathering.

This book is an expression of the necessity for playfulness, an appreciation for beauty, and respect for balance in life. Maria understands we are sustained emotionally and physically by what we eat. She reminds us of the child in us as she creates her Chocolate Shortbread with Vanilla Cream Filling, about as close as she could get to her favored Oreos. She gives a lesson in elegance in her recipe for Brandied Pears, combining them with sugar and butter to create sweet golden morsels, or as she says, "opaque jewels." She reaches into the earth for her grilled porcini recipe, meaty and pungent, served with Parmesan, lemon, and pepper.

In other words, this book presents food for all who appreciate the senses and life for what they have to offer in all their simplicity and natural beauty. It is a reminder of gardens in summer and orchards in autumn. It is a celebration. I hope you enjoy it as I do.

Thomas Keller

introduction

Nana DiGregorio, my great-grandmother on my mother's side, was an immigrant from Bari, Italy. She spoke little English and she could neither read nor write. But it was of no consequence; she had a memory as sharp as a tack and her hands were magic in the kitchen. I can't remember a time when she wasn't standing in front of the stove, wearing a flowered house dress, wooden spoon in hand, stirring a big pot or pulling a fragrant pan from the oven. I could smell the tomato sauce before I crossed the threshold of the front door. I would be met with a huge pinch on the cheek and hurriedly escorted to the table, for not to eat immediately and copiously upon arrival at Nana's house was a sin. She would bring forth bowls of delicately scented broth with tiny veal meatballs light as air. Trays of manicotti with their whisper-thin pancakes holding together a cloud of ricotta. Braciola so tender the meat would lie open at the mere touch of a fork. Of course at the time I did not know exactly what I was eating. But over the years, after Nana passed away, my mother would fill in the blanks as I described the dishes. My mother would recall Papa DiGregorio's fig tree. The figs that grew on his tree in his small backyard in Queens were, in memory, huge unwieldy teardrops of soft white skin filled with a juicy burst of magenta flesh and popping seeds. How could this gnarled tree pruned to a twisted stump in winter produce such sweet weighty orbs of summer delight?

In late summer at their country house, Papa DiGregorio would pick all of the tomatoes from the garden and Nana would light her outdoor woodstove and can her tomatoes for the winter. Her pantry would be filled with shelf upon shelf of brilliant red tomatoes in jars. These were the secret to her wonderful sauce. Winter tomatoes were not welcomed in her house. She would buy loaves of crusty bread from the Italian bakery around the corner. Happiness was sitting on a stool in the corner, legs swirling around, with a heel of bread and a bowl of sauce in which to dip.

My mother's father came from a very old New England family. His ancestors had settled on Nantucket in the late 1700s, where they became whaling captains. This was odd since their family name was Baker and they had come from England, which meant that somewhere along the line someone most likely had been a baker. My grandfather was raised in house where everything was made from scratch, including the daily bread.

My great-grandmother Baker took great pride in her ability to manage a household. When my grandfather married my mother's mother he married a modern woman. She was not going to stay home to cook and bake, she was going to work and make her way in the world. Her days were spent at work and every evening, when she arrived home, she prepared dinner. She would put it together in the space of an hour without opening one can or jar. It was quick and it was fresh. With the birth of her five children she became a full-time mother. Dinners became more expansive and a time to catch up on everyone's activities

during the day. She expanded her nightly repertoire for holidays when she had more time, and more help, to flex her culinary muscles. Italian dishes were always included as a course but as a first-generation American she also embraced the American traditions of turkey, steak, and baked potatoes. We consumed all for they were equally tasty.

My father's mother was from Strasbourg and his father from the Black Forest. Geographically close but culinary worlds apart. Grandma Helm's kitchen was the culinary equivalent of a safari. Strange meats and sea creatures abounded. The table was always piled with strong-smelling cheeses, meats, hot mustard, and coarse-textured breads. She served dark red sausages thick with spices and a curious-looking cured meat thinly sliced with chunks of fragrant white fat in undulating gelatin—the names of which I later learned were blood sausage and headcheese. These bits of newly acquired knowledge conjured up thoughts of the unimaginable in my young head. Eels swam once again in simmering pots of vegetables and broth. Viewing a very large cow's tongue on the tip of a carving fork, just wrestled from its pot of poaching liquid, was a culinary epiphany. My stomach felt sick at the realization that the silky moist squares of meat, rich with flavor, were, in reality, an identifiable body part. My trust had been betrayed. Tongue, however, remained in my food repertoire; tripe, kidneys, and brains dropped out. On holidays, there would be salt-cured hams and geese with copious amounts of sauerkraut and a shiny quarter for any grandchild cleaning his or her plate. Lentils, simmered with the remainder of a ham bone, would be served with steaming spaetzle, freshly scooped from a boiling pot of salted water.

My grandfather tended two gardens, where he would disappear for hours. A wild tangled one behind his house yielded Swiss chard, cabbage, onions, rhubarb, cucumbers, pole beans, and tomatoes. The one at his house on Fire Island yielded spicy white icicles and flaming red balls of radishes that were easily pulled from the sandy soil, and even more tomatoes. We ate from the gardens in the summer and the pantry in the winter where potatoes, turnips, pickles, and sauerkraut were found in abundance.

This was how I grew up in an endless parade of food and celebrations. Bleak winters of upstate New York were weathered with hearty stews, potpies, roast chicken, and the ever-present pot of tomato sauce simmering on the stove. In wintertime, comforting desserts such as custard warm from the oven, baked with a sprinkling of nutmeg, chased away the chill.

We eagerly awaited the opening of the local farm stand. It heralded the arrival of summer. My mother would whirl common cream cheese into a delectable crust for a plum tart. The sweet flesh of the fruit melting with the puckery sourness of the skin made for a wonderful mouth dance of flavors. My father would create sugar-dusted cinnamon-scented doughnuts warm from the fryer whose smell would wake us from our sleep. Other mornings we would fight for a stack of orange-laced crepes slathered with butter and jam.

These are memories that I hope my children will enjoy too. During my lifetime, food has become faster and faster, far removed from its natural state. I have tasted glimpses of my childhood memories throughout my work and travels in France and Italy. There, small villages still rely on what is cultivated locally. Meals are a time for both sustenance and celebration. Artisans create cheeses that are delivered to the back door of restaurants each morning. Bread is baked twice daily. Chickens come with feet and feathers. Rabbits with fur. Herbs are selected from the ground, not the grocery rack. The link between earth and table is still intact.

Home cooking is a disappearing craft; what was once commonplace has now become a luxury as time becomes more precious in our busy world. These seasonal recipes are designed to inspire you to make time in your busy schedule to step back into kitchen. The menus and recipes respect the merits of the seasons, reflecting a sense of time and place. They remind us that we should rejoice in the warm sweet tomatoes of summer and revel in the stoic, earthy root vegetables of winter, that the bright colors of summer vegetables should gracefully fade to the brown, gold, and dark green of fall and winter ones.

Choose how lofty or humble your meals will be. Some recipes are simple and basic; others require more diligence on the part of the cook. The recipes and menus are created to provide pleasure not torment. Preparation of these recipes should be done with the best ingredients available to you. Best does not mean the most expensive, but the freshest and most wholesome ones you can find at your market.

The menus are meant to be guidelines for preparing a three-course meal. They are not set in stone. Menus can be combined and dishes substituted or dropped. Salads can be expanded to make a summer luncheon entrée. Soup can become a meal in itself with a crusty heel of bread. Replace a salad with a tart or a roast with a risotto, whatever your whim dictates or your time frame accommodates. All of the recipes, with the exception of some desserts, can be halved to serve four without consequence.

I hope this book will teach you take a step back and appreciate a just-picked, fully ripened peach in its simplicity—the creaminess of a perfectly aged goat cheese and the fruitiness of a newly pressed olive oil. May each foray to the market be an adventure and the enjoyment that preparing a meal also brings a sense of accomplishment. For many of the meals you create for family and friends will provide memories to last for years and years to come, as they did during my childhood and continue to do to this day.

fresh, in season, local, and organic

When I began cooking professionally in the early eighties my interest was that the food be fresh, in season, and as local as possible. The term organic was still relatively foreign to me. It conjured up thoughts of the local health food store with its myriad of leaking grain bins and paltry bits of rather weak-looking vegetables with store clerks to match. (Mind you we are talking upstate New York.)

Walking into a Bread & Circus Market in Boston altered the course of my life forever. The notion that you could actually find beautiful organic produce, crusty breads baked from organic grains, and chickens that weren't raised in cages was an epiphany. Soon after my Boston encounter, I visited my sister, who was living in Berkeley. Of this, I can say two words: Berkeley Bowl, a massive hoop barn of a store, with its many beautifully imperfect perfect vegetables, endless arrays of artisanal dairy products, and meats that actually saw the outside of a barn. Suddenly it was as if all the great food in America was on the West Coast. Life seemed unfair.

I eventually made it to the West Coast in 1986. I envisioned California as the land of plenty, where purveyors would be at my door plying me with organic produce, meats, and cheeses at the snap of a finger. This was not the case. There were a few produce companies at the time that had small lists of organically farmed vegetables and a couple of small companies that supplied organic dairy products and naturally raised poultry and meat, but the supplies were inconsistent and prices expensive. I used what organics I could afford, but always kept my menus fresh, in season, and as local as possible.

During this time I made contact with a few small farmers and artisan producers, some organic, some not, that would let me know what they were picking or producing a day or two ahead of time so I could plan my menus accordingly. Buying directly from the farmer was more cost effective, but it had its drawbacks. I had to plan for the unexpected—too much compost, thrown on by a neophyte assistant, burning the entire lettuce crop, a cherry-splitting rain, and ewes that weren't producing enough milk to satisfy all the cheese orders. Delivery times were shaky and many substitutions were made without notice. These problems could be dealt with in a small restaurant but as my venues changed and the number of covers went from 50 to 150 it became more and more difficult to work in the unexpected. With a larger staff, I needed to depend on a steady supply to keep menus consistent and affordable.

Times have changed. Across the country, small local farmers and artisan producers of breads, cheeses, olive oils, and other items too numerous to list are in the spotlight. Every year more organic producers, small and large, enter the market. Their products offer quality and flavor and provide an alternative choice to consumers. Advanced technology and less expensive, more efficient shipping have given restaurateurs and consumers easier access to the fruits of their efforts. It is a heady time for those who appreciate good food.

Take advantage of what your region offers. Oftentimes it's a lot more than you think. Prepare meals that convey a sense of the season at hand. Buy local and organic when you have the opportunity. Naturally it's easier to buy local produce in the summer when it is abundant. It becomes more difficult as the weather becomes colder and farms shut down for the winter. I remember my winter days in upstate New York, where there was nary a fresh leafy vegetable to be seen, but there were all types of root vegetables, squashes, and dried beans—fall produce harvested, cured, and stored to last until spring. Even in northern California we turn to hardy greens, squashes, broccoli, and root vegetables to carry us through the winter.

Make your choices based on what is available to you. Find out where your local farmers' market is and visit it when it's open. Use seasonal produce year-round and get creative with what is available. This book is here to help. Keep things fresh, in season, local, and organic—in that order. Do not become seduced by the strawberries, tomatoes, and corn proffered in winter. Let their memory sustain you and the expectations of their impending arrival thrill you. It's the way a slower life used to be and perhaps shall be once again.

wine for food

Wine should enhance, not overpower the food you are eating. Likewise food should enhance not overpower the wine you are drinking. There needs to be a balance between the food and wine. Otherwise, they will not work together.

Why the interest in food and wine? Why not food and lemonade or food and milk? Modern-day pairing of food and wine springs from the agricultural traditions of Europe and certainly can be traced further back to other regions.

Certain grape varieties thrived in specific regions with specific soil and climate. Vegetables, fruits, and grains grown in these regions were also dictated by what would thrive in the same soil and climate. Animals raised on the same land were chosen based on their adaptability to the climate and terrain. Food and wine grew up together hand in hand.

A good way to approach food and wine pairings is to look at historical pairings of food and wine in Europe. The pairing of European (Old World) wines with regional foods can then be translated to similar cuisine and wines produced in other parts of the world. The key is to identify the grape varietals from which the wines are made. Old World wines usually bear the name of the town or region—Rioja, Chianti, Chablis, Pomerol—where they are produced. New World wines produced in the United States, Australia, and South America are identified by grape varietals—Tempranillo, Sangiovese, Chardonnay, and Merlot. Once identified, Old World grape varietals can be matched to their New World counterparts and the wine and food pairing can begin.

The following are some examples of historical food and wine pairings. The dry white wines of Bordeaux pair well with seafood, especially shellfish. This is no surprise as the Bordeaux region borders the Atlantic Ocean. White Bordeaux are largely a blend of Sauvignon Blanc and Sémillon. New World Sauvignon Blanc and Sémillon also tend to go well with seafood. Red and white Burgundy pair well with foods of the region—rabbit in mustard, coq au vin, squab with roasted fruits, mushrooms and classic beef bourguignon. These dishes are rich but not heavy, therefore an elegant pinot noir or chardonnay with a balance of fruit and acid and a hint of oak is the perfect accompaniment. Many New World Pinot Noirs and Chardonnays will pair with like cuisine. If the dish has Italian roots I look for those regions that produce the type of dish that I am cooking. Tuscany produces Chianti from the widely planted Sangiovese grape. It is a red wine that pairs well with cooked tomatoes, simple grilled meats, and good peppery olive oil.

A New World Sangiovese would also pair well with dishes bearing similar ingredients. The examples could go on forever.

The first questions to ask when choosing a wine are what color and what characteristics are you looking for? I prefer dry white wines with a crispness that comes from bright acidity for seafood, poultry, light meats, and salads. The acidity should balance and carry the fruit notes of the wine, be they pear, melon, tropical fruit, or citrus. It should have a mouth feel that enlivens your palate and causes you to salivate. White wine can handle oak if it is in balance with the acid and fruit. White wines that are ripe with fruit, heavy with a buttery mouth feel, and sweet with oak can be awkward with food. There is nothing wrong with this style of wine but they are better consumed without food because of their richness. White wines with a hint of sweetness pair well with meats cooked with fruit and with foods that have a bit of hot spice.

French Chardonnays are a fine example of what makes a good food wine. They typically have crisp acidity and have been made with a discreet use of oak. Many people consider them to be some of the finest food wines in the world. Sometimes it is hard to believe that the wines of Pouilly-Fuissé and Chablis, where wine makers use very little or neutral oak, and the richer wines of Meursault and Puligny-Montrachet, where oak use is more prolific, are all made from the same grape varietal. The stylistic range is profound and the potential number of dishes they pair with is endless.

Other Old World white varietals, such as the Albariño from Spain, Pinot Blanc, Gewürztraminer, and Riesling from Alsace, Riesling from Germany, Pinot Grigio and Tocai from Italy, and Sauvignon Blanc from France have gained a foothold in food and wine circles. They have all the characteristics of a great food wine—acidity balanced with fruit, spice, and/or mineral notes, some with residual sugar, most unfettered by oak. They are priced considerably less than most white Burgundies.

Red wines make admirable food partners. The tannins, produced from the contact of juice against the skins and seeds of the grapes, provide another layer of complexity as well as longevity. Light, medium, or heavy-bodied red wines that have a balance of fruit, acidity, and oak are ideal food companions. Overripe and heavily oaked reds may taste great during cocktail hour but they become a meal in themselves when paired with food.

Wines made from red grapes run the gamut from the delicate rosés of Provence to the heavier reds of Bordeaux and the meaty Barolos of northern Italy. As a rule of thumb, lighter-bodied reds made from Pinot Noir, Grenache, Tempranillo, and Sangiovese can accompany heavier seafood dishes and light meats such as pork, poultry, rabbit, and squab. Heavier reds made from Syrah, Cabernet Sauvignon, Cabernet Franc, and Merlot go well with game such as venison, wild boar, and elk and with a good steak. Most reds, with the exception of a few juicy high acid rosés, do not hold up when matched with vinegar.

Some fantastic European food-loving red grape varietals, listed by varietal/region, include Tempranillo and Garnacha/Rioja, red Gamay/Beaujolais, Cabernet Franc/Chinon, Syrah and Grenache blends/Côtes du Rhone, Sangiovese/Chianti, Dolcetto/Alba and Barbera/Alba. These wines can be considerably less expensive than the grand cru wines of Burgundy and Bordeaux.

It is more challenging to pair New World wines with food because New World growing regions do not have established agricultural traditions of food and wine. Characteristics of many Old World wines are influenced by the concept of *terroir*. *Terroir* is the effect climate and soil have on grapes grown in a specific location in combination with the wine makers craft. Wine-making techniques support, not overpower, the inherent flavors of the grapes in the resultant wine. Most New World wines are not driven by *terroir*, but by wine-making technique and style. Many wine makers bend the inherent flavor of the grapes to fit a predetermined style of wine making regardless of where they are grown. The wines are not produced with regional foods in mind.

The New World has many different grapes growing and styles of wines being produced within the same region. Growing conditions are often warmer than in Europe. This results in wines that have riper fruit, more body, and lower acidity. New World cuisine is often a fusion of ethnic flavors and not region specific. New World pairings can become elusive. Once you have identified your preference for Old World grape varietals and the foods that pair well with them, New World pairings are much easier. This is one case where familiarity does not breed contempt. It may instead pique your interest and turn you on to other varietals.

We cannot discount outside influences such as weather on food and wine pairings. During the summer we tend to eat lighter. The wines we drink are lighter-bodied and often served chilled, even reds. We tend to lean toward whites and rosés that are fruity and crisp to balance the warmth of the weather. I call them noncerebral, fun food wines. Fruity white and rosé wines give beer a run for its money and pair great with barbecue. Cold weather lends itself to heavier food and richer sauces. Cold weather cuisine is better suited to heavier-bodied white and red wines; many of the light chilled wines of summer would seem out of place except as an aperitif.

All in all, wine purchases should be dictated by what you enjoy or what you would like to try. Perhaps a certain varietal or producer is intriguing. The only way to find out what grape varieties and style of wine you enjoy is to taste. The wine suggestions for each menu are just that. They serve as a guideline when you must choose from a whole wineshop of wines. Start from the suggestions. If you don't care for them, make your own. Experiment with food pairings. If worse comes to worse you can always open another bottle.

a note on salt

There are many varieties of salt available to the home cook. I prefer sea salt or flaked kosher salt (such as Diamond Crystal) for both savory and sweet dishes. I use Fleur de Sel for finishing dishes (see Notes on page 49). I shy away from common iodized table salt because of its medicinal taste. If you don't see the salt you want at your local grocer's, ask them to order you some or order some by mail.

fall

Ruby apples hang merrily, crisp and tart,

Nearby, stoic pears in their golden wraps await,

Pumpkins giddily, yellow and plump, tumble forth,

Ripened grains bow their heads, heavy with anticipation,

For Harvesttime has come.

I beckon thee to the table.

—MARIA HELM SINSKEY, 1989

The first time you smell that cool snap of air with the earthy scent of dry rustling leaves, you stop and close your eyes, as if it were imagined. The breath you draw to capture it is deep, as if with its expulsion, it might release the pent-up memories of autumns past. The carrying breeze is not cold and abrupt, but warm in its center and chilled on the edges. It conjures up thoughts of newly sharpened pencils and books covered just so. It sounds of the laughter of friendships rejoined after a sweltering separation and birds flying south. It brings with it crisp apples and yellow jackets crowding the cider press, and the camaraderie of a freshly pressed jug passed from hand to hand. Pumpkins are ripening, fields are browning, and the scent of cinnamon fills the air. There is a sense of urgency and of anticipation. Bees gorge on pollen. Squirrels gather nuts. Combines work in fields of grain without pause. We eat the last of the summer vegetables from the waning garden knowing it will be a while before we see them again. Like dear old friends, they'll leave without fanfare and, upon their return, pick up where they left off. The days are growing shorter and colder. Indian summer, in a mocking fit of heat, reminds us one last time of not so distant summer days. Fall gives us fair warning that winter will soon be upon us.

The first frost sweetens carrots, beets, and other edible roots. It turns radicchio's bitter green head into a tight fist of ruddy red leaves with brilliant ribs of white. As we ready ourselves for our descent into winter we change the way we eat. Soups and stews are heartier. Greens become more rugged. Tender summer shoots are replaced with leaves of more substance. We no longer fear the heat from an oven left on to braise or roast. Salads offer warm components. Figs, apples, pears, and quinces abound on menus, savory or sweet. Fall is the play and our plates the stage. What a play indeed, the characters of shelling beans, late corn, and chard dance about. Plump squashes curing in cool darkened storerooms await their turn to strut the stage. There is time for all, for most of what we harvest now will keep for months to come.

Fall is the last time to appreciate freshly picked local fruits and vegetables. The further we travel down the road toward winter the longer our apples, pears, and root vegetables have been in storage. Use as much as you can now, while they're fresh. Those who live in year-round growing seasons embrace late fall fruits and vegetables. The rest of us will bide our time until the frozen earth softens once again.

fall menus

Fall Menu I

spinach and sheep's milk ricotta "pie"   8

roast pork loin with figs   12

toasted pine nut couscous   14

pear fritters   15

WINES: The ricotta pie calls for a crisp Pinot Grigio or a fruity Chianti Classico. The pork loin with the sweetness of the figs would pair nicely with a juicy Dolcetto or Beaujolais.

spinach and sheep's milk ricotta "pie"

Ricotta pie is the Italian equivalent of French quiche. My great-grandmother always mixed the fresh ricotta she bought from the Italian market on the corner with spinach from Papa DiGregorio's small garden. The flavors of the sweet curds were grounded by the earthiness of the spinach and enhanced by a pinch of nutmeg. Spinach ricotta pie was something we looked forward to when we visited her house. There always seemed to be a wedge of it on the counter.

This "pie" sits in a crust of thinly sliced potatoes. When the pie is turned out onto a plate, the potatoes make a beautiful golden petal-like crust. My great-grandmother would make another version of this pie by lining a casserole with a mixture of bread crumbs, olive oil, and cheese. She would sprinkle the extra bread crumbs on top to form a crunchy topping. The resulting "pie" would be scooped out warm with a spoon or left to cool to room temperature so that it could be sliced and served more elegantly. The bread crumb crust can be substituted for the potato crust.

Fresh sheep's milk ricotta is heavenly white clouds of freshly made curd, with the whey still oozing from the cheese. The ricotta should be consumed within a short time of being made, as it does not contain any stabilizers or fillers. (See Headnote on page 283.) The flavor of the fresh ricotta is delicate and rich and tastes of sweet ewe's milk, which pairs beautifully with the spinach. The grocery store variety of ricotta, sheep's or cow's milk, will work in this recipe though the flavor and texture will be less delicate because of the added fillers used in its making.

SERVES 8; MAKES ONE 10-INCH DEEP-DISH PIE

1   Destem the spinach. To remove the large stems, fold the leaf in half with one hand so that the center rib is exposed and the stem is pointing toward the ground. Grab the stem with your other hand and pull upward. The stem will tear the leaf to the point where it becomes tender, leaving a leaf that is tender and stem-free.

Small stems can be left intact. Fill a large bowl or sink with cold water and add the spinach leaves. Swish the leaves around. Lift the leaves from the water so that all the dirt falls to the bottom of the bowl or sink. Repeat the process until the leaves are free of grit. Taste a leaf to see if there is any dirt remaining. Drain the leaves well before sautéing.

2 Heat a large sauté pan over medium-high heat; add 2 tablespoons of the extra virgin olive oil. Add the spinach; take care, as the damp spinach added to the hot oil will spatter. Sauté the spinach until it's completely wilted; season with salt and pepper to taste. Place the spinach in a large colander and let cool. When the spinach is cool enough to handle, squeeze out any excess liquid with your hands and chop finely. You should have approximately 1 cup of chopped spinach. Reserve the spinach until ready to use.

3 Preheat the oven to 350 degrees F.

4 Heat a medium sauté pan over medium heat. Add 2 tablespoons of olive oil and then the diced onion. Sauté the onion until it is golden, about 5 minutes. Add the minced garlic and cook a few minutes more; season with salt and pepper to taste. Reserve the mixture at room temperature until ready to use.

5 In a large bowl, beat the eggs lightly to combine the yolks and the whites. Add the cream and whisk to incorporate. Fold in the ricotta, chopped spinach, reserved onion-garlic mixture, and ¼ cup of the grated Parmesan cheese. Season with 1½ teaspoons salt, a few grinds of fresh black pepper, and the nutmeg.

2 pounds spinach

4 tablespoons extra virgin olive oil

Salt

Freshly ground black pepper

1 medium yellow onion, peeled, trimmed, and finely diced

1 large garlic clove, peeled, trimmed, and minced

2 large eggs

½ cup heavy cream

1 pound sheep's milk or cow's milk ricotta

½ cup grated Parmesan cheese

⅛ teaspoon grated nutmeg

One 10-inch deep-dish pie plate prepared with Potato Crust or Bread Crumb Crust (recipes follow)

6   Fill the reserved potato or bread crumb–lined pie plate with the ricotta mixture and sprinkle the remaining Parmesan cheese over the top.

7   Place in the preheated oven and bake until the top of the pie is golden and the filling has set, about 45 to 50 minutes. On a wire rack, cool the pie to warm before slicing. If you have baked the pie with the Potato Crust, cool to room temperature and turn out onto a serving plate so that the golden potato crust is exposed. Serve in wedges.

NOTE: The onion-garlic mixture and the spinach steps may be prepared 1 day in advance of serving, combined, and stored in the refrigerator until ready to use.

VARIATION: For a variation on the spinach filling, such aromatic vegetables as sautéed leeks and caramelized onions and a little diced smoked ham or sausage can be substituted for the spinach and onion-garlic mixture. Use the same proportion of ricotta, eggs, and cream and add your choice of cooked, well-drained vegetables and meat, up to 2 cups total.

potato crust

Use this crust to cradle the savory filling of quiches and frittatas, instead of a pie crust. The crust can be made a day ahead and left covered at room temperature until ready to use.

MAKES ONE 10-INCH PIE CRUST

1   Preheat the oven to 400 degrees F.

2   Brush a pie plate or casserole dish heavily with the room temperature butter.

3   Peel the potatoes and slice thinly on a Japanese mandolin or by hand. The slices should be the thickness of thin cardboard and almost translucent. Starting at the

2 tablespoons unsalted butter, at room temperature

2 large Russet potatoes

2 tablespoons melted butter

Salt

Freshly ground black pepper

center of the pie plate, line the plate with the sliced potatoes, overlapping the slices by half to form a crust. Form a spiral with the slices until they are used up. The slices should be tightly packed and can be doubled over to use all of the slices. Be sure that the potatoes generously overlap the lip of the pie plate, as they will shrink as they bake.

4   Brush the layered potatoes with the melted butter and season evenly with salt and pepper. Place the potato-lined plate in the preheated oven and bake for 35 to 45 minutes until the potatoes are golden. Remove from the oven and cool before filling. Cool and leave covered at room temperature for up to a day.

bread crumb crust

This quick, simple crust can be substituted for the Potato Crust.

MAKES ONE 10-INCH PIE CRUST

1   Preheat the oven to 400 degrees F.

2   Butter the pie plate thickly with a brush or your fingers.

3   Mix together the bread crumbs, olive oil, and Parmesan cheese; season with salt and pepper to taste. Press the mixture into the butter using your fingers. The bread crumbs should be a thin layer about ⅛ inch thick. Excess bread crumbs can be reserved to sprinkle over the top of the pie after it is filled.

2 tablespoons unsalted butter, at room temperature

1 cup coarse bread crumbs

¼ cup extra virgin olive oil

¼ cup finely grated Parmesan cheese

Salt

Freshly ground black pepper

4   Bake the crust in the preheated oven for 10 minutes until the bread crumbs are lightly toasted and golden.

roasted pork loin with figs

After their brief appearance in early summer, figs come on strong in the fall. They make a wonderful addition to sweet and savory preparations alike. This recipe balances the sweetness of the figs with the saltiness of the brined pork and the mellow tanginess of the balsamic used to finish the dish. Use good-quality balsamic vinegar. Quality varies widely by producer so if you have a chance to taste them do. If you can afford an aged *tradizionale,* fantastic—there are also many 10- to 12-year-old balsamics with good flavor that will work at much friendlier prices. The pork roast is brined for extra flavor and added moisture. Pork loin roasts are very lean and have a tendency to dry out if they are the slightest bit overcooked. Brine is a cheap insurance policy for slight overcooking. Keep in mind that for maximum effectiveness, the pork loin should spend 2 days in the brine.

The pork can be served with simple roasted potatoes or Toasted Pine Nut Couscous (recipe follows), which makes a wonderful textural bed in which to tuck the pork and figs. Prepare the couscous while the pork is roasting (step 9) and cover to keep warm or serve at room temperature.

SERVES 8

1   Prepare the brine: Place 5 cups of water in a large pot. Add all of the brine ingredients and stir well.

2   Bring to a boil, reduce the heat to a simmer, and simmer for 5 minutes. Remove the pan from the heat. Cool the brine thoroughly before using.

3   Marinate the pork roast in the cold brine for 2 days in the refrigerator. Remove the loin from the brine and drain it well. Blot it dry with a paper towel.

4   Peel, halve, and slice the onions into ¼-inch wedges. Reserve. Trim the very tip of the stem off the figs. Reserve.

5   Preheat the oven to 400 degrees F.

6 Heat a heavy-bottomed sauté pan over medium-high heat. Add enough olive oil to coat the bottom of the pan and sear the pork loin, fat side down, until it is nicely browned. Turn the loin to brown on all sides. Lower the heat if the pan gets too hot and smoky. Because of the brine no additional seasoning is necessary.

7 Remove the loin to a plate. Drain the fat from the pan. Add 1 tablespoon of olive oil to the hot pan and add the onions. Sauté them until they begin to caramelize, about 5 minutes. Drizzle the onions with the honey and season them with salt and pepper.

8 Place the loin on top of the onions in the pan and roast in the preheated oven for 25 minutes. Add ½ cup of water. Toss the figs lightly with olive oil and season them with salt and pepper. Add them to the pork roast and onions.

Brine

½ cup kosher salt

¾ cup sugar

4 medium garlic cloves, peeled and sliced

1 teaspoon chile flakes

1 bay leaf

One 4-pound boneless pork loin, cut crosswise into 2 equal pieces

2 medium yellow onions

24 ripe figs, Black Mission or Calimyrna

Extra virgin olive oil

2 tablespoons honey

Salt

Freshly ground black pepper

1 to 2 tablespoons aged balsamic vinegar (see Headnote opposite)

9 Continue roasting for 25 to 30 minutes or until a thermometer reads 145 degrees F when inserted into the center of the roast. Remove the loin from the pan and place on a cutting board or plate. Cover it with foil and let it rest for 10 to 15 minutes before slicing. The roast will continue to cook while it rests.

10 Remove the figs from the roasting pan and drizzle them with balsamic vinegar. Stir the onions in the pan and taste for seasoning. Season them with salt and pepper to taste and place in a serving bowl with the figs on top.

11 Slice the pork and serve on a platter accompanied by the roasted figs and onions. Serve couscous, simple roasted potatoes, or rice as a side.

toasted pine nut couscous

Preparing couscous the traditional way by steaming is a time-consuming task. The couscous must be dampened and rolled between your hands several times to allow it to bloom before steaming. This method gives the couscous a wonderfully firm yet fluffy texture. The technique below is a tasty compromise between the traditional method and quick-cooking boiled couscous. Its texture is light and fluffy and full of flavor.

SERVES 8

1 cup pine nuts

1 medium red onion

3 tablespoons extra virgin olive oil

Salt

Freshly ground black pepper

2 cups couscous

2 tablespoons chopped Italian parsley

1   Preheat the oven to 350 degrees F.

2   Spread the pine nuts on a sheet pan and toast for 15 minutes in the oven until golden; cool and reserve.

3   Peel, trim, and finely dice the red onion. Heat 1 tablespoon of olive oil in a medium sauté pan over medium heat. Add the red onion and sauté until tender and golden, about 5 minutes; season to taste with salt and pepper; cool and reserve.

4   In a large bowl, combine the couscous with 2 tablespoons of olive oil and the chopped parsley. Stir in the onions.

5   Bring 2¾ cups of water to a boil and add 2 teaspoons of salt. Pour the boiling water over the couscous, making sure all of the couscous is moistened. Cover the bowl tightly with plastic wrap and let it sit for 10 minutes.

6   Fold in the toasted pine nuts and fluff with a fork. Season to taste.

pear fritters

Taste with your imagination: moist, delicate little puffs of dough filled with bits of succulent pear, sprinkled with powdered sugar, and you've successfully developed the sensory picture of these fritters. They can be made as small or as large as you like, just bear in mind that the larger the fritter gets the longer it will take to cook through. Little bite-sized fritters can be served alongside a big scoop of Vanilla Ice Cream (page 289) or Caramel Ice Cream (page 336). Serve the hot fritters as soon as possible after frying.

SERVES 8

1 Peel, halve, core, and dice the pears into ½-inch cubes right before making the batter.

2 In a large bowl, combine the flour, baking powder, brown sugar, and salt.

3 Separate the eggs. In a large bowl, whisk the egg yolks with the vanilla, milk, and the melted butter until thoroughly incorporated.

4 Add the egg yolk mixture to the dry ingredients and stir well. Fold in the diced pears. Let the batter relax for 20 minutes at room temperature.

5 In a very clean bowl of a standing mixer with a whisk attachment or by hand, whip the egg whites to soft peaks and fold them gently, half at a time, into the pear mixture. The whites should be added just before frying.

2 large ripe pears, 1½ pounds

1 cup all-purpose flour

2 teaspoons baking powder

2 tablespoons brown sugar

½ teaspoon salt

2 large eggs

½ teaspoon pure vanilla extract

½ cup whole milk

2 tablespoons unsalted butter, melted and cooled

2 quarts expeller pressed vegetable oil for frying (see Note on page 16)

Confectioners' sugar for dusting

6　Heat the oil in a deep 4-quart pot to 375 degrees F. The oil should fill the pan halfway. Test the temperature of the oil with a little drop of dough. The dough should sizzle merrily when it hits the hot oil. Using two tablespoons, drop a heaping tablespoon of the batter into the hot oil, taking care not to spatter yourself. Cook until the fritters float and are golden on both sides. Turn them over if they need help browning on both sides. Adjust the heat if the oil gets too hot and the fritters get dark too quickly. You need a medium-hot steady heat to cook the fritters evenly and to prevent them from soaking up too much of the fat. Remove the fritters from the fat with a slotted spoon and drain them on a clean lint-free cloth or paper towel. Sprinkle with confectioners' sugar and serve in an open basket lined with a cloth napkin or towel or alongside a scoop of ice cream.

NOTE: Expeller pressed oils are mechanically extracted at cool temperatures. Most commercial oils, with the exception of expeller and cold-pressed, are extracted through a harsh chemical process that adulterates the oil's flavor. You can find expeller and cold-pressed oils at most natural food stores and some of the larger chain stores. Look for the extraction method on the label. For more information on culinary oils visit www.spectrumnaturals.com.

The batter can be held at room temperature for 4 hours before folding in the beaten egg whites. Do not refrigerate or the batter will become too thick and cold. Once the whites are added the batter should be used immediately.

Fall Menu II

fuyu persimmon, candied almond,
and goat cheese salad   18

——

wild mushroom risotto   20

——

honey walnut cake   23

WINES: Salads make wine pairing difficult because of the vinegar. A crisp Sancerre or a New Zealand Sauvignon Blanc would work well with the goat cheese in the salad. The sweetness of the fruit in this salad balances the acid of the vinegar, making it more wine-friendly. The meatiness of the wild mushrooms calls for a full-bodied Pommard or American Pinot Noir. The walnut cake pairs lusciously with Malmsey Madeira.

fuyu persimmon, candied almond, and goat cheese salad

A persimmon tree in late fall is a haunting sight. The leaves have fallen yet the bare branches still clutch their vivid burnt orange fruit. They hang like Christmas ornaments on a forgotten tree.

Persimmons were introduced to the United States from China and Japan in the late 1800s. The two commercially grown varieties are Hachiya and Fuyu. The acorn-shaped Hachiya is astringent when hard and unripe. It turns custard soft when it is ripe and sweet enough to eat. The squat round Fuyu, used in this salad, is nonastringent and retains its firm texture when ripe. Its sweet firmness makes it great for slicing into salads, eating out of hand, and drying. Look for fruit that gives slightly under pressure.

This salad is full of bright flavors and textures: The sweet crunch of the persimmons and almonds contrasts with the salty soft pungency of the goat cheese. If you cannot find persimmons, pears make an excellent understudy. Slice them just before tossing the salad to avoid browning.

SERVES 8

1 Toss the almonds with ¼ teaspoon of olive oil in a medium sauté pan. Heat the almonds over medium heat until you hear one pop. Sprinkle the 2 tablespoons of sugar over the almonds and toss. Keep the pan over the heat while tossing. Season with ¼ teaspoon of salt and a few grinds of black pepper and remove the pan from the heat. Continue to toss the almonds until the sugar hardens. Cool and chop coarsely. Reserve in a tightly sealed container at room temperature. The almonds can be prepared up to 2 days in advance.

2 Trim the tough and discolored leaves from the frisée. Tear the leaves into fork-sized pieces. Wash and spin dry. Wash the baby spinach and spin dry. In a large salad bowl, toss the greens together and cover with a damp towel. Store in the refrigerator until ready to use. Place a piece of plastic wrap over the greens to store overnight.

3   Wash the persimmons and cut out the core. Cut the fruit into quarters and then slice each quarter into ⅛-inch-thick slices. Place the slices in a small bowl and toss with 1 tablespoon of vinaigrette to keep the slices from sticking together. It is best to slice the persimmon just before tossing the salad.

4   To finish the salad: Toss the greens with ¼ cup of the vinaigrette. Add the persimmons and toss again. Taste the greens and add more vinaigrette to taste. Toss, season with salt and pepper, then toss a final time. Sprinkle the almonds and crumble the goat cheese over the top.

½ cup whole almonds

¼ teaspoon extra virgin olive oil

2 tablespoons sugar

Salt

Freshly ground black pepper

½ pound frisée

½ pound baby spinach

4 (1 pound) Fuyu persimmons

¼ to ½ cup Champagne Vinaigrette (recipe follows)

½ pound fresh goat cheese

champagne vinaigrette

MAKES ¾ CUP

1   Whisk together the vinegar and shallot. Season to taste with salt and pepper. Let the shallots marinate for 10 minutes.

2   Whisk in the olive oil and season to taste with salt and pepper.

NOTE: The vinaigrette may be made up to 2 days in advance of serving. Store covered in the refrigerator; bring to room temperature and whisk well before serving.

¼ cup Champagne vinegar

1 small shallot, peeled, trimmed, and finely minced

Salt

Freshly ground black pepper

½ cup extra virgin olive oil

wild mushroom risotto

A few notes on rice for risotto: You will find two main types of rice for risotto at your market, Arborio and Carnaroli. Arborio is a standard short-grained Italian rice with a high starch content that makes it very good for risotto. It cooks faster than Carnaroli and has a softer texture. Carnaroli is the finest aged Italian short-grained rice for risotto. It is known for its superior silken and creamy texture when cooked. The grains of rice are very round, almost barrel-shaped. Arborio rice can be substituted, but as mentioned above, requires a shorter cooking time.

Wild mushrooms freshly picked from the forest are showcased in this dish. They often come complete with pine needles and dirt; therefore, they need to be cleaned as thoroughly as possible. If fresh wild mushrooms are unavailable, high-quality dried wild mushrooms can be rehydrated and substituted. If wild mushrooms, fresh or dried, are out of the question, cultivated mushrooms such as clamshell, hen-of-the-woods, oyster, and crimini can be substituted. Avoid shiitakes if you dislike strong flavors.

A cautionary note: As the rice begins to thicken it has a tendency to spit hot starchy liquid, which can be painful. Use a long thick wooden spoon or paddle to take your hand as far out of spitting range as possible. While this will not prevent the spitting, it should reduce your pain.

SERVES 8 AS A MAIN COURSE; 12 AS AN APPETIZER

1 Clean the mushrooms thoroughly. Keep each variety separate. The dirty stem end should be trimmed with a small sharp knife and the pine needles should be gently brushed away with a semi-stiff brush. If the mushrooms are so dirty as to warrant a bath, fill a large bowl with cold water. Quickly dip and swish the mushrooms in the water two handfuls at a time. Repeat if necessary and then drain the mushrooms in a colander or on top of an absorbent towel. Never allow the mushrooms to soak. They are like sponges and will quickly become water-logged if allowed to sit in water for any amount of time. Their sodden state will make it

almost impossible to get a good golden caramelization when they are sautéed or roasted. Slice the larger mushrooms into bite-sized pieces and cut the smaller mushrooms in half or, if they are very small, leave them whole.

2   Heat a large sauté pan over high heat; add 1 tablespoon of olive oil and then one type of mushroom. Each variety must be cooked separately as they cook at different speeds. Sauté the mushrooms until they are golden and their juices are almost dry, 5 to 10 minutes. Stir some of the shallots, garlic, and fresh thyme leaves into the mushrooms (be sure to reserve equal amounts for the rest of the mushrooms) and season the mixture with salt and pepper to taste. Sauté the remaining mushrooms following the same procedure.

3   After all of the mushrooms have been sautéed, mix them together and reserve them in a warm place until ready to use or, if you prepare them in advance, cover and store them in the refrigerator. Reheat the cold mushrooms before adding to the risotto.

4   Bring the stock to a boil in a large pot and reduce to a simmer.

5   Heat a large heavy-bottomed saucepan over medium-high heat, add the butter and cook until it is lightly browned and bubbling. Add the diced onion and sauté them until they are translucent, about 4 minutes. Season them with 2 teaspoons of salt and a few grinds of black pepper.

3 pounds assorted wild mushrooms— hedgehogs, chanterelles, and porcini (see Headnote)—or 12 ounces dried wild mushrooms (see Note on page 22)

Extra virgin olive oil

2 large shallots, peeled, trimmed, and minced

1 large garlic clove, peeled, trimmed, and minced

1 tablespoon chopped fresh thyme leaves

Salt

Freshly ground black pepper

12 cups chicken stock

2 tablespoons unsalted butter

1 medium yellow onion, peeled, trimmed, and finely diced

4 cups Carnaroli or Arborio rice

1 cup dry white wine

¼ cup chopped Italian parsley

Grated Parmesan cheese for sprinkling

6   Add the rice and stir until it is thoroughly heated. Add the white wine and bring everything to a boil while stirring constantly. Stir until the wine is completely absorbed by the rice. Set the timer for 12 minutes.

7   Using a 6-ounce ladle, add the simmering stock to the rice one ladleful at a time; stir the rice constantly while adding the stock. Add more stock as the rice absorbs the liquid. When the timer goes off, stir in the warm mushroom ragout and continue cooking for 6 to 8 minutes, stirring constantly. I prefer my risotto with a little tooth so I cook it a little less. The grains should be silky and slide easily over one another when a spoon is drawn through. If this is not the case, add a little more stock to loosen them up. The rice should have enough liquid so that the texture is creamy. If the rice is not cooked enough the texture will be starchy and crunchy. If the rice is overcooked the grains will be bloated and stick together. Add more liquid until it reaches the texture you desire. Add the chopped Italian parsley immediately before serving.

8   Garnish with a little grated Parmesan cheese and serve with additional Parmesan cheese on the side. The rice should be served soon after it has finished cooking or it will continue to cook in its own heat and clump together.

NOTE: To use dried wild mushrooms, substitute 4 ounces of dried for each pound of fresh. To reconstitute, cover the mushrooms with a generous amount of boiling water and let them soak for 30 minutes. Be sure to lift them out of the water after they are rehydrated to prevent contamination by any dirt that has fallen to the bottom. The rehydrating juices may be strained through fine cheesecloth and reduced to ½ cup. Add the reduced juices to the chicken stock for extra flavor. Cut the rehydrated mushrooms in the same manner as the fresh mushrooms.

The mushroom ragout can be made a day or two ahead of time and reheated to add to the rice.

honey walnut cake

Alsatians are fiercely proud of their honey. It shows up in their cakes and pastries and gets drizzled on cheese. Nothing expresses a region's character more than a spoonful of wildflower honey. The flavor varies depending on what flowers are indigenous to the area. A hive full of bees did a lot of hard work only to have their cache robbed so every spoonful consumed should be appreciated. My Strasbourg-born grandmother would combine honey and walnuts in the fall to produce a cake similar to this one. It is delicate and moist with the scent of honey, orange peel, and walnuts. Serve it in wedges unadorned or with softly whipped cream.

SERVES 8 TO 10

1 Preheat the oven to 350 degrees F.

2 Butter and flour a 9-inch cake pan.

3 Spread the walnuts on a sheet pan and toast in the preheated oven for 6 minutes. Cool and rub the nuts in a towel to remove the loose skins.

4 Grind the nuts in a food processor with ½ cup of the flour until very fine. In a medium bowl, combine the ground nuts, remaining flour, baking powder, and salt. Reserve.

5 In a standing mixer with a paddle attachment or with an electric hand mixer, beat the butter with the honey and sugar until light and fluffy, about 3 minutes. Scrape down the sides of the bowl.

1½ cups walnut pieces

1 cup all-purpose flour

1½ teaspoons baking powder

¾ teaspoon salt

12 tablespoons (1½ sticks) unsalted butter, at room temperature

½ cup honey

¼ cup sugar

3 large eggs

1 teaspoon grated orange zest

½ teaspoon pure vanilla extract

10 nice walnut halves and 2 tablespoons honey for garnish

6   In a small bowl, beat the eggs lightly with the orange zest and vanilla. Add it in thirds to the butter mixture. Beat well to incorporate after each addition. Scrape down the sides of the bowl. Add the dry ingredients and mix until fully incorporated.

7   Spread the batter evenly in the prepared cake pan. Bake in the preheated oven for 35 to 40 minutes, until a toothpick inserted into the center comes out clean.

8   While the cake is baking toast the ten walnut halves on a sheet pan for 8 minutes. While they are still warm rub the nuts in a towel to remove the excess skin and place them in a small bowl. Add the 2 tablespoons of honey and stir until the walnuts are coated. Reserve the walnut halves at room temperature to garnish the cake when it is finished.

9   Cool the cake in the pan for 5 minutes and then turn out onto a cake rack to cool. Garnish the edge of the cake with the walnut halves.

Fall Menu III

prosciutto with figs and arugula   26

—

nana's tomato sauce with potato gnocchi   28

—

brandied pears   33

—

nut brittle   35

—

WINES: Enjoy the figs with a sweet Moscato d'Asti. The gnocchi call for a Chianti or American Zinfandel. Malmsey Madeira would suit the richness and flavors of the brandied pears and toasted nuts.

prosciutto with figs and arugula

Fall is the season for the second and lengthier outing of figs. They show themselves and tease us briefly in early summer. There are several varieties of figs. The dark-skinned and intense Black Missions, large amber-colored Calimyrna, and the firm-fleshed green Kadota are wonderful to eat out of hand. One of the most amazing dishes I have had the pleasure to consume was a plate of perfectly ripe, peeled Calimyrna figs with thinly shaved prosciutto. Both were perfect in texture and flavor, nothing else was needed on the plate. This dish takes that idea one step further by adding a little salad of simply dressed tender baby arugula and a drizzle of aged balsamic to the plate. A good aged balsamic, twenty years or more, is expensive but a little goes a long way (see Headnote, page 12). The flavor is really worth the expense and you will find many other things to drizzle it on. Gather a little of each ingredient on your fork to experience the full flavor spectrum.

There is a difference in the taste and texture of domestic and imported prosciutto. Prosciutto di Parma, from the Parma region of Italy, is considered to be one of the finest. Thinly sliced, prosciutto should be light, with a hint of salt that complements the sweetness and flavor of the pork. If it is sliced too thickly it can become chewy, but it should never be leathery or mushy.

SERVES 8

1   Trim the very tip of the stem off the fig. Peel the figs, if desired. Cut them almost all the way in half starting at the bottom of the fig. The fig will still be attached at the top. Set them aside until you are ready to plate the salad.

2   Wash the baby arugula and spin it dry. Toss the leaves with a little olive oil, salt, and black pepper.

3   Place the arugula in the center of the individual plates. Arrange three slices of prosciutto on each plate so that it lies in waves around the arugula. Fan the figs slightly and tuck them into the waves of prosciutto.

4   Drizzle the figs and the arugula with drops of aged balsamic vinegar. Sprinkle each fig with a few grains of salt. Grind a little black pepper over all and serve immediately.

24 soft ripe figs

½ pound baby arugula

Extra virgin olive oil

Salt, preferably Fleur de Sel (see Notes on page 49)

Freshly ground black pepper

24 thin slices of prosciutto di Parma

Good aged balsamic vinegar, twenty years or more

nana's tomato sauce with potato gnocchi

Two of my favorite comfort foods are combined in this dish. The rich tomato sauce gently baths the soft pillows of potato gnocchi. Each delicious bite will tantalize, gratify, and provide warmth from head to toe. Serve the sauce-covered gnocchi on a large platter, topped with a snow of finely grated Parmesan cheese and some good crusty bread.

SERVES 8

nana's tomato sauce

My great-grandmother Nana DiGregorio would make this sauce and can it over an outdoor wood-fired stove at her summerhouse in Rocky Point, New York. It was an end of summer ritual that would provide her with summer tomato sauce all winter. Use the last of your summer tomatoes for this sauce. If you have the wherewithal, make a ton of sauce and freeze it in small containers to last you through part of the winter, or if you have the time, can it so that you can store it on your shelf. It makes a great gift for family and close friends. Make sure you follow the guidelines of a good canning manual so that your efforts are preserved safely.

If you opt to use canned tomatoes for your sauce, look for a brand that contains only tomatoes and juice. There should be no salt or citric acid. If your canned tomatoes do have salt, adjust or omit the salt in this recipe until the final seasoning. Canned San Marzano plum tomatoes from Italy are famous for their flavor. They frequently come packed with the addition of basil leaves, which is fine for use in this recipe. It is far better to use good canned tomatoes than inferior fresh tomatoes.

YIELD: 4 QUARTS

1   Core the fresh tomatoes and make an "X" on the bottom with a sharp knife.

2   Bring a large pot of water to a boil. Add the tomatoes without crowding them. Boil them for 20 seconds, remove them from the water with a slotted spoon, and place in a bowl. Repeat with the remaining tomatoes. Let them cool until you are able to handle them.

3   Peel the tomatoes and divide them into two equal parts. Take the first part, cut the tomatoes in half, and squeeze out the seeds over a strainer and bowl to catch the juices. Chop the flesh coarsely. Pour the strained juice from the seeds over the chopped flesh and reserve. Puree the remaining tomatoes in a food processor or blender and strain out the seeds. Reserve together. Continue on to step 4 of the recipe.

8 pounds fresh Roma or plum tomatoes
    or 7 pounds canned tomatoes

6 large garlic cloves, peeled, trimmed,
    and minced

¼ cup extra virgin olive oil

3 medium yellow onions, peeled,
    trimmed, and finely chopped

1 cup red wine

2 tablespoons tomato paste

1 tablespoon toasted whole fennel seed

¼ cup chopped fresh oregano or
    1½ tablespoons dried

1 cup loosely packed Italian parsley leaves

1 bay leaf, fresh or dried

¼ teaspoon chile flakes

Salt

1 tablespoon sugar for canned tomatoes,
    if you are using them

Or, if you are using canned tomatoes:

1   Open the cans and drain the tomatoes into a strainer over a bowl to catch the juices.

2   Use your hands to remove most of the seeds and the hard tomato core over the strainer and bowl containing the juices.

3   Break the tomatoes into chunks with your hands or coarsely chop them with a knife and place them in a bowl. Pour the bowl of collected juices over the tomatoes. Reserve the tomatoes in the juice.

4   Heat a large stockpot over medium-high heat and lightly brown the garlic in ¼ cup of olive oil, about 2 to 3 minutes. Add the finely chopped onion and sauté it until it is lightly browned.

5   Add the red wine and reduce it until it is almost evaporated, about 5 minutes. Add the tomatoes, tomato paste, herbs, chile flakes, and 2 teaspoons of salt. Add the sugar if you are using canned tomatoes. Simmer over low heat for 1½ hours for canned tomatoes; add water if the sauce becomes too thick before the cooking time is up. Simmer up to 2 hours for fresh tomatoes until the sauce has thickened and flavors have developed. Season the sauce to taste with salt. Remove the bay leaf before serving.

6   Optional: If you prefer a smooth versus a chunky sauce, puree the sauce in a blender. Remove the bay leaf before pureeing. When you puree hot liquids, do not fill the blender more than two-thirds full or you risk having the contents explode. Allow the steam to escape by removing the center plug in the lid and covering the hole with a thick towel to protect your hand. Hold the lid down securely and lift the towel slightly to allow the pressurized air to escape as you blend.

NOTE: The sauce can be made in advance and stored for up to 1 week in the refrigerator or up to 6 months in the freezer.

potato gnocchi

Gnocchi are very versatile and can be served many ways (see Variations below) but my favorite way is napped in tomato sauce with a little grated Parmesan on top. It's comforting and simple.

SERVES 6 TO 8

1   Preheat the oven to 350 degrees F.

2   Wash the potatoes, prick them with a fork, and place them on a sheet pan. Bake them in the preheated oven for 1½ to 2 hours, until they are very soft. Resist roasting them at a higher temperature to speed the process. This will cause the

skin and flesh just inside the skin to become crusty. Cool them slightly and scoop out the insides. Rice the scooped-out potato with a ricer or mash them with a fork. Place them in a bowl and cover with a damp cloth to retain their heat. The potatoes must be used while they are still very warm.

3 pounds large baking potatoes

2 large eggs

1 large egg yolk

2 teaspoons salt

Freshly ground black pepper

A pinch of nutmeg

2 cups all-purpose flour

1 cup grated Parmesan cheese for garnish, optional

4   In a small bowl, beat the eggs and yolk lightly together. Add them to the potatoes along with 2 teaspoons of salt, a few grinds of freshly ground black pepper, the nutmeg, and flour. Mix gently with your hands until all the ingredients are well incorporated and the dough is smooth.

5   Turn the dough out onto a lightly floured flat surface. Knead lightly and add a little more flour if the dough is overly sticky. Let the dough rest for 10 minutes, uncovered.

6   Roll the dough into thin ½-inch logs and cut into ½-inch pieces. Using a generous amount of flour, press each piece against your thumb tip to make a hollow or roll it over the back and off the tip of a floured fork to make the traditional ridged shape. Place the finished gnocchi on a lightly floured sheet pan. Cook them as soon as possible in boiling salted water, 2 tablespoons of salt per 5 quarts of water.

7   Lower the gnocchi into the boiling water; when they rise to the top let them cook for a minute or two and then remove them with a slotted spoon. Drain well and toss with the tomato sauce and grated cheese.

NOTES: If the gnocchi are not to be cooked right away, they should be frozen. To cook the frozen gnocchi, throw them directly into the boiling salted water without thawing. Their cooking time will be slightly longer than unfrozen but their preparation should be completed in the same manner as with fresh unfrozen gnocchi.

The gnocchi can be made up to 2 weeks in advance and frozen on sheet pans. Once they are frozen solid they can be transferred to a Ziploc bag or wrapped tightly to avoid freezer burn. Do not thaw them before cooking or they will stick together.

VARIATIONS: The dough can be scented with chopped fresh rosemary or thyme (1 tablespoon of chopped herb per recipe).

Finely chopped Italian parsley (about ¼ cup) kneaded into the dough lends jewel-like emerald flecks to the cooked gnocchi.

The fresh uncooked gnocchi can be sautéed to a crisp golden brown in butter and used to accompany roasted meats.

Boiled gnocchi are fabulous tossed with butter and showered with fresh white truffle shavings.

For a homey spin, toss boiled gnocchi with butter and a little cream to moisten, top with grated Parmesan, and broil until the Parmesan is golden and the cream bubbles.

brandied pears

A dish's superlative taste does not often rival its incredible beauty. These opaque brandied pears glisten like golden jewels. The heat of the oven toasts the tops of the pears turning them into bronze-capped peaks. They're soft and juicy, redolent of brandy, caramel, and butter. The pears are quite easy to make, although they do need some attention during their baking time. The results are worth it. Serve the pears warm with Vanilla Ice Cream (page 289) and Nut Brittle (recipe follows) or on their own. They are fabulous either way.

Bosc pears are best for this recipe because of their size and texture. They tend to be firmer than most pears when ripe. Because of their size and anatomy their seeds sit lower in the core, which makes them easier to remove and prevents the entire pear from collapsing when roasted.

SERVES 8

1 Peel the pears and leave them whole, keeping the stem intact if possible. Core them from the bottom using a dual-sized melon baller or a ¼-teaspoon measuring spoon. First remove the bottom of the core with the small end of the baller, taking out the surface with about a quarter inch of flesh, then plunge the larger end of the melon baller into the same hole to remove the core and seeds. Slice the very bottoms off so the pears stand flat.

2 Preheat the oven to 400 degrees F.

3 Add the butter to a large sauté pan over medium-high heat. When the butter starts to brown, add the pears and sauté, turning them frequently, until they are golden all over, about 5 to 10 minutes. Adjust the heat if necessary.

4 Sprinkle the pears with the sugar and continue cooking, rolling the pears around, until sugar is caramelized and thick, about 5 to 10 minutes.

8 large Bosc pears, ripe but firm

4 tablespoons (½ stick) unsalted butter

1 cup sugar

1 cup brandy

5   Remove the pan from the heat and, away from the heat, add the brandy. Place the pan back on the heat and reduce the brandy, being careful as the liquid might flame up at any moment. When the brandy and caramelized sugar have reduced to a thick bubbly syrup, about 10 to 15 minutes, add 1 cup of very hot water and stand the pears upright in the pan.

6   Bring the liquid to a boil and place the pan in the preheated oven for 1 to 1½ hours, basting every 15 minutes until the pears are tender and caramelized and the liquid has reduced to a thick syrup. Add more water, ¼ cup at a time, if the liquid reduces too quickly.

7   Remove the pears from the oven and leave them in the pan. Cool the pears to warm, periodically basting them with the syrup. The pears can be cooled and rewarmed to serve.

8   To serve the warm pears, place one pear each on individual plates or in shallow bowls. Serve the pears alone with the syrup drizzled over or place one scoop of ice cream next to each pear, spoon the syrup over, and sprinkle with crushed Nut Brittle. Additional Nut Brittle can be served in a big bowl.

nut brittle

This Nut Brittle can be eaten out of hand as candy and makes a great gift when placed in an airtight tin and wrapped in ribbon. You can use one variety of nut or any combination of your favorites instead of the ones listed below. Use a candy thermometer for this recipe if you feel more comfortable or until you get the hang of caramelizing the sugar. Be sure to use very clean cane sugar, a newly opened bag that hasn't been contaminated by flour or dust. Always have a bowl of ice water next to the stove in case any hot sugar splatters on your skin. If this happens plunge the affected area into the ice water immediately and not in your mouth or that will burn as well. Keep all unnecessary people, especially children, out of the kitchen when you prepare the nut brittle as it requires complete focus. Boil water in the caramel pan until the residual caramel has melted for easy clean up.

MAKES 6 CUPS

1   Preheat the oven to 350 degrees F. Line a sheet pan with parchment paper.

2   To remove the hazelnut skins, toast the hazelnuts on a sheet pan for 12 minutes in the preheated oven. Cool and rub the nuts between your hands to remove most of the skins. Crush the hazelnuts lightly and mix with the remaining nuts. It is not necessary to toast or remove the skin of the other nuts. The hot caramel will toast them thoroughly.

½ cup hazelnuts

1 cup slivered almonds

½ cup pine nuts

½ cup pecans

3 cups sugar

12 tablespoons (1½ sticks) unsalted butter

1 teaspoon salt

¼ teaspoon baking soda

3   Pour the sugar into a heavy-bottomed saucepan and stir with a wooden spoon over high heat until sugar begins to melt. Lower the heat slightly and continue stirring until sugar is completely melted and is a dark caramel (295 degrees F) in color. Quickly mix in the nuts and then the butter, salt, and baking soda. The baking soda adds flavor and an airy crunch to the brittle. Stir well to incorporate thoroughly.

4   Turn the brittle out onto the prepared sheet pan. Spread the brittle with the back of a wooden spoon into a thin sheet or pull it even thinner with your hands if you have a brand-new pair of rubber dish gloves. Spread the brittle as thin as you can with the wooden spoon, then lift it with your gloved hands and pull into thin sheets quickly. Have another parchment paper–lined sheet pan nearby on which to lay the pulled brittle. Break the brittle into pieces when cooled and store in an airtight container for up to a week. Crush 2 cups rather finely to serve with the pears.

Fall Menu IV

tart flambé   38

roasted duck breast with quince compote   40

spiced pumpkin custard   44

WINES: The flambé will pair classically with a dry Alsatian Pinot Blanc or Riesling. The sweetness and spice of the duck make it a match for an refreshingly sweet Alsatian Gewürztraminer Vendange Tardive. You can carry the Gewürztraminer on through dessert.

tart flambé

My good friend Emile Jung, the chef and owner of the three-star restaurant Au Crocodile in Strasbourg, introduced me to this Alsatian soul food at a local *winstub*. He was a kind and generous man who made me fall in love again with the cooking of my Alsatian grandmother. I worked with him for a few months and learned a tremendous amount about Alsatian wine and food. Their beautiful food-friendly wines pair perfectly with their regional dishes such as this Tart Flambé, made all the more special by the yeasted tart dough. I like to serve one of these thin, crisp tarts per person. For smaller appetites divide the recipe in half and have two people share one.

MAKES 8 VERY THIN AND CRISP 8-INCH TARTS

1   To prepare the tart dough, whisk together 8 ounces of warm water and the yeast in a small bowl.

2   Combine the flour and salt in a large bowl.

3   Add the yeast mixture to the flour mixture. Mix together until combined—the dough will look dry; add the butter. Knead to a smooth and elastic dough and let rise, covered, for 1 hour until doubled.

4   While the dough is rising, peel, halve, and thinly slice the onion lengthwise so that you have very thin wedges. Reserve in a bowl.

5   Julienne the ham into thin ¼-inch-wide strips. Reserve.

Yeasted Tart Dough

1 tablespoon dry yeast

3½ cups all-purpose flour

2 teaspoons salt

4 tablespoons (½ stick) unsalted butter, softened

Topping

1 large red onion

1 pound thinly sliced applewood-smoked ham or German Speck

2 large eggs

2 cups Crème Fraîche (recipe follows)

Salt

Freshly ground black pepper

½ cup finely ground cornmeal for sprinkling on the sheet pans

¼ cup chopped chives

6　In a small bowl, beat the eggs well and fold in the Crème Fraîche; season with salt and pepper to taste.

7　After the dough has risen, preheat the oven to 500 degrees F. Lightly sprinkle two or three sheet pans with cornmeal.

8　Divide the dough into eight equal pieces (2 ounces each). Roll each round of dough as thinly as possible and place them on the sheet pans. Let them rise covered with a cloth for 10 minutes, then prick them well with a fork.

9　Use the back of a spoon to spread ¼ cup of the Crème Fraîche mixture on each circle, leaving a ¼-inch border. Sprinkle each tart liberally with the onions and ham, dividing them equally among the tarts; season with salt and pepper.

10　Bake in the preheated oven until the crust turns golden and the Crème Fraîche is set, about 10 minutes. Garnish with the chopped chives.

crème fraîche

Substitute this delicious homemade Crème Fraîche for the more expensive commercial variety.

MAKES 2 CUPS

1　Combine the cream and buttermilk in a very clean glass container.

2　Cover with cheesecloth secured by a rubber band or a piece of plastic wrap that has been perforated with a toothpick twenty times or more.

3　Let the mixture sit at room temperature overnight or for up to 2 days. If you prefer a mild Crème Fraîche with just a bit of tang, stop the culture by refrigerating the Crème Fraîche after one night. If you prefer more tang, let the cream sit for one more night. Transfer to an airtight container and refrigerate.

2 cups heavy cream

4 tablespoons cultured buttermilk

roasted duck breast
with quince compote

This dish has few components. But the components it has are a delicious marriage. Try to secure the magret of Muscovy duck though your butcher or mail order. *Magret* is the name given to a breast taken from a duck that has been fattened for foie gras. It is rich in flavor and steaklike in texture. The large breast size (1 pound per breast piece) is equal in proportion to the exaggerated size of the fattened duck liver. Smaller duck breasts such as the Pekin or regular Muscovy can be substituted but the meat is not as dark or rich so the contrast with the Quince Compote is not the same. If you cannot locate quince, substitute apples or pears for an equally satisfying compote. Serve the duck and compote accompanied by wild rice or simple sautéed spinach to capture the juices.

SERVES 8

1   Clean the duck breasts of any excess fat and silver skin—the silvery-looking fan of nerves on the underside of the breast. Remove the tenders from the breasts. The tender is a strip of meat with a silver stripe of tendon that can be easily pulled away from the underside of the breast with your fingers. Sauté them separately for a snack while you are preparing dinner. Trim the edges of any overhanging skin and tidy them up. Score the skin almost to but not into the breast meat in a crisscross diamond pattern. This will help render the fat and crisp the skin. Reserve the breasts well wrapped in the refrigerator until you are ready to cook them. Have the quince compote prepared before you cook the duck.

2   To cook the breasts, preheat the oven to 400 degrees F. Warm the compote in the oven, if necessary, while the breasts are cooking and resting.

3   Heat a large sauté pan over medium heat so that the pan is warm but not too hot. The duck should sizzle when it is placed in the pan but not smoke. Season the duck breasts with salt and pepper. Place them skin side down in the pan and begin rendering off the fat. Be sure that the fat in the pan doesn't smoke. Reduce the heat if necessary. As the pan fills with fat, carefully pour it off into a heatproof

container so that the breasts do not deep fry in their fat (see Notes below). Hold the breasts in place with a carving fork or metal spatula. Keep rendering the skin side until no more fat is released and the skin is crisp, about 15 to 20 minutes.

4 magrets of Muscovy duck
(4 pounds total) (see Notes below)

Quince Compote (recipe follows)

Salt

Freshly ground black pepper

4   Turn the breast over and place the pan in the preheated oven to roast for 5 minutes for medium rare, more if you like your breast less rare. Remove the breasts from the pan and let them rest for 10 minutes before slicing to allow the juices to distribute evenly throughout the breast.

5   To serve, slice the breast starting at the small pointed end. Slice the meat at a 45-degree angle thinly across the grain. If you see long striations of muscle in the slice cut it the opposite way, or taste a piece. It should be tender not chewy. If it's too chewy, slice it at the opposite angle. Serve the sliced duck with the Quince Compote on the side. Drizzle the compote juices over the duck.

NOTES: Clean the duck breasts up to 2 days in advance. Wrap well and store in the refrigerator. The Quince Compote can be prepared 1 day in advance and stored in a tightly sealed container in the refrigerator. Reheat in the oven while the duck breasts are cooking.

The rendered duck fat can be strained and stored in an airtight container in the refrigerator for 1 month or frozen for 6 months. Use it in place of butter or oil to sauté potatoes for extra flavor.

quince compote

Quince is a very odd fruit. It has the incredible heady smell of pineapple, apple, pear, and vanilla, but biting into this fragrant fruit will have you quickly spitting it out. The raw flesh is tannic and hard. In order to be eaten with enjoyment, it must be cooked. Quince is magical in that when it is poached or simmered into marmalade it turns a beautiful deep pinkish red. It dons this color to a lesser degree when sautéed.

The flavor principles of this compote are based on the classic French *gastrique* sauce. *Gastrique* sauces have the yin-yang of sweetness and acidity and are used in conjunction with fruit. If not enough vinegar is used to balance the sugar, the effect can be cloying rather than seductive. Think of the classic duck à l'orange. Taste your compote to make sure that the sweetness and acidity are balanced. If the compote needs more sugar or vinegar, add it until you achieve the right balance.

SERVES 8

1   Peel and halve the quinces. Quinces are very hard so you will need a sharp peeler or a small sharp thin-bladed knife to do this. Scoop out the seeds with a melon baller. Remove both ends of the core with a sharp knife.

2   Preheat the oven to 400 degrees F.

3   Heat the butter in a large sauté pan over medium-high heat until it begins to turn brown and then add the quince halves. Sauté them until they are golden on all sides, about 10 minutes; season with salt and pepper.

4 medium quinces (1½ pounds)

2 tablespoons unsalted butter

Salt

½ cup sugar

½ cup cider vinegar

Two 3-inch strips orange peel

6 whole cloves

One 3-inch cinnamon stick

¼ teaspoon coarsely crushed black peppercorns

6 cups chicken or duck stock

4   Add the sugar to the quinces and cook until the sugar is bubbly, thick, and caramelized to a golden brown, about 5 to 10 minutes. Adjust the heat if necessary. Add the cider vinegar, orange peel, and spices and reduce until the mixture bubbles thickly, about 10 to 15 minutes. Add the stock to the pan and bring it to a boil.

5   Remove the pan from the heat and place it in the preheated oven. Roast the quinces until they are meltingly tender and the juices are reduced and viscous, about 1 hour. Remove from the oven and check the seasoning; season to taste with salt. The cracked black pepper added at the beginning should be enough pepper for the dish. Cover the quinces to keep warm. Remove the whole spices and orange peel before serving.

spiced pumpkin custard

Warm thoughts of pumpkin and cinnamon-scented custard draw you to this dish. It's like eating a very light pumpkin pie without the crust. Serve it with soft whipped cream on top or turn the custard out of the dish and serve with a drizzle of Caramel Sauce (recipe follows). Freshly roasted pumpkin puree is wonderfully light and delicate in flavor. Canned pumpkin is a little more intense and sweeter. If you choose to use canned pumpkin, be sure to buy the solid pack pumpkin without any added spices or other ingredients.

SERVES 8

1   Place eight 6-ounce ramekins in a deep roasting pan. Reserve.

2   Preheat the oven to 350 degrees F. Place an oven rack on the lowest rungs.

3   Whisk together the eggs, salt, and brown sugar in a large bowl.

4   In a large saucepan, bring the cream and milk to a boil with the cinnamon, cloves, and ¼ teaspoon grated nutmeg. Remove it from the heat and pour it over the egg mixture in thirds, while whisking constantly.

5   Fold the pumpkin puree into the egg-cream mixture. Mix until smooth.

6   Strain the custard into a large pitcher. Ladle or pour the custard slowly into the ramekins, filling them ¼ inch from the top. Grate a little fresh nutmeg over the top of each custard.

5 large whole eggs

Pinch of salt

¾ cup brown sugar

1½ cups heavy cream

1½ cups whole milk

½ teaspoon ground cinnamon

⅛ teaspoon ground cloves

¼ teaspoon grated nutmeg plus more for topping

1 cup Fresh Pumpkin Puree (recipe follows) or equal amount canned solid pack

½ cup heavy cream, whipped to soft peaks

7   Pour enough hot, not boiling, water into the roasting pan to come three-fourths of the way up the sides of the ramekins. Cover the ramekins with a piece of parchment paper. Bake the custards on the low oven rack in the preheated oven until set, 30 to 40 minutes. To test to see if the custards are done, jiggle one gently with your hand. They are done if the custard is set in all but the very center, a circle about the size of a dime. Carefully remove the ramekins from the water bath. Cool the custards before placing them in the refrigerator, uncovered, until they are completely cold. Then cover tightly with plastic wrap. Serve with soft whipped cream sprinkled with a little freshly grated nutmeg.

VARIATION: If you would like to serve the custards turned out of their baking dishes, run a hot wet knife around the edge of the custard, turn it upside down over a plate, and tap the edge of the baking dish at an angle until the custard falls out. Garnish with softly whipped cream and Caramel Sauce (recipe follows).

fresh pumpkin puree

MAKES 2 TO 2 ½ CUPS

1   Preheat the oven to 400 degrees F.

One 2-pound sugar pie pumpkin or other small pumpkin (see Note below)

2   Place the pumpkin on a sheet pan and prick it all over with a knife. Roast in the preheated oven until soft, about 1 hour. Cool.

3   Cut the pumpkin in half. Scoop out the seeds with a spoon and peel off the skin with a paring knife. Puree the pumpkin flesh in a food processor until smooth. Do not add liquid to puree the pumpkin, you want the flesh as dry as possible.

NOTE: Extra puree can be tightly sealed in a plastic container and frozen for up to a month.

caramel sauce

The sugar, the pan, and all of the utensils you use for this sauce should be sparklingly clean. Open a new bag of sugar to ensure there is no debris such as flour in it. Dirt of any kind can cause the sugar to crystallize and ruin the sauce. Keep a bowl of ice water next to you at all times in case you get hot caramel on you by accident.

MAKES 2 CUPS

1   Bring the cream to a boil in a small saucepan and turn off the heat.

1 cup sugar

1½ cup heavy cream

2   Pour the sugar into a heavy bottomed saucepan. Stir the sugar constantly over high heat until it begins to melt and form lumps. Crush the large lumps with the edge of your spoon. Keep heating until the lumps have melted and the sugar is dark gold in color.

3   Remove the pan from the heat and slowly pour the hot cream into the sugar a little at a time to prevent the sugar from hardening into solid lumps. Continue to stir as you add the cream. After all the cream has been added stir until the sauce is smooth and bring to a simmer. Remove from the heat and strain into a storage container. Store at room temperature overnight or in the refrigerator for up to two weeks. Rewarm to sauce consistency before serving.

Fall Menu V

frisée salad with a poached egg, lardons,
and dijon vinaigrette   48

—

pumpkin tortellini with sage brown butter   5I

—

heirloom apple pie   54

—

WINES: Salads are difficult for wines. If you would like to serve a wine with the salad, try a fruity Beaujolais. The pumpkin tortellini, scented with earthy sage and nutty brown butter, call for a Barbera d'Alba or Chianti. The pie does well with a sweet but crisp Coteaux du Layon or New Zealand late harvest Chenin Blanc.

frisée salad with a poached egg, lardons, and dijon vinaigrette

French bistros embrace this common peasant salad in its many forms by listing it simply as a Salade Frisée aux Lardons. Be forewarned, not all of these salads are the same, although the ingredients are similar. The best one I ever had, hands down, was at the Chat Noir *winstub* in Strasbourg. The sweet and crunchy frisée had just enough tangy shallot-perfumed vinaigrette clinging to its curls, the fat pieces of lardons were crunchy on the outside and tender-chewy at their centers. The egg, bursting with laid-that-morning flavor and texture, was poached to a perfect softness. I punched the yolk with my fork and sighed as the rich yolk melted into the tangled, pale green web. After the first bite I was silenced until the last. I shared with no one at the table, as they all looked on with envy. That was the best; the one below follows closely.

SERVES 8

1   Clean the tough green ends off the greens and any tough outer leaves. Trim off the root end. Wash and spin dry. Tear the leaves into fork-sized pieces. Wrap the lettuce in a large kitchen towel and shake well to remove any clinging drops of water. Do it in batches to match the size of your towel. Transfer the lettuce to a towel-lined bowl and lightly cover the greens with another towel. Refrigerate until ready to use.

2   Unroll the pancetta and slice it ½ inch thick. Cut the slices into ¼-inch pieces. Place them in a pot of cold water and bring to a boil. Drain the water from the pancetta and let the pancetta drip dry in a strainer.

3   Place the well-drained pancetta in a pan over medium heat and slowly render the fat from it until the pieces are almost crisp but retain some chew. The pancetta has now become lardons. Reserve them in a warm place near the stove or reheat them briefly before using.

4 Bring 3 quarts of water to a boil. Add 2 tablespoons of white wine vinegar and 1 tablespoon of salt.

5 Toss the frisée lightly with the Dijon Vinaigrette, season with salt and pepper. Add the crisped lardons and parsley leaves and toss again. Divide the salad among eight plates.

6 One at a time, working quickly, crack an egg into a small bowl and slide it into the water. Allow the water to simmer but do not let it boil. Adjust the heat if necessary. Poach the eggs for 3 to 4 minutes (see Note below) and then remove them gently with a slotted spoon.

7 Drain the eggs on a paper towel one at a time. Place one egg on top of each salad.

8 Grind black pepper on top of the egg and sprinkle with a little bit of Fleur de Sel. Serve with good crusty bread.

1½ pounds frisée, chicory, or escarole

1 pound pancetta

2 tablespoons white wine vinegar

Salt

Dijon Vinaigrette (recipe follows)

Freshly ground black pepper

½ cup Italian parsley leaves

8 large farm-fresh organic eggs

Fleur de Sel (see Notes below)

NOTES: Fleur de Sel, or "flower of the sea" in English, is a natural unrefined sea salt from the Brittany region of France. It is the purest of all sea salts and tastes the least salty. Its flaky, delicate, sometimes moist, crystals taste of the sea and contain traces of many minerals. Use it to finish dishes at the last moment before serving to retain its delicate crunch.

Eggs should be cooked well done for people whose health might be seriously compromised by salmonella. These people include young children, the elderly, and those with weakened immune systems.

dijon vinaigrette

The Dijon mustard exported to the United States is not as hot as its French counterpart. The real stuff will make your eyes water and your nose tingle and in some cases cause shortness of breath. The best way to ensure that you always have the genuine product on hand is to stuff a few large jars into your suitcase before leaving France. It is important not to add too much oil to the dressing. This will take away the punch of the vinegar and mustard and make your salad taste flat. Err on the more acidic side when adding the oil. The yolk from the egg as it drips through the lettuce will mellow the vinaigrette.

MAKES 1 CUP

1   Whisk together the mustard, shallots, and white wine vinegar in a large bowl. Season the mixture with 1 teaspoon of salt and a couple of grinds of black pepper. Let the mixture marinate for 10 minutes.

2   Whisk in the olive oil to the desired amount of tanginess. Check the seasoning and adjust with salt and black pepper to taste.

2 tablespoons Dijon mustard, the hotter the better

2 medium shallots, peeled, trimmed, and minced

¼ cup white wine vinegar

Salt

Freshly ground black pepper

½ to ¾ cup extra virgin olive oil

pumpkin tortellini with sage brown butter

I have designated the sugar pie pumpkin as the pumpkin of choice for this recipe. The small sugar pie pumpkin has been bred specifically for use in pie making, hence its name. Another type of pumpkin, butternut squash, or baked mashed sweet potatoes may be substituted. A 2-pound pumpkin yields about 2½ cups of puree. The extra puree can be tightly sealed and frozen for up to a month. If you use canned pumpkin, buy the solid pack without anything added. Canned pumpkin is usually much sweeter and thicker than fresh pumpkin.

These tortellini can be filled and shaped up to a week in advance. Freeze them on a sheet pan. Once they're frozen they can be placed in a Ziploc bag and stored in the freezer until ready to use. Place the frozen tortellini directly into a pot of boiling water—do not defrost. Cook a few minutes longer than fresh.

SERVES 8

1   For the pasta dough, mix the flour, semolina, and salt together in a mixing bowl. Whisk the eggs and the olive oil together in a separate bowl.

2   Make a well in the flour and add the egg mixture. Mix until combined. If the dough is too dry add a few drops of water. Knead until the dough is smooth and elastic. Turn out onto

Pasta Dough

2 cups all-purpose flour

1½ cups semolina

2 teaspoons salt

5 large eggs

1 tablespoon extra virgin olive oil

Pumpkin Filling

2 cups pumpkin puree (one 2-pound sugar pie pumpkin or one 15-ounce can solid pack pumpkin)

2 teaspoons chopped fresh thyme

2 teaspoons chopped fresh sage

½ cup grated Italian Fontina

½ cup mascarpone

4 tablespoons brown sugar

Salt

Freshly ground black pepper

Sage Brown Butter

16 tablespoons (2 sticks) unsalted butter

64 medium sage leaves

Salt

a wooden board and knead a few times. Cut it into two equal pieces and let the dough rest wrapped in plastic at room temperature for 1 hour or in the refrigerator overnight. Bring the dough to room temperature before rolling out.

3   For the pumpkin filling, preheat the oven to 400 degrees F. Skip to step 6 if you are using canned pumpkin.

4   Prick the pumpkin all over with a knife and place it on a sheet pan. Roast the pumpkin until soft, about 1 hour.

5   Cool the pumpkin and cut it in half. Scoop out the seeds with a spoon and peel off the skin with a paring knife. Puree the pumpkin flesh in a food processor until smooth. Do not add liquid to puree the pumpkin, you want it as dry as possible.

6   Place 2 cups of the pumpkin puree in a bowl. Add the remaining filling ingredients and mix thoroughly. Season the mixture with salt and pepper to taste. Refrigerate in a tightly sealed container until you are ready to use it, up to 2 days in advance.

7   To roll the pasta dough with a machine (for hand rolling see Note below), flatten the dough as much as possible with a rolling pin before kneading in the machine. Knead the dough by passing it through a pasta machine three times on the widest setting (see Headnote, page 118). Fold the dough in half lengthwise each time it is passed through the machine. Let the dough rest covered with plastic wrap for 10 minutes after its initial kneading. Divide the dough into three equal pieces.

8   Roll each piece of the pasta dough to the second thinnest setting on the pasta machine. Dust the dough lightly with flour as needed.

9   Lay the rolled pasta out on a counter that has been lightly dusted with flour. Cut out circles with a 2¾-inch round cutter.

10   Place ½ teaspoon of the pumpkin filling in the center of each pasta circle. Using your finger, dampen half of the edge of the circle with a small amount of cold water. Fold the dough over and press the two pieces of pasta together to seal, starting from the folded edge. Push out any air bubbles as you go so that the

filling sits firmly between the two sheets of pasta. Dampen one point of the folded edge and bring the other point over, press together.

11   Place the tortellini on a sheet pan that has been dusted with flour or semolina. Cover them with a dry towel until you are ready to cook them.

12   Preheat the oven to 250 degrees F.

13   Bring a large pot of lightly salted water to a boil, using 2 tablespoons of salt to 5 quarts of water. Add half the tortellini to the pot. Do not allow the tortellini to boil or they might burst. Keep the water at a steady simmer. Reduce the heat if necessary. After the tortellini rise to the top continue cooking them for 1 or 2 more minutes.

14   Remove the tortellini from the water with a slotted spoon and place them on a sheet pan drizzled with olive oil. Cover the pan with foil to keep the heat of the tortellini contained. Cook the remaining tortellini in the same manner and add them to the sheet pan. Place them in the preheated oven to keep warm while you prepare the Sage Brown Butter.

15   To make the sauce, melt the butter in a heavy saucepan over medium heat.

16   Add the sage leaves and cook until the butter turns light brown and begins to foam, 2 to 3 minutes. Shake and stir the sage leaves so that they cook evenly. The sage leaves should be crisp.

17   Remove the sage-scented butter from the heat and immediately sprinkle with a little salt. Drizzle the hot butter over the pasta, making sure that everyone gets equal amounts of the crisp sage leaves.

NOTE: To roll the dough by hand, lightly flour a large flat surface. Roll the dough ¼ inch thick with a lightly floured rolling pin. Fold the dough in half and repeat twice. Let the dough rest covered with plastic wrap for 10 minutes.

   Unwrap the dough and cut it into three equal pieces. Lightly flour your work surface and roll the dough to the thickness of thin cardboard with a lightly floured rolling pin. Proceed with step 9 of the recipe.

heirloom apple pie

Using heirloom apples is like taking a step back in history. They have wonderful names like D'Arcy Spice, Ashmead's Kernel, Seek-No-Further, Summer Rambo, and Wealthy. Heirloom apples are best right off the tree, so enjoy them throughout the fall and early winter. Bid them adieu when winter envelopes us and turn to the hard, hearty, and tart varieties to tide you through until spring.

SERVES 8 TO 12; MAKES ONE 10-INCH DEEP-DISH PIE

1   To make the pie crust, combine the flour and the salt in a mixing bowl.

2   Add the butter and mix with a paddle in a standing mixer or by hand with a pastry cutter until the mixture is the size of small peas.

3   Add the water gradually and mix until the dough starts to come together. Add only enough water to bring the dough together. The dough should be moist but it will not be completely uniform and its texture will be slightly crumbly.

4   Turn the dough out onto a lightly floured surface. Press it together gently to form a flat 1-inch-thick patty and wrap it tightly with wax paper or plastic wrap. Let it rest in the refrigerator for at least 30 minutes before rolling to firm up the butter and allow the dough to relax. The dough can be made ahead and frozen for up to 3 months well wrapped. Thaw in the refrigerator before rolling out.

5   For the filling: Peel and halve the apples. Core the halves with a melon baller and remove the rest of the core at either end with a sharp knife. Cut the apple halves into quarters and slice them thinly.

6   In a large bowl, mix all of the filling ingredients together.

7   Place the oven rack on the lowest rung and preheat the oven to 400 degrees F.

8   Roll half of the pâte brisée into a large circle ⅛ inch thick. Roll the circle large enough to allow the dough to hang over the edge of a 10-inch deep-dish pie plate by 2 inches. Turn the pie plate over and place it on top of the rolled dough to measure. Line the pie plate with the rolled dough. Press it securely against the pie plate before filling.

9   Pile the apple mixture into the pie plate. The apples will be piled very high; as they cook they'll lose half their volume.

10   Roll the second piece of dough ⅛ inch thick, 2 inches larger than the diameter of the pie dish.

11   Dampen the exposed edges of the pie dough around the edge of the pie plate with a little cold water. You can use a pastry brush or your finger. Cover the pile of apples with the second circle of brisée dough.

12   Press the top crust against the lower crust to seal the edges and trim them to 1 inch from the edge of the pie plate. Fold the sealed dough under so that the folded edge is even with the outside edge of the pie plate. Use a fork or your fingers to crimp the edge of the dough. Brush the entire crust with the whole milk and make a slit in the center to allow the steam to escape.

13   Bake on the lower rack of the preheated oven for 10 minutes.

14   Lower the oven heat to 350 degrees F. Place a piece of aluminum foil on the floor of your oven, taking care not to cover any vents. The foil will catch any juices that bubble over. Continue baking the pie for another 1½ hours. The crust should be golden and the apples should be very tender when poked with a knife through the slit in the top of the crust. Allow the pie to cool before serving.

VARIATION: Prepare the filling with half apples and half pears—1 pear equals 1 apple.

Pâte Brisée

2½ cups all-purpose flour

1½ teaspoons salt

20 tablespoons (2½ sticks) unsalted butter, cubed and chilled

4 to 6 tablespoons ice water

Filling

8 heirloom apples (3 pounds)

¾ cup sugar

2 tablespoons all-purpose flour

2 teaspoons ground cinnamon

1 teaspoon pure vanilla extract

1 tablespoon lemon juice

2 tablespoons whole milk

Fall Menu VI

roasted tomatoes with pecorino toscano and olives   58

fried cod   60

lemon risotto   62

orange-laced buckwheat crepes   63

WINES: Pair the tomatoes with a crisp Sauvignon Blanc or simple fruity Chianti. The cod calls for a white Bordeaux or Chablis. The orange scent and nuttiness of the buckwheat crepes would strike a balance with a Malmsey Madeira.

roasted tomatoes with pecorino toscano and olives

The last of the tomatoes in the garden hang lonely on the vine. This dish was created just for them. Slow roasting the tomatoes concentrates their sweetness and perfumes them with herbs and olives. The pits are left in the olives so warn your guests, or, if you have the time, remove them. You can use any variety of olives you like. The black buttery Niçoises are a nice contrast to the green, nutty pickled Picholines. Pecorino Toscano is a soft Italian sheep's milk table cheese. It is not hard like a Pecorino Romano. If you can't find the Toscano you can substitute an Italian Fontina or fresh mozzarella. Use a rustic crusty bread to soak up the juices.

SERVES 8

1   Bring a large pot of water to a boil. Fill a large bowl with ice water. Core the tomatoes and make an X in the bottom. Dip them into the boiling water for 30 seconds (or a little longer for less ripe tomatoes). Remove with a slotted spoon and plunge them into the ice water to cool. Slip the skins off and leave the tomatoes whole.

2   Preheat the oven to 350 degrees F.

3   Place the peeled tomatoes in an ovenproof dish. Push a garlic clove into the core indentation of each tomato top.

4   Drizzle the tomatoes with 1 cup of extra virgin olive oil, season well with coarse salt and black pepper, then sprinkle the sugar evenly over all.

5   Add the olives and bay leaves to the pan. Lay the thyme sprigs over the tops of the tomatoes.

6   Place the pan in the preheated oven and roast the tomatoes for 1½ hours until the tops are lightly caramelized and slightly puckered.

7   Bring the cheese to room temperature while the tomatoes are roasting.

8   Remove the bay leaves and the thyme sprigs from the tomatoes before serving.

9   Place one or two tomatoes, depending on their size, in individual bowls. Divide the cubed Pecorino among the dishes. Spoon the hot pan juices and olives over the tomatoes and cheese. The cheese will melt into soft little pillows. Serve with thick slices of grilled or toasted bread.

8 large tomatoes or 16 small

8 to 16 garlic cloves, peeled, trimmed, and left whole, 1 for each tomato

1 cup extra virgin olive oil

Coarse sea salt

Freshly ground black pepper

2 teaspoons sugar

1 cup Niçoise olives

1 cup Picholine olives

4 bay leaves, fresh or dried

12 fresh thyme sprigs

½ pound Pecorino Toscano cheese, cut into ¼-inch cubes

8 thick slices of bread, grilled or toasted with extra virgin olive oil

fried cod

Cod has never been a rarefied fish. Years ago, before it became fashionable, I had cod on the menu at PlumpJack Café in San Francisco. Diners turned their noses up at it. If I substituted halibut or salmon for cod, with the same preparation, it sold like hotcakes. I thought that maybe on the West Coast cod was out of place; years later I was proved wrong. Cod may not have a fancy name but you'd be hard-pressed to find another fish with the same huge sweet tender snowy white flakes. Serve the cod with the accompanying risotto recipe: the crunchiness of the bread crumb crust, the steaming tender flakes of fish, the creaminess of the rice, and the snap of acid from the lemon all come together to make the pairing a gustatory delight, a study in contrasts. If you have the urge for fish and chips, pair this cod with crispy fries and you'll be in fried-food heaven.

SERVES 8

1   Whisk the egg whites with 1 teaspoon of salt and a grind of black pepper in a shallow bowl or pan.

2   Place the bread crumbs and chopped parsley in a shallow bowl or pan and season with the remaining 2 teaspoons of salt and a few grinds of black pepper.

3   Preheat the oven to 250 degrees F.

4   Pat the fillets dry with a paper towel to remove any juices. Remove any bones with a sharp knife or pliers.

5   Dip the cod in the egg whites, and then roll them in the bread crumbs. Place them on a cake rack. The fish may be held in the refrigerator at this point, unwrapped, for a few hours before frying. (Prepare the risotto at this step before frying the fish if you will be using it as an accompaniment.)

6   Heat a heavy-bottomed sauté pan over medium-high heat and add ½ inch of olive oil. To test to see if the oil is hot enough to fry, dip the edge of a piece of breaded fish into the oil. If the oil sizzles immediately and vigorously, it is ready. Carefully add the breaded fillets to the pan so as not to splash the hot oil, taking care not to crowd them.

7   Fry the fillets until they are golden on both sides. Add more oil to the pan if necessary after the first batch is fried. Heat the oil for a few minutes and then retest the temperature to make sure it is hot enough to fry before adding more fish. Drain the fried fish on a cake rack to retain their crispiness and keep them warm in the preheated oven until all of the fish is fried.

8   Serve two pieces of fish per person with the accompaniments of your choice.

NOTE: At this writing net-caught Atlantic cod is an endangered fish. Choose line-caught Atlantic cod or substitute Pacific cod or Alaskan halibut. Halibut won't have the same moist succulent flakes but it will still be tasty, especially if you can find halibut cheeks.

4 large egg whites

3 teaspoons salt

Freshly ground black pepper

3 cups fine dry bread crumbs

2 tablespoons chopped Italian parsley, plus whole leaves for garnish

Eight 6-ounce cod fillets, cut in half (see Note below)

Extra virgin olive oil for frying

lemon risotto

Serve this risotto on its own as an appetizer or light entree.

SERVES 8

1 Bring the stock to a boil in a saucepan and reduce the heat to a simmer.

2 Peel, trim, and dice the onion finely while the stock is warming.

3 Melt the butter in a heavy-bottomed stockpot; when it turns golden, add the onion and sauté it, about 4 minutes. Season with salt and pepper.

4 Add the rice to the pot and sauté it until it is hot. Add the white wine, bring to a boil quickly, and stir briskly until the wine is absorbed.

6 cups aromatic vegetable stock or chicken stock

1 medium yellow onion

2 tablespoons unsalted butter

Salt

Freshly ground black pepper

2 cups Carnaroli or Arborio rice (see Headnote, page 20)

1 cup white wine

½ lemon, juice and grated zest

3 tablespoons chopped Italian parsley leaves

5 Start adding the simmering stock one ladleful at a time. Wait until the rice absorbs the stock before adding more. Continue to cook, adding the stock and stirring the rice constantly, for 16 minutes, to prevent it from sticking on the bottom of the pan.

6 Add the lemon juice and zest, cook for another 2 to 4 minutes until the rice is tender but not mushy. The rice should be creamy with the individual grains holding their shape. I prefer my risotto with a bit of tooth so I cook it a little less. The grains should be silky and slide easily over one another when a spoon is drawn through. If this is not the case, add a little more stock to loosen the rice grains. The rice should have enough liquid so that the texture is creamy but not soupy. If the rice is not cooked enough the texture will be starchy and crunchy. If the rice is overcooked the grains will be bloated and stick together. Add enough liquid and cook the rice long enough to reach the texture you desire.

7 Season the risotto with salt and pepper to taste and then fold in the parsley. Cover the risotto to keep warm while you quickly fry the fish. If the risotto stiffens thin it with a little hot stock.

orange-laced buckwheat crepes

When I was young, my father would make crepes for the family on many a Sunday morning. We would fight over the stacks of orange-scented crepes and drizzle them with the mysterious tangy orange sauce he prepared. This experience almost forever cemented crepes as a breakfast food in my mind until I lived in France during high school and discovered that savory and sweet crepes, served from a cart, were suitable for any time of day. I never took well to the savory fillings although I loved to eat the buckwheat crepes. I craved their nuttiness and the crunch of their crisp golden edges. I later learned that for ten dollars more than the price of a crepe from a cart, plus the cost of a meal, you could sit in swishy surroundings and get your crepes flambéed with Grand Marnier and served on fine china. These memories set the premise for these simple orange-laced crepes. You don't have to deal with an exotic presentation, enjoy them just as they are.

MAKES THIRTY 7-INCH CREPES

1   Melt 3 tablespoons of butter in a small pan. Add 1½ teaspoons of orange zest and cool slightly.

2   Place the eggs and milk in a blender. Add the salt, 1 tablespoon of granulated sugar, and the flours; blend until smooth. Add the melted butter and zest mixture and blend until smooth. Let the batter rest for 30 minutes at room temperature before using. The batter may also be made a day in advance, covered, and stored in the refrigerator overnight.

3   Brush a 7-inch nonstick pan lightly with soft butter and heat over medium-high

11 tablespoons (1 stick plus 3 tablespoons) unsalted butter, plus soft butter for brushing frying pan

1½ teaspoons plus 1 tablespoon finely grated orange zest

4 large eggs

2 cups whole milk

½ teaspoon salt

3 tablespoons granulated sugar

⅔ cup all-purpose flour

½ cup buckwheat flour

1 cup Grand Marnier

Confectioners' sugar for dusting

heat. It usually isn't necessary to rebutter the pan after every crepe. Whisk the batter lightly before using. Using a ¼-cup measure three-quarters full, place 1½ ounces of crepe batter in the center of the pan and roll the pan around to coat the bottom evenly. The crepes should be thin and uniform. Cook until the crepe is golden on the edges and batter is set and cooked through, about 1 to 2 minutes in a very hot pan.

4   Loosen the crepe with a heatproof rubber spatula and flip over to cook for 5 seconds on the other side. The first crepe is usually greasy, so eat or discard it and continue with the remaining crepes. Rebutter the pan lightly every six crepes. Adjust the heat as necessary to keep the crepes cooking quickly but not burning. Flip the crepes onto a plate with the pale side up and pile one on top of the other. The crepes may be used immediately or allowed to cool. They may be prepared up to 1 day in advance, cooled, and stored well wrapped at room temperature.

5   When ready to serve, preheat the oven to 450 degrees F. Lightly butter a cookie sheet.

6   Heat the remaining 2 tablespoons of sugar in a 3-quart pan. Stir constantly until it is melted and golden brown. Remove the pan from the heat, turn off the heat, and add the Grand Marnier slowly. Stir constantly to keep the sugar from hardening into clumps. Return the pan to the heat and add the remaining 1 tablespoon of orange zest. Keep your face and other combustibles away from the pan. Bring the liquid to a boil and flame the Grand Marnier. There will be *big* flames. When the flames die down, stir the liquid over low heat until any hardened sugar has dissolved. Whisk in the remaining 8 tablespoons (1 stick) of butter. Turn off the heat and reserve on the stove top. Reheat gently to serve.

7   Fold each crepe in half and then in half again. Use two or three crepes per serving depending on the size. Place the crepes on the prepared cookie sheet. Put the sheet on the bottom rack of the oven and reheat the crepes for 5 minutes. Divide the warm crepes among serving plates and drizzle generously with the orange butter. Dust with confectioners' sugar and serve immediately. Leftover crepes can be eaten for breakfast.

Fall Menu VII

grilled porcini with extra virgin olive oil
and shaved parmesan   66

—

black pepper–crusted new york steak   68

—

oven-roasted potatoes and shallots   70

—

caramel nut tart   71

—

WINES: The rich meatiness of the porcini would pair wonderfully with a Rosso or
Brunello di Montalcino or Chianti Classico. The peppery steak calls for Châteauneuf-
du-Pape or New World Syrah. Caramel and nuts are heaven with a Malmsey Madeira.

grilled porcini with extra virgin olive oil and shaved parmesan

There is nothing more magnificent and awesome than coming upon a porcino growing in the forest, as I experienced in Italy. A spotlight of sun illuminated it, a solitary sentry guarding fallen leaves. As I found out during my days of foraging, it can take a whole day to discover two or three. Meaty and pungent, the best way to enjoy them is simply, for too much fussing will overpower and distort their flavor.

Purslane, also known as pigweed, a foraged green, is a wonderful accompaniment to grilled porcini. It was favored as a vegetable by the ancient Egyptians, Romans, and Greeks. Popular today in Middle Eastern and Indian dishes, it grows wild all over northern California. Purslane's tender and juicy leaves are mild in flavor and delicious eaten raw with a drizzle of good olive oil and a sprinkle of salt and pepper or blanched lightly and served as a vegetable, drizzled with olive oil.

The porcini that you buy will most likely be cut in half and held together with a rubber band. They are sold this way so that you can examine the stem for worm tracks. Maggots consider the porcino a delicacy as much as we do, so sometimes we must share the mushroom with them. Mushrooms that have the remains of a considerable amount of feasting should be rejected, as they most likely will be worm-filled. A good porcino will show no signs of consumption, be firm of flesh and free of slime, and smell like the forest that it comes from.

SERVES 8

1   Preheat the grill to medium / medium-high heat.

2   Clean any large spongy gills from the mushrooms by scraping them gently with the rounded edge of a spoon. If the gills are firm, pale, tight, and small they can be left on.

3   Cut the large mushrooms into ½-inch-thick slices. Cut the smaller ones in half. In a large bowl, toss them with enough olive oil to lightly coat and season well with salt and pepper.

8 large (3- to 4-inch-diameter) porcini or 3 pounds mixed sizes

Extra virgin olive oil

Salt

Freshly ground black pepper

1 lemon, cut in half

4 ounces Parmesan cheese

¼ pound purslane sprigs or ½ cup whole Italian parsley leaves for garnish, optional

4   Grill the porcini until they are golden and juicy, about 5 to 7 minutes per side. Divide them among individual plates. Drizzle the grilled mushrooms with extra virgin olive oil and a squeeze of lemon. Shave Parmesan cheese over with a vegetable peeler. The plates can be garnished with purslane or whole Italian parsley leaves that have been dressed with olive oil and lemon juice and seasoned to taste with salt and pepper.

NOTE: The mushrooms may also be roasted in a 450 degree F oven until lightly golden, about 15 to 20 minutes. Turn the mushrooms over halfway through roasting.

black pepper–crusted new york steak

A New York is the most flavorful of the prime cuts of steak. People often complain about the toothiness of a New York, expecting the tenderness of a filet. If a choice were to be made between the two, steak lovers would choose a thick New York for its flavor over the blander filet, or for the best of both worlds, a porterhouse, the thick-cut combination of a New York and a filet. You might think that 12 ounces seems like a lot of meat for one person, but if a New York is cut any lighter the steaks turn out thin and difficult to cook properly. Because the steak is crusted with peppercorns it must be thick enough to withstand the intense searing required to toast the peppercorns so that they lose their "raw" heat. A thinly cut steak would be overcooked by the time the desired effect is achieved. Any leftover steak will make a great sandwich. For smaller portions cut the steak into two equal portions before cooking. Marinate the steaks overnight for the best flavor. Serve the steaks with the Oven-Roasted Potatoes and Shallots (recipe follows) or a good baked potato.

SERVES 8

1 Place the peppercorns on a large cutting board. Crack them with the heel of a small frying pan. Hold the pan at a 45 degree angle with one hand on the front of the pan and one hand on the handle. Press the rounded heel of the pan against the peppercorns, rolling as you press. The peppercorns will crack into coarse pieces. Continue to crush and roll until all the peppercorns are cracked.

2 Rub the steaks with olive oil and then the cracked peppercorns, using ½ teaspoon of peppercorns for each side of the steak. If you really like a lot of pepper you can double the amount to 1 teaspoon per side. Sprinkle the steaks with the thyme sprigs, cover well, and marinate them overnight in the refrigerator.

3 Remove the steaks from the refrigerator 30 minutes before cooking to allow them to come to room temperature. Remove the thyme sprigs and season the steaks well with salt.

4   Heat two large heavy-bottomed sauté pans or cast-iron skillets over high heat. Add 2 tablespoons of butter to each pan. When the butter starts to brown add the steaks and sear them until crisp and golden on both sides, about 4 to 7 minutes for each side. Reduce the heat if the pans get too hot; you don't want the butter to burn, as you will be using the pans to make the sauce. Cook four steaks per pan at a time, do not crowd them. The peppercorns should be crisp and toasted. Let the steaks rest on a rack for 10 minutes before serving so that the juices do not run out when they are cut. Reserve both pans without washing for the sauce.

8 teaspoons whole black peppercorns

Eight 12-ounce New York strip steaks or four cut in half

Extra virgin olive oil

16 fresh thyme sprigs

Salt

14 tablespoons (1 stick plus 6 tablespoons) unsalted butter, at room temperature

2 medium shallots, peeled, trimmed, and minced

1 cup brandy

1 cup strong veal or chicken stock

5   Make the pan sauce while the steaks are resting. Pour off any fat in the pans. Over medium-high heat, add 2 tablespoons of butter to one of the pans. When the butter starts to brown add the shallots. Sauté the shallots until they are golden.

6   Remove the pan from the heat and add the brandy. Lower the heat. Place the pan back on the heat. Take care that the brandy does not flame up into your face. Simmer to reduce the brandy by half, about 5 minutes. Pour the brandy mixture into the other pan, scraping the bottom with a rubber spatula as you go so that you have all the spicy caramelized bits from both pans in one. Add the stock and bring it to a boil. Reduce the heat and simmer the sauce for 5 minutes until it is slightly reduced.

7   Lower the heat and add the remaining 8 tablespoons of butter. Whisk it into the sauce over low heat until it is fully incorporated. Do not boil the sauce again after the butter has been added, otherwise the butter will separate. Drizzle the sauce over the steaks and serve with Oven-Roasted Potatoes and Shallots or the accompaniment of your choice.

oven-roasted potatoes and shallots

SERVES 8

1   Preheat the oven to 450 degrees F.

2   Wash the potatoes with a stiff brush to
    remove any stubborn dirt. Drain them
    well and cut them in half. Toss them with
    ¼ cup of olive oil to coat well and season
    with salt and pepper. Pour them into a
    roasting pan and roast in the preheated
    oven for 20 minutes.

3 pounds small Yukon Gold or
    red potatoes

¼ cup extra virgin olive oil

Salt

Freshly ground black pepper

8 medium shallots

3   While the potatoes are roasting, peel, trim, and slice the shallots into ¼-inch rings.

4   After 20 minutes, reduce the oven heat to 400 degrees F and add the sliced shallots
    to the potatoes. Stir the potatoes well. Roast for another 40 to 50 minutes, stirring
    occasionally, until the potatoes and shallots are golden.

caramel nut tart

Fall brings the nut harvest. I know it's walnut season when I hear the ping of fallen walnuts being crushed beneath my tires. We gather and husk them to reveal the sturdy nut within. The crows join us and drop their share on the road to crack the shells. It's not uncommon to be caught in a rain of walnuts.

This tart showcases crunchy nuts swathed in a silken cover of caramel. It's rich and delicious so a little goes a long way. The tart can be served on its own or with ice cream and Bittersweet Chocolate Sauce (page 241) for pure decadence.

SERVES 8 TO 12

1 Remove the Pâte Brisée from the refrigerator and let it sit for 10 minutes before rolling. Roll out the dough ⅛ inch thick, using as little flour as possible, large enough to line a 12 by 1-inch tart pan. Turn your tart pan over on top of the dough and use the edge as a measure to cut out a circle 2 inches larger than the pan all of the way around. Lift the dough and place it in the pan. Press it firmly into the corners and trim the edges. Chill the lined pan in the refrigerator until the dough is firm, about 40 minutes. The lined tart shell can be wrapped in plastic and chilled overnight in the refrigerator or frozen for up to 2 weeks.

½ recipe Pâte Brisée (page 55)

1 cup walnut halves

1 cup pecan halves

½ cup whole almonds

1½ cups sugar

1 tablespoon honey

16 tablespoons (2 sticks) unsalted butter, at room temperature

1 cup heavy cream

½ teaspoon salt

2 Place an oven rack on the bottom rung and preheat the oven to 400 degrees F.

3 Remove the pan from the refrigerator. Prick the dough well with a fork. Line the dough with a square of aluminum foil that has been cut larger than the diameter of the pan. Press it into the corners well. Fill the tart shell with dried beans or pie weights and bake in the preheated oven for 25 minutes. Remove the beans using caution. They will be very hot. Carefully peel off the foil. Place the tart shell on a sheet pan to cool. Reserve at room temperature until ready to fill. The tart shell may be baked up to 1 day in advance and stored well wrapped at room temperature.

4   Mix the nuts together and spread them on a sheet pan. Toast the nuts for 8 minutes while the tart shell bakes. Cool and rub them lightly between your hands to remove any loose skins.

5   Reduce the oven heat to 375 degrees F.

6   Combine the sugar, honey, and butter in a medium-sized heavy-bottomed saucepan. Heat over a medium-high heat stirring constantly until the sugar has caramelized and the color is golden brown, about 10 minutes. Remove the pan from the heat and pour the cream in slowly while stirring constantly. The mixture will bubble vigorously. Be careful of the rising steam; it can cause a painful burn. Stir until the caramel stops bubbling and becomes smooth. Stir in the salt.

7   Place the pan back on the heat and bring to a boil. Stir in the nuts to coat well with caramel and turn off the heat. Use a slotted spoon to transfer the nuts to the tart shell. Pour enough caramel over the nuts to fill the tart shell ⅛ inch beneath the top edge. Extra caramel can be eaten or discarded.

8   Place the tart on the bottom rack of the preheated oven and bake for 15 to 20 minutes until the caramel bubbles and the crust is golden. Cool before serving. Store loosely wrapped at room temperature for up to 2 days.

Fall Menu VIII

butternut squash soup

buttermilk biscuits

roasted guinea hen

sautéed savoy cabbage with golden raisins

caramelized apple galette

WINES: The soup brings out the sweetness of the squash, making it a nice pairing with a Vouvray Demi-Sec or a slightly sweet German Riesling Spätlese. The Guinea hen served alone is wonderful with a red Burgundy or American Pinot Noir. If you serve it with the cabbage try a dry Alsatian Riesling or Beaujolais. Caramelized apples are a wonderful match with a Coteaux du Layon or a German Riesling Beerenauslese.

butternut squash soup

Butternut squashes are a fall and winter staple. Roast them with brown sugar, butter, and salt as a side dish, use them to perk up mashed potatoes, or stuff them into ravioli. This recipe showcases the most simple and gratifying use of butternut squash, a warm, satisfying soup scented with sage.

For a wonderful homey accompaniment bake the Buttermilk Biscuits (recipe follows) 15 minutes before serving the soup. Or serve the soup with a good loaf of crusty bread.

SERVES 8

1   Preheat the oven to 400 degrees F.

2   Prick the squash with a fork and place it whole on a sheet pan. Roast for 45 minutes in the oven until the squash has softened. Cool the squash, then cut it in half and remove the seeds. Peel the halves and cut into 2-inch chunks. Reserve.

3   Peel, trim, and coarsely chop the onion. Reserve.

4   Melt the butter in a large saucepan over medium heat. When the butter starts to brown, add the onion and sauté until it is translucent and starts to brown, about 4 to 5 minutes.

5   Add the honey to the onions and cook until it bubbles. Add the squash chunks and sage; season with salt and pepper.

6   Add the chicken stock and enough water to cover the squash by an inch. Bring the soup to a boil and lower the heat to a simmer. Cook the soup until the onions and squash are very tender, about 45 minutes to 1 hour. Add more liquid if necessary to keep the squash submerged. Remove the pan from the heat and cool for 15 minutes.

7   Puree the soup in a blender. Do not fill the blender more than two-thirds full or you risk having the contents explode. Allow the steam to escape by removing the center plug in the lid and covering the hole with a thick towel to protect your hand. Hold the lid securely down and lift the towel slightly to allow the pressurized air to escape as you blend. Strain through a coarse strainer if you want a smoother soup or return it directly to the pan; season it with salt and pepper to taste. Bring the finished soup back to a boil. Ladle it into bowls and serve with a dollop of Crème Fraîche, about 1 tablespoon per bowl.

1 butternut squash, 4 pounds

1 medium yellow onion

1 tablespoon unsalted butter or olive oil

1 tablespoon honey

6 sage leaves

Salt

Freshly ground black pepper

4 cups chicken stock

1 cup Crème Fraîche (page 39)

buttermilk biscuits

Buttermilk biscuits pair wonderfully with the soup. They are as light as air with the tanginess of buttermilk. They need a hot oven to puff up and turn golden without being overbaked. Have plenty of good sweet butter to slather on the hot hastily halved biscuits. Leftover biscuits can be toasted and served with jam or stuffed with fried ham and eggs.

MAKES TWELVE 2-INCH BISCUITS

1   Place an oven rack on the top rung and preheat the oven to 450 degrees F. Line a sheet pan with parchment paper.

2   Combine the dry ingredients in a mixing bowl. Add the cold butter. Using the paddle attachment of a stand mixer or by hand with a pastry cutter, mix the butter and the flour mixture together until it resembles coarse cornmeal. Add the buttermilk to bring the dough together.

> 2 cups all-purpose flour
>
> 1 tablespoon sugar
>
> 1 tablespoon baking powder
>
> ½ teaspoon kosher salt
>
> 8 tablespoons (1 stick) cold unsalted butter, cut into chunks, plus 4 tablespoons unsalted butter, melted to brush the tops
>
> 1 cup buttermilk

3   Turn the dough out onto a lightly floured board and knead it a couple of times to combine the ingredients uniformly. Pat the dough into a 1-inch-thick round and cut with a 2-inch round cutter.

4   Transfer the biscuits to a parchment-lined sheet pan. Space them 1½ inches apart on all sides. Brush the tops with melted butter and bake on the top rack of a preheated oven for 10 minutes, turning the pan once midway through the baking. Serve warm.

NOTE: The biscuits can be cut, placed on a parchment-lined sheet pan, and refrigerated, well wrapped, overnight before baking.

roasted guinea hen

Guinea hens are very odd and very loud birds. They are frequently used as watch birds on country properties because of the racket they make when someone approaches. Their redeeming feature is that they make wonderful eating. The breast has a lot of nice yellow fat under the skin that crisps beautifully when sautéed or roasted and stays crisp for some time after being taken from the heat. The gray-skinned legs are remarkable not only in color, but in flavor. They yield succulent and tender dark meat. If, for the life of you, you can't locate a guinea hen, this recipe will work well with chicken or game hens.

SERVES 8

1   Remove the wing tip at the second joint of the wing from the tip with a knife or poultry shears. Cut off the tail. Season the cavity of the birds with salt and pepper and stuff each with half an onion, a bay leaf and 6 thyme sprigs. Rub the skin with olive oil and then season it well with salt and black pepper. Truss the birds (see method on page 96).

2   Preheat the oven to 400 degrees F.

3   Prepare the Savoy Cabbage (recipe follows) or another accompaniment while the birds are roasting.

2 guinea hens, 3 to 4 pounds each

Salt

Freshly ground black pepper

1 medium yellow onion, peeled and halved

2 bay leaves, fresh or dried

12 fresh thyme sprigs

Extra virgin olive oil

2 cups strong chicken stock

4   Heat a heavy-bottomed ovenproof skillet over high heat and add a little olive oil to coat the bottom of the pan. Sear the birds until the skin is golden and crisp, about 15 minutes. Reduce the heat if the pan gets too hot and smokes. Arrange the birds in the pan and roast in the preheated oven for 1 hour until the juices of the thigh run clear when pricked with a sharp knife. Remove the birds from the pan and let them rest on a plate for 15 minutes before cutting up.

5   Skim or pour the fat from the roasting pan and add the chicken stock. Bring it to a boil and scrape the bottom of the pan to remove any caramelized bits. Strain the stock into a pan; season with salt and pepper to taste. Cover the pan and keep warm over low heat until ready to use.

6   Cut the breasts into two pieces so that one half has the wing and the other half is completely bone-free. Remove the thighbone from the thigh. Serve one piece of breast and one thigh or leg per person accompanied by the cabbage or the accompaniment of your choice. Serve the hot pan juices in a pitcher on the side.

sautéed savoy cabbage with golden raisins

Savoy cabbage is a wonderful accompaniment to the crisp-skinned guinea hen. The smokiness of the bacon is juxtaposed against the sweetness of the raisins and the cabbage. This cabbage also makes a great accompaniment for pork, chicken, squab, and game birds.

SERVES 8

1   Remove the large tough or blemished outer leaves from the cabbage. Cut the cabbage in half and remove the core in a triangular wedge. Slice the remaining leaves into strips ¼-inch wide.

2   Coarsely chop the raisins and reserve. Cut the bacon into ¼-inch pieces. Render the bacon in a heavy-bottomed sauté pan over medium heat until almost crisp. Remove from the pan with a slotted spoon and drain on a paper towel. Reserve.

3   Pour the fat from the bacon pan; increase the heat to medium-high. Add 1 tablespoon of butter to the pan. When the butter starts to brown, add the diced onion and brown. Season to taste with salt and pepper. Transfer the onion to a large pot.

4 Add 2 tablespoons of butter to the same pan. Add the sliced cabbage and sauté it quickly until it is golden; do it in two or three batches if the pan cannot accommodate all the cabbage at once. Transfer the cabbage to the pot with the onion.

5 Add the raisins, bacon, and thyme to the cabbage and onion. Season the mixture with salt and pepper and add the chicken stock. Bring the stock to a boil and reduce the heat. Cook partially covered over medium heat until the liquid has almost completely evaporated but the pan is still moist and the cabbage is tender, about 20 minutes. If the pan gets dry too soon add a little bit of water.

6 Cover to keep the cabbage warm until ready to serve with the guinea hen. If the cabbage cools reheat in a 400 degree F oven before serving.

2 pounds Savoy cabbage

½ cup golden raisins

8 strips thick-cut applewood-smoked bacon

6 tablespoons unsalted butter

1 medium yellow onion, peeled, trimmed, and finely diced

Salt

Freshly ground black pepper

1 tablespoon fresh thyme leaves

1 cup strong chicken stock

caramelized apple galette

Oh, the pure delight of apples, sugar, butter, and flaky pastry. This galette is a study in simplicity. The sugar, apples, and crust must bake to a caramelized golden brown in order to achieve the correct contrast of flavor and texture. The juices leaking from the galette might burn but it is of no consequence, so do not worry. One bite proves that simplicity reigns supreme in an otherwise complex world.

SERVES 8 TO 10

1   Peel, halve, and core the apples with a melon baller or small knife. Slice them thinly across (perpendicular to) the core.

2   Roll the dough into a 16-inch circle, ⅛ inch thick, and place it in the middle of a parchment-lined sheet pan. The dough will hang over the edge. This is fine as you will be folding it over to bake.

3   Place an oven rack on the top rungs, and preheat the oven to 400 degrees F.

4   Starting 2 inches from the edge of the dough overlap the apple slices by half in a circle around the perimeter so that the straight core side is facing the center and the rounded crescent side is facing the edge. Keep them spaced tightly. After the outer circle is complete repeat until concentric circles fill the tart. Each row should tightly overlap the previous one. The tart should look like a flower, with the apple slices the petals. As you get closer to the center the apples will become elevated. Fill the space underneath with small ends and pieces of apple. The apples will soften as the tart bakes and become level.

5   Sprinkle the tart evenly with ¼ cup of the sugar. Fold the edges over the apples, making a pleat with the dough every couple of inches. They should lie flat and all fall in the same direction. Brush the dough lightly with cold water to seal each pleat before pressing together. Brush the dough with the milk just to moisten and dot the apples with butter.

8 tart medium-sized baking apples

½ recipe Pâte Brisée (page 55)

¾ cup sugar

2 tablespoons whole milk

3 tablespoons unsalted butter

6   Place the galette on the top rack of the preheated oven. Bake for 30 minutes. Sprinkle the remaining ½ cup of sugar over the tart and continue baking 1 hour more, until the crust is golden, the apples are tender, and the sugar has caramelized. If the crust seems to be browning too quickly lower the oven heat to 375 degrees F.

7   Remove the galette from the oven when it is golden. Loosen the crust from the caramelized sugar on the edges while it cools. Cool to warm. Transfer the galette from the sheet pan to a serving plate. If the caramelized sugar on the sheet pan has hardened so that you can't remove the galette to a serving plate, place the galette back in the oven for 5 minutes to soften the sugar. Loosen the edges with a thin metal spatula to release the crust.

Fall Menu IX

escarole and belgian endive salad
with lemon anchovy dressing   84

braised beef shanks with rough-cut pasta   86

figs poached in port   90

WINES: The strong flavors of the salad make it difficult to pair with wine. Move on to the main course and choose an American Zinfandel or Barolo to go with the meaty rich beef shanks. Serve the figs with a tawny port.

escarole and belgian endive salad with lemon anchovy dressing

Though similar to a Caesar, this salad has more character. The escarole and Belgian endive have more dimension than romaine. The inner pale leaves of the escarole are sweet and juicy. The leaves become increasingly bitter as they darken to a deep green. Add some of the tender green tips for contrast but trim away the tough majority. Brush any dirt gently from the Belgian endive and pull away blemished outer leaves. It is unnecessary to wash them. Cut the endive as close to serving time as possible to prevent it from browning. Do not soak the cut leaves in lemon water to prevent browning. They are like sponges and their wonderful bittersweet essence will be diluted and lost.

The dressing has a Caesar-like character but doesn't use raw egg. The dressing is also good as a dip for raw vegetables.

SERVES 8

1   To make the dressing, put the garlic, shallot, mustard, lemon juice, capers, and anchovies in a blender, blend until the mixture is smooth. Turn off the blender and season with salt and pepper to taste.

2   Turn the blender on and drizzle in the olive oil until thickened. Fold in the chopped parsley by hand. Let the dressing sit for an hour to allow the flavors to marry before using. Store in the refrigerator for up to 2 weeks.

3   Trim the escarole of its tough outer leaves. Cut off the root end and separate the leaves. Tear the leaves into bite-sized pieces. Wash and dry them thoroughly.

4   Peel the dirty or bruised outer leaves from the Belgian endive. It is not necessary to wash the endive. Slice them in half lengthwise. Remove the core by cutting it out in a triangular wedge with a sharp knife. Cut the leaves crosswise into 1-inch pieces. They will look like little crescents when they fall apart. Toss the escarole and endive together and store in a bowl or plastic bag, well wrapped, in the refrigerator until ready to use.

5   Preheat the oven to 350 degrees F.

6   Trim the crust from the bread and cut into ½-inch slices. Cut the slices crosswise into ½-inch cubes.

7   Place the cubed bread in a large bowl and toss with the olive oil and ⅓ cup Parmesan cheese, season with salt and pepper.

8   Spread the bread cubes evenly on a sheet pan and bake in the preheated oven until the croutons are golden and crisp, 10 to 15 minutes. The croutons will keep well for a week or two stored in an airtight container. Use them to top hearty soups and salads for that extra sensory experience, crunch.

9   In a large bowl, toss 1 cup of croutons with a little of the dressing, add the escarole and the endive, toss lightly with the dressing. Add more croutons, as many as you'd like, and the remaining ½ cup Parmesan cheese and toss again, season with salt and freshly ground pepper to taste.

Lemon Anchovy Dressing

2 garlic cloves, peeled, trimmed, and minced

1 medium shallot, peeled, trimmed, and minced

1 tablespoon Dijon mustard

½ cup lemon juice

1 tablespoon capers, chopped

8 anchovy fillets, chopped

Salt

Freshly ground black pepper

¾ cup extra virgin olive oil

1 teaspoon chopped Italian parsley

1 pound escarole

1 pound Belgian endive

½ loaf firm peasant bread, 4 cups cubed

¼ cup extra virgin olive oil

⅓ cup finely grated Parmesan cheese, plus additional ½ cup for finishing

Salt

Freshly ground black pepper

braised beef shanks with rough-cut pasta

As the days become shorter and cooler I crave heartier soul-satisfying meals. The warmth of the sun is exchanged for the warmth of the meal. I like to use up any tomatoes left on the vine for this dish. They're usually not very pretty. These shanks can also be prepared with good-quality canned tomatoes. If you like your juices to be thick with tomatoes, add more and the dish will become more like an Italian *sugo*—meat braised with vegetables in tomato sauce. Because of the massive size of beef shanks the meat should be removed from the bone before serving. Serve the marrow-filled bones as a side dish so that marrow lovers can indulge themselves. If you have it, offer Fleur de Sel (see Note, page 49) to season the rich marrow. This dish is also wonderful in the winter; substitute dried thyme when fresh is no longer available.

SERVES 8

1   Preheat the oven to 450 degrees F.

2   Peel and trim the carrots and onions. Chop into ½-inch pieces. Wash, trim, and slice the celery thinly. Toss the vegetables, including the garlic, together with 2 tablespoons of olive oil. Season with salt and pepper.

3   Spread the vegetables out in a deep roasting pan and roast in the preheated oven until they are golden, about 30 to 40 minutes. Stir the vegetables halfway through roasting.

4   Prepare the tomatoes while the vegetables are roasting. Peel, seed, and chop the tomatoes into ½-inch pieces. If you are using canned tomatoes, remove the core and most of the seeds with your hands over a strainer and bowl to catch the juices. Break the tomatoes into pieces and reserve in another bowl. Pour the strained juices over the tomatoes and reserve.

5   Remove the pan from the oven and add the prepared tomatoes, bay leaves, thyme sprigs, and the 1 cup of parsley leaves. Stir to incorporate.

6. Place some flour in a large shallow pan or bowl. Season the beef shanks well with salt and pepper, dip into the flour, and shake off the excess.

7. Heat a large heavy-bottomed sauté pan or two smaller pans over medium-high heat; add enough olive oil to lightly cover the bottom. Sear the beef shanks on both sides until browned and crisp, about 10 minutes. Adjust the heat if necessary to keep the flour from burning. Remove the shanks from the pan and place them in the roasting pan with the vegetables.

8. Drain off the fat from the pan. Add the wine and bring to a boil. Reduce the heat and simmer for 10 minutes to reduce the wine by half. Pour the wine over the beef shanks in the roasting pan.

9. If there is enough liquid from the wine and the tomatoes it is not necessary to add additional water to the pan. The liquid should rise halfway up the shanks.

10. Place the pan in the preheated oven for 30 minutes.

4 medium carrots

2 medium yellow onions

4 celery stalks

12 garlic cloves, peeled, trimmed, and left whole

2 tablespoons extra virgin olive oil, plus more for searing

Salt

Freshly ground black pepper

4 large ripe tomatoes or one 2-pound can whole peeled tomatoes

2 bay leaves, fresh or dried

12 fresh thyme sprigs or 1 tablespoon dried

1 cup Italian parsley leaves, plus more leaves for garnish

All-purpose flour for dusting

8 pounds meaty beef shanks, cut 2 inches thick

4 cups red wine

Rough-Cut Pasta (recipe follows) or dried papardelle

Fleur de Sel for bone marrow (optional)

11   Reduce the heat to 350 degrees F and cook for 3½ hours. Prepare and roll the pasta according to the recipe below while the shanks are braising. Turn the shanks over after 1½ hours. Check the liquid level in the pan occasionally. Add more water, if necessary. When the shanks are done they should be meltingly tender with the meat falling off the bone. Cool the shanks to warm and remove them from the braising liquid.

12   Remove the meat from the bone in large chunks. Remove and throw away any fat, cartilage, membranes, and sinew. Reserve the meat and the bones containing marrow.

13   Skim the fat off the juices in the pan. Add the meat back to the pan with the vegetables and juices. Pull out any herb stems and the bay leaves. Bring to a simmer and reduce the juices slightly if they are thin; season with salt and pepper to taste.

14   Serve the shanks and vegetables over the Rough-Cut Pasta. Serve the warm marrowbones on the side with Fleur de Sel. Garnish with parsley leaves.

NOTE: The beef can be braised a day or two ahead of time. The flavors get better as it sits. After refrigeration, any fat will harden on top of the juices. Scrape this off with a spoon and discard before reheating. Do not serve the marrow bones if they've been cooked and reheated; they just don't taste the same.

rough-cut pasta

I like to roll this pasta thicker so that it stands up to the heartiness of the braised beef. The pasta has a nice tooth because it uses equal parts of semolina and flour. If you like softer pasta add more flour and less semolina; do the opposite for firmer pasta. This pasta can be cut into any shape desired. If you are going to use it for ravioli, continue to roll the dough through the second thinnest setting, otherwise the ravioli will be thick and clunky.

MAKES 2 POUNDS

1   Mix the flour, semolina, and 2 teaspoons of salt together in a large bowl.

2   Whisk the eggs, 2 tablespoons olive oil, and 2 tablespoons of cold water together in a separate bowl.

3   Make a well in the flour and add the egg mixture. Mix until combined. If dough is too dry add a few drops of water a little at a time. If it is too wet add a little bit of flour. Knead until the dough is smooth and elastic. Cut it into three pieces and let them rest, well wrapped with plastic, for at least 45 minutes at room temperature or overnight in the refrigerator. If the dough has been refrigerated, bring it to room temperature before rolling.

4   Roll the dough out with a rolling pin so that it will pass through the pasta machine. (To roll dough by hand, see Note, page 53.)

5   To knead the dough, pass each piece three times through the pasta machine. Fold the dough in half lengthwise each time it is passed through. After the kneading is completed, let the dough rest for 10 minutes.

6   Roll the dough through the third thinnest setting, do not fold it after passing it through the machine; keep it in one long sheet. If the sheet gets too long, cut it in half and roll each half separately. Dust the sheets of pasta lightly with flour to keep them from sticking.

7   Roll the sheets up and cut into all different widths with a sharp knife. Dust the cut ribbons with flour.

8   Cook in a huge pot of boiling salted water, 2 tablespoons salt to 5 quarts of water, for 3 to 4 minutes. Drain and toss lightly with olive oil. Serve with the beef shanks.

2 cups all-purpose flour

2 cups semolina

2 teaspoons salt

5 large eggs

Extra virgin olive oil

2 tablespoons cold water

figs poached in port

Poached figs can be eaten alone or as a simple and light dessert with a scoop of ice cream and biscotti. Serve them with a wedge of Stilton to add a savory note to the end of your meal. Do not overcook the figs. You don't want them so soft that they burst open when you touch them. Black Mission figs work best for this recipe, as they tend to be firmer in texture. Other varieties may be substituted but the cooking time should be reduced to 5 minutes if they are very soft and ripe. If you can't find good figs poach small pears instead (see Note below).

SERVES 8

1   Combine the port, sugar, vanilla bean and seeds, cinnamon, orange peel, and peppercorns in a large saucepan. Bring to a boil and reduce the heat to low.

2   Simmer until the liquid has the consistency of a light syrup, about 40 minutes. You will have about 3 cups of syrup.

3   Add the figs and simmer for 15 to 20 minutes. Turn off the heat and cool the figs in the syrup.

6 cups tawny port

3 cups sugar

1 vanilla bean, split and scraped

Two 3-inch cinnamon sticks

Two 3-inch strips of orange peel

16 whole black peppercorns

24 Black Mission figs, ripe yet firm

Vanilla Ice Cream (page 289) and Anise-Scented Almond Biscotti (page 319)

4   Serve the figs warm or cool with any of the accompaniments mentioned above.

NOTE: The port syrup may be made several days in advance and stored in the refrigerator. The figs may also be poached several days ahead and stored in the syrup under refrigeration. To substitute pears, peel and core them in the same manner as for Brandied Pears (page 33). Poach the pears for 40 minutes or until tender.

Fall Menu X

minestrone with shelling beans   92

—

sage-roasted chicken with sweet potatoes
and cipollini onions   96

—

apple spice cake   98

—

WINES: If you would like to serve a wine with the soup choose a Chianti or Beaujolais.
The chicken is wonderful with a Riesling, either Alsatian or German. Choose a
Gewürztraminer Vendange Tardive or New Zealand Late Harvest Chenin Blanc
for the apple cake.

minestrone with shelling beans

Minestrone can be a meal in itself, so when served as a first course it must be doled out lightly. Since minestrone is a hearty vegetable soup, many different vegetables can be substituted. Swiss chard or escarole can stand in for kale, and chunks of summer squash for Romano beans. Base your choices on what is available in the market. Vegetables that need little cooking time should be added at the end. If shelling beans are not available substitute cooked dried beans. Remember this soup for a warm sustaining lunch on a cold fall day.

SERVES 8 TO 10

1　Shell the fresh beans.

2　Peel, seed, and coarsely chop the fresh tomatoes. Reserve in their juices. If you are using canned tomatoes, remove the core and most of the seeds with your hands over a strainer and bowl to catch the juice. Break the tomatoes into pieces and reserve in a bowl. Pour the juice over the tomatoes.

3　Wash the kale and cut the thick tough ribs from the larger leaves. The ribs can be left on the tender leaves. Slice the leaves into ½-inch strips.

4　Clean the Romano beans and cut on the diagonal into 1-inch pieces. Chop the carrots and onions into pieces about the same size as the shelling beans. Slice the celery thinly. Peel and slice the garlic thinly. Reserve the vegetables separately.

5　Heat a large soup or stockpot over medium-high heat. Add 2 tablespoons of olive oil to the pot and sauté the garlic until it is toasted and the oil is perfumed. Add the carrots, onions, and celery. Cook until the onions are translucent, about 4 minutes, then add the sliced kale; season with salt and pepper. Cook until the kale has wilted, then add the peeled chopped tomatoes.

2 pounds fresh shelling beans, cranberry or white, about 2 cups shelled, or 3 cups Basic Bean Recipe (recipe follows)

3 ripe medium tomatoes or 2 cups canned

1 pound kale (see Headnote)

½ pound Romano beans, green or yellow or both (see Headnote above)

3 medium carrots

2 medium yellow onions

2 celery stalks

4 medium garlic cloves

2 tablespoons extra virgin olive oil

Salt

Freshly ground black pepper

1 bay leaf, fresh or dried

3 small fresh sage leaves

½ cup Italian parsley leaves

1 large piece Parmesan cheese rind, optional

2 cups cooked tubettini or other small round pasta

Grated Parmesan cheese for garnish

Peasant bread

6   Cover the vegetables with water by 2 inches and add the herbs and Parmesan rind, if you're using it. Simmer for 30 minutes. Add the shelling beans and simmer until they are tender, 30 to 40 minutes. If you are using cooked dried beans simmer for 20 minutes so the beans absorb some of the flavor of the broth. Add the Romano beans and simmer for 10 more minutes. Check the seasoning and add the pasta. Salt and pepper to taste. Discard the bay leaf. Ladle into bowls and sprinkle with grated Parmesan cheese. Serve with bread to soak up the broth.

NOTE: This soup can be made a day or two in advance. Do not add any quick-cooking vegetables, such as Romano beans, until you reheat the soup to serve.

basic bean recipe

In addition to using this basic recipe for soups, dried white beans can be cooked, drained, and pureed with roasted garlic and olive oil for a wonderful spread for crusty bread.

MAKES 6 TO 8 CUPS

1   Place the beans in a large bowl and cover with water by 5 inches. Let them soak overnight.

2   The following day drain the beans and place in a large pot. Fill it with cold water to cover the beans by 2 inches and bring to a boil. Turn off the heat and let the beans sit for 15 minutes. Drain the beans and reserve.

1 pound dried beans

1 medium yellow onion

1 medium carrot

1 celery stalk

2 garlic cloves

1 tablespoon extra virgin olive oil

1 bay leaf, fresh or dried

Salt

Freshly ground black pepper

3   Peel the onion and carrot. Cut the onion into quarters and leave the carrot whole. Wash the celery and leave whole. Peel the garlic and leave whole.

4   In a large stockpot over medium-high heat, sauté the garlic in the olive oil until golden, 3 to 4 minutes. Add the onion, carrots, and celery. Cook until the vegetables begin to wilt, about 2 to 3 minutes. Add the beans and enough water to cover by 3 inches. Add the bay leaf and bring to a boil. Reduce the heat and simmer for 30 minutes.

5   Add a generous amount of salt to the beans and continue to simmer for another 30 minutes or more until the beans are tender. Dried beans can take up to an hour or more depending on the type and age of the beans. If the beans absorb all of the liquid before they are tender, add more boiling liquid to the beans. When the beans are tender, remove from the heat and cool.

NOTE: If you are going to save the beans for a few days, store them in their cooking liquid. If you will use them immediately, drain them and remove and discard the chunks of vegetables and herbs.

sage-roasted chicken with sweet potatoes and cipollini onions

Sage is a wise and beautiful herb. For centuries, people have consumed it for medicinal as well as culinary purposes. The shimmery green leaves with delicate silver fur are powerfully flavored. When used in proper combinations sage is a showcased beauty. Stuffing would be amiss without it. Butter mellows its intensity and fries it to a crunch for topping gnocchi, soups, and risotto. Here it perfumes the meat of the chicken while roasting in the fat of the skin. It blends seamlessly with the golden caramelized cipollini and the roasted sweet potatoes. The flavors smolder in every earthy bite.

SERVES 8

1   Peel the sweet potatoes and cut into four pieces each. Peel the onions and if they are large cut in half to form half moons.

2   In a large bowl, toss the onions and the sweet potatoes with the brown sugar, 2 teaspoons of salt, ¼ teaspoon of black pepper, and just enough olive oil to moisten. Place the vegetables in a large roasting pan.

3   Preheat oven to 475 degrees F.

4   Cut off the tail and the excess skin and fat on the chickens. Separate the skin from the meat by gently working from the front and back of the breasts with your fingers. Move down the breasts and over the tops of the thighs and legs. Separate the skin as far as your fingers can reach. Slide the sage leaves between the skin and the meat. Position one on top of each of the legs, one on each of the thighs, and two on each breast. Season the cavity of the chickens well with salt and pepper; stuff the sage stems into the cavity. Tie the birds with kitchen twine: Cut a string measuring 24 inches long or measure a piece of string three times the length of the bird. Loop the center of the string over the neck bone and under the shoulders. Run the string over the wings and along the bottom of the breast so that it is tucked in between the breast and the thigh. Cross the string at the point

of the breast and tie once, pulling the string tightly. Loop each end of the string around the end of each drumstick and tie once to pull the legs snugly against the point of the breast. Tie a second time to form a knot. Trim the ends of the string.

To do a quick truss, make a slit on either side of the breast just above the thigh/leg joint, parallel to the breast meat in the space where the breast meat ends and the thigh meat begins. It should be wide enough to stick the ends of the legs in. The slit should be about 2 inches from the edge of the cavity. Turn the bird so that the cavity is facing toward you. Grab the end of the drumstick and push the leg thigh joint back toward the wing. Tuck the end of the drumstick into the slit and pat the leg back into position, repeat with the other leg.

Rub the chickens with olive oil and season their skin well with salt and pepper. Place the birds on top of the prepared vegetables in the roasting pan.

6 medium (3 pounds) sweet potatoes

16 cipollini onions or small white onions

½ cup brown sugar

Salt

Freshly ground black pepper

Extra virgin olive oil

Two 4- to 6-pound roasting chickens

16 sage leaves, with stems reserved for stuffing cavity

5   Oven-sear the chickens in the preheated oven for 20 minutes.

6   Turn the oven down to 400 degrees F and add 1 cup of water to the roasting pan. The water will mix with the caramelized juices of the chicken and vegetables and produce a wonderful pan juice. Roast for 1¼ to 1½ hours; add more water if the pan juices become dry. The chickens are done when a thermometer reads 145 degrees F when inserted into the thigh or when the juices run clear from the thigh and leg when pierced. Remove the chickens and place them on a cutting board or platter.

7   Let the chickens rest covered lightly with a foil tent for 15 minutes before carving. They will continue to cook as they rest. Cut the chickens into eight pieces each (cut the large breasts in half). Serve with onions and potatoes on the side and the degreased pan juices spooned over.

apple spice cake

The flavors of this moist homey apple-studded cake get better with each passing day as they have time to settle into one another. Heirloom varieties of apples grown specifically for cooking, such as the Swaar, do very well in this recipe. Golden Delicious also work quite well. Pears can be substituted for apples or a mixture of both can be used. Serve this cake with ice cream and caramel sauce, or a spoonful of soft nutmeg-scented whipped cream, or a wedge by itself with a cup of coffee. It will fittingly rise to the occasion whenever and however served.

SERVES 8 TO 12

1   To prepare the apples, peel, halve, and core them. Dice into 1-inch pieces.

2   Heat the butter until golden in a large sauté pan over medium-high heat. Add the apples and sauté them until they are golden. Sprinkle with the sugar and cook until all the liquid has evaporated from the pan. Cool. Prepare the apples up to 3 days in advance, tightly wrap, and store in the refrigerator.

3   Butter and flour a 12-cup Bundt pan.

4   Preheat the oven to 350 degrees F.

5   In a standing mixer fitted with the paddle attachment or with an electric hand mixer, beat the butter and sugar together until fluffy.

6   In a small bowl, combine the eggs and the vanilla. Add to the butter mixture in two parts, beating well after each addition.

7   Combine the dry ingredients in a medium bowl and add to egg/butter mixture, half at a time, alternating with the buttermilk.

8   Fold in the cooled cooked apples and spoon into the buttered and floured Bundt pan. Bake in the preheated oven for 45 to 50 minutes until a toothpick inserted into the center comes out clean.

9   Cool for 10 minutes and then turn upside down onto a rack. Leave the pan on the rack and cool to warm. Remove the pan and dust with confectioners' sugar. Serve with ice cream or alone.

Sautéed Apples

4 tart medium-sized baking apples

2 tablespoons unsalted butter

2 tablespoons granulated sugar

Cake Batter

12 tablespoons (1½ sticks) unsalted butter, at room temperature

1½ cups granulated sugar

4 large eggs

2 teaspoons pure vanilla extract

1 tablespoon baking powder

1 teaspoon baking soda

3 cups all-purpose flour

¾ teaspoon salt

½ teaspoon nutmeg

1 teaspoon ground cinnamon

¼ teaspoon ground cloves

1 cup buttermilk

Confectioners' sugar for dusting

winter

Winter lays its heavy cover upon the land.

The frozen ground cradles promise of the future,

While we reap the stores of seasons past.

Gather ye round the hearth,

Fragrant with crusty bread,

For warmth and pleasant company.

Until spring doth tap us on the shoulder.

—MARIA HELM SINSKEY, 1989

The landscape turns still and cold. A hard, cold sky swells with pregnant gray clouds. We long anticipate winter's arrival, which happens in an instant. Whether heralded with the heavy drum of raindrops or the silence of floating snowflakes, the effect is the same. It forces us to retreat into the warmth and comfort of our homes.

The earth is frozen in some parts, sodden in others. No tractor will tread in either. The air becomes brittle. Deep breaths sputter with surprise as the cold stabs our lungs. Birds flee to the welcoming South. Animals burrow and sleep. Seeds lie dormant. In areas where the earth is not frozen winter crops are planted. Hardy greens, broccoli, and cauliflower are the stars of the winter show. Garlic and onions winter over, ready to sprout with prodding by the grounds first warming. Citrus thrives in temperate zones. Bananas reveal their glaring year-round permanence, made more spectacular by the lack of other fruits to distract.

Winter is a time for root vegetables, cabbages, hard squashes, and dried beans for they are harvested from the closest season. Apples and pears are welcome companions through January until their texture and flavor suffer from storage and are no longer good eating. Persimmons and pomegranates keep company through early winter to perk up salads, roasted meats, and desserts, but they too abandon us, and leave us to dried fruits, citrus, and the efforts of summer canning. Like Sirens, fruits and vegetables out of season tempt us in the marketplace. Buy them and you will be sorely disappointed, their taste and texture a mere shadow of their spring, summer, and fall cousins.

Meals become heavier to offer protection from the cold. Their inviting smells relieve us of the dreariness of winter. Crisp duck confit with a bubbling pot of tiny green lentils, and short ribs braised in red wine, provide comfort. Warm cakes and puddings tame our sweet tooth. We add a few pounds and cover them with the bulk of our sweaters.

Children occupy themselves with sugar cookie shapes and golden bread dolls baked on cold snowy days. A hot stove no longer tortures, but adds fragrant warmth to the house enticing us to bake, braise, and stew. Winter is a time of holidays and celebrations. It carries within it the beginning of a new year. It is a season to enjoy visiting with family and friends as they linger around the table, bathed in the glow of a memorable repast.

Contemplate the wonders and stillness of the winter from the warmth of your kitchen. Wipe your hand across a steamy window to appreciate the fullness of a sun-sparked day. As the days slowly become longer, look forward to the first warm breath of spring.

winter menus

Winter Menu I

caramelized onion and smoked bacon tart   108

steamed mussels in red wine and shallots   110

nutmeg custard   112

WINES: A fruity red Spanish Rioja or French Beaujolais would complement the intense flavors of the onion tart and the sea-sparked acidity of the mussels. Choose an Alsatian Gewürztraminer Vendange Tardive for the custard.

caramelized onion
and smoked bacon tart

A warm, savory tart makes a nice start for a winter meal. The hint of sweetness from the onions and the scent of thyme deliciously complement the smoky bacon. This onion tart is reminiscent of those served in bistros throughout France.

SERVES 8 TO 10

1   Remove the Pâte Brisée from the refrigerator and let it sit for 10 minutes before rolling. Roll out the dough ⅛ inch thick, using as little flour as possible, large enough to fit a 12 by 1-inch tart pan. Turn your tart pan over on top of the dough and use the edge as a measure to cut out a circle 2 inches larger than the pan all of the way around. Lift the dough and place it in the pan. Press it firmly against the bottom and sides of the pan and trim the edges. Chill the lined pan in the refrigerator until the dough is firm, about 40 minutes. The lined tart shell can be wrapped in plastic and chilled overnight in the refrigerator or frozen for up to 2 weeks.

2   Preheat the oven to 400 degrees F.

3   Remove the pan from the refrigerator. Prick the dough well with a fork. Line the dough with a square of aluminum foil that has been cut larger than the diameter of the pan. Press it into the corners well. Fill the tart shell with dried beans or pie weights and bake in the preheated oven for 25 minutes. Remove the beans using caution. They will be very hot. Carefully peel off the foil. Place the tart shell on a sheet pan to cool. Reserve at room temperature until ready to fill. The tart shell may be baked up to 1 day in advance and stored well wrapped at room temperature.

4   Peel and halve the onions. Remove the core on the root end by cutting it out in a triangular wedge. You want the onion slices to separate when they are sliced. Slice the onions into very thin wedges from top to bottom, parallel with the natural lines in the onion. You should have about 6 cups of sliced onions. Reserve.

5   Slice the bacon into ¼-inch pieces. Heat a large sauté pan over medium heat. Add the bacon and cook, stirring occasionally until it is crisp. Remove the bacon with a slotted spoon and drain on a paper towel. Pour off all but about 1 tablespoon of the bacon fat from the pan.

6   Add the sliced onions to the pan and sauté over medium-high heat until they are lightly browned on the edges, about 5 minutes. Season them with salt and pepper and add the chopped thyme. Reduce the heat to medium/medium-low and continue to cook, stirring occasionally, until the onions are soft and their juices have evaporated, about 10 minutes. Remove the onions from the heat, season to taste with salt and pepper, and spread them out on a sheet pan to cool. The onions and bacon can be prepared up to 2 days in advance. Mix them together and store well wrapped in the refrigerator.

7   Move the oven rack to the bottom rung. Preheat the oven to 400 degrees F.

8   In a large bowl, lightly whisk together the Crème Fraîche and the flour; season with salt and pepper to taste. Add the onion-bacon mixture and stir to combine. Spread the mixture evenly over the bottom of the crust.

9   Bake on the bottom rack in the preheated oven until the filling has set and the top and the crust are golden, about 40 to 50 minutes. Cool to warm before slicing into wedges.

½ recipe Pâte Brisée (page 55)

3 medium yellow onions

½ pound sliced smoked bacon

Salt

Freshly ground black pepper

1 tablespoon chopped fresh thyme or 1 teaspoon dried

1½ cups Crème Fraîche (page 39)

3 tablespoons flour

steamed mussels in red wine and shallots

Classically mussels are steamed in white wine. Steaming them in red wine makes them heartier and more robust in flavor. The fragrant broth, finished with butter, is rich and satisfying—perfect to soak up with toasted hunks of garlic-scented bread. When I prepare this dish I prefer to use the small intensely flavored black Prince Edward Island (PEI) mussels to the flashy, flabby New Zealand green-lipped mussels.

It is not necessary to serve the mussels with a fork. Instead, remove one mussel from its shell and use the shell as a pincer to pluck the remaining mussels from their shells. It's a rustic and fun way to eat them and saves on cleanup. Be sure to put out extra bowls in which to put the empty shells. The broth can be finished using the bread as a mop. Encourage your guests to do so with gusto. Plan on about a dozen mussels per person, a half dozen or so more if you have hearty eaters or mussel-loving fanatics.

SERVES 8

1   Preheat the oven to 350 degrees F.

2   Rub the sliced bread with the whole peeled garlic clove. Rub the clove first all over the rough crust to get the juices flowing and then on the sides of the bread. Keep rubbing the clove along the crust as necessary to keep the garlic juices flowing. Drizzle the garlic-scented bread with enough olive oil to lightly moisten the slices.

3   Spread the bread slices on a sheet pan. Toast in the preheated oven until the bread is golden on the outside but still soft on the inside, 10 to 15 minutes. You don't want the bread to be completely crisp. Reserve on the sheet pan or in a basket until ready to serve.

4   Scrub the outside of the mussels with a stiff brush under running water. Throw away any that are open and do not close, have broken shells, or are light and feel hollow. Using a clean cloth, grasp the beard of the mussel and pull it off. The

beard hangs off the hinge of the mussel and looks like a tangle of green-brown threads. Reserve the mussels in a large bowl, cover with a few sheets of damp newspaper, and refrigerate.

5   Heat 2 tablespoons of butter in a large stockpot over medium-high heat. Add the shallots and sauté until their perfume is released and they are golden and tender, about 5 minutes. Add the red wine, 1½ teaspoons of salt, bay leaf, thyme sprigs, and ½ cup of the parsley leaves. Bring to a boil. The steaming liquid may be prepared ahead of time and reheated to cook the mussels. Cool and store well covered in the refrigerator.

6   Add the mussels to the steaming liquid and cover tightly. Shake the pan to mix the mussels, which will open after 3 to 4 minutes. After they have opened, continue to cook for 3 to 4 minutes more. Discard any mussels that are still closed. Remove the pan from the heat.

7   Remove the mussels from the pot with a slotted spoon and place them in a large bowl. Remove the bay leaf and thyme stems. Bring the steaming liquid to a boil and whisk in the remaining 4 tablespoons of butter; season to taste with salt and black pepper. Pour the broth over the mussels and sprinkle the remaining parsley leaves over the top. Serve the bread in a basket to be passed.

Sixteen 1-inch slices of peasant bread

1 large garlic clove, peeled and left whole

Extra virgin olive oil

8 to 12 dozen PEI mussels, plus some more in case a few don't open

2 tablespoons plus 4 tablespoons unsalted butter

8 medium shallots, peeled, trimmed, and finely sliced

One 750-ml bottle good fruity red wine such as Beaujolais

Salt

1 bay leaf, fresh or dried

6 bushy thyme sprigs or 1½ teaspoons dried

½ cup Italian parsley leaves, plus an additional ½ cup for garnish

Freshly ground black pepper

nutmeg custard

I always knew when my mother was baking these custards. The scent of nutmeg would rush to greet me as soon as I opened the mudroom door. It would wrap around me as I entered the kitchen where my mother would be busily preparing dinner. I would beg her to tell me when the custards would be done, hoping for an early taste. She would pull them slowly and ceremoniously out of the oven to avoid splashing them with water from their bath. I would stare longingly at the cooling custards dusted with fresh nutmeg, safely tucked inside their earthenware pots. The custards would be served with a bit of warmth still clinging to them. I would carefully break the delicate skin and gather a bit of the nutmeg dust along with the warm custard. The flecks of dry sandy nutmeg were stark in contrast to the smooth silky custard. The exotic flavor of the grains would explode as they softened in my mouth. It was pure delight then and remains the same every time I plow my spoon through the shimmering brown-speckled top of a warm nutmeg custard. The custards are also wonderful served chilled.

SERVES 8

1   Place eight 1-cup ramekins or custard cups in a deep roasting pan; reserve until ready to use.

2   Preheat the oven to 350 degrees F. Place an oven rack on the lowest rungs.

3   In a large bowl, whisk together the sugar, eggs, and egg yolks.

4   Bring the milk to a boil in a medium saucepan and add the 1½ teaspoons nutmeg. Turn off the heat and let the milk and nutmeg steep for 10 minutes.

5   Pour the hot milk slowly into the egg mixture, whisking constantly. Strain the custard into a pitcher.

6   Pour or ladle the custard into the prepared ramekins or custard cups. Fill them to ¼ inch below the top edge. Sprinkle or grate nutmeg lightly over the tops.

7   Pour enough hot, not boiling, water, into the roasting pan to come three-quarters of the way up the sides of the ramekins. Bake the custards in the preheated oven on the low oven rack, covered, but not sealed, with a flat piece of parchment paper or foil until set, 30 to 40 minutes. To test to see if the custards are done, jiggle one gently with your hand. They are done if the custard is set. Carefully remove the ramekins from the water bath. Cool the custards to warm to serve or serve chilled. To chill, cool the custards to room temperature and place them in the refrigerator, uncovered. When they are cold, cover them tightly with plastic wrap. The custards can be prepared up to 2 days in advance if you are serving them chilled.

¾ cup sugar

5 large eggs

2 large egg yolks

4 cups whole milk

1½ teaspoons freshly grated nutmeg, plus some to sprinkle

Winter Menu II

WINES: Many people prefer to eat their salads without an accompanying wine. Acid in vinegar is challenging to most wines. This salad is more wine-friendly because of the acid-dispersing pancetta and croutons. If you would like to have a white wine to start, a French or New Zealand Sauvignon Blanc will hold up to the acidity of the vinaigrette. Otherwise go directly to a red wine for the papardelle. The meatiness of the mushrooms and the zing of the tomato in the sauce make the dish an ideal match for a Chianti or fruity American Zinfandel.

salad of two endives with pancetta and tiny croutons

The two endives in this salad are members of the chicory family, but come from two different branches. The curly endive comes from the *Cichorium endivia* curly-leaved branch and the Belgian endive from the *C. intybus* blanched-leaved branch. Two important nuggets of information should you ever find yourself in an argument over salad greens.

The ruffled leaves of the curly endive capture the Dijon Vinaigrette and keep it from pooling in the bottom of the salad bowl, and the juicy pale yellow crescents of Belgian endive provide bursts of juicy crunch. They are a refreshing contrast in textures.

The Tiny Croutons can be made anytime you want to use up day-old artisan bread. They keep at room temperature up to a week stored in an airtight container.

SERVES 8

1   Preheat the oven to 350 degrees F.

2   Slice the bread ½ inch thick (see Note below). Rub a whole garlic clove against the rough crust to get the garlic juices flowing, then lightly rub the soft surface of the bread. The effect you want is garlic-scented not saturated. Cut the bread into ½-inch cubes. Toss them lightly with the olive oil and season with salt and pepper.

3   Spread the bread in one layer on a sheet pan and toast in the preheated oven for 15 to 20 minutes until golden and crunchy. Cool before using.

4   Unroll the pancetta and slice it into ¼-inch-thick strips; cut the strips crosswise into ¼-inch pieces. This may be done up to 2 days in advance. Wrap and place in the refrigerator. Cook the pancetta just before serving so that it is warm when tossed with the salad.

5   Pull off the tough outer leaves of the curly endive and trim off any tough green ends. Wash the leaves and then spin dry. Tear them into bite-sized pieces.

6   Remove any dirty or bruised leaves from the outside of the Belgian endive. It is not necessary to wash it. Trim off the end and cut the endive in half lengthwise. Cut out the core in a long triangular wedge. Cut the leaves crosswise into ½-inch-thick pieces.

7   Place the endive in a large salad bowl and cover with a damp towel. Refrigerate until ready to toss the salad.

8   To finish the salad, cook the pancetta over medium-high heat in a large sauté pan until the pieces are crisp and brown on the edges and chewy at the center, about 5 minutes. Remove from the pan with a slotted spoon and drain well.

9   Toss the endive with a little of the Dijon Vinaigrette to moisten and season with salt and black pepper. Sprinkle the greens with the Tiny Croutons and the warm pancetta. Add more vinaigrette to coat the croutons and pancetta and toss again; season with salt and pepper to taste. Leftover vinaigrette can be stored under refrigeration in a tightly sealed container for up to 2 weeks.

Tiny Croutons

½ loaf day-old artisan bread, 4 cups diced

1 garlic clove, peeled and left whole

¼ cup extra virgin olive oil

Salt

Freshly ground black pepper

Salad

1 pound pancetta

1½ pounds curly endive or frisée

1 pound Belgian endive—red, white, or both

1 recipe Dijon Vinaigrette (page 50)

Salt

Freshly ground black pepper

NOTE: It is very easy to cut slices of bread from a loaf with a serrated knife. It is another story when you then have to neatly cube the slices with the same blade. A serrated edge will pull and tear the soft inside of the bread rather than cut it cleanly. To solve this problem I switch knives and use a smooth-edged chef's knife to slice the bread into cubes neatly. Make sure that your knife is sharp and cut down firmly with one or two strokes. Do not saw.

papardelle with mushrooms

The thick wide noodles and the earthy-flavored mushroom sauce make a heartwarming meal. Because the mushrooms are so meaty this dish satisfies both meat and non-meat eaters alike. Vegetable stock may be substituted for chicken stock for strict vegetarians. Use whatever domesticated or wild mushrooms you can find in the market. Dried wild mushrooms may be used after they have been rehydrated. Look for domesticated mushrooms such as clamshell, oyster, and hen-of-the-woods. Each will provide a different taste and texture. Avoid shiitakes unless you are in love with their pronounced flavor.

This pasta dough is delicate yet has a nice tooth when it is cooked. The semolina may cause the dough to crumble when it is first rolled through the pasta machine. Do not despair. Press the pieces together and keep folding and rolling until you have a smooth sheet. The dough will be smooth and firm on its final pass through the machine. You can substitute 2 pounds of dried pasta for the fresh.

SERVES 8

1   Prepare the pasta: In a large bowl, combine the flour, semolina, and salt.

2   In a separate bowl, whisk together the eggs, 4 tablespoons water, and the olive oil. Make a well in the flour and add the egg mixture. Mix until combined.

3   Turn the dough out onto a flourless counter and knead until the dough is smooth and elastic; it will seem dry. The dough will become more moist and pliable as it rests.

4   Press the dough into a flat round, cut it into three pieces, and let it rest, well wrapped, at room temperature for 45 minutes or in the refrigerator overnight.

5   Prepare the mushroom sauce: Trim the dirty tips of the mushroom stems. Dip and swish the mushrooms in cold water if they are dirty and drain well. The dirt can also be brushed off with a small stiff brush such as a toothbrush. Cut the cleaned mushrooms into bite-sized slices. It is not necessary to keep the mushroom varieties separate, as they will be used in a sauce.

6   In a large sauté pan over medium heat, lightly toast the garlic until it is golden in 2 tablespoons of olive oil, and then add the prepared mushrooms. Increase the heat and cook until the mushrooms are golden and the juices have evaporated, about 10 to 15 minutes. Season the mushrooms with salt and pepper to taste.

7   Add the shallots and cook 2 to 3 minutes, then add the red wine and simmer for 5 minutes to reduce the wine by half. Add 3 cups of chicken stock, the tomato paste, bay leaf, thyme, and parsley. Simmer for 20 minutes; season with salt and pepper. Turn off the heat and reserve, covered, in the pan. Remove the bay leaf and reheat just before serving. The sauce may also be made a day or two ahead of time and rewarmed to dress the pasta.

8   Roll the pasta dough while the sauce is simmering. Remove the dough from the refrigerator 20 minutes before rolling to allow the dough to warm up. Roll one piece of the dough with a rolling pin so that is will pass through the widest setting on the pasta machine. Pass three times through the pasta machine. (To roll the pasta by hand, see Note on page 53.) If the dough breaks press it together and pass through the widest setting until it is smooth. Fold the dough in half after each pass. Let the dough rest for 10 minutes before rolling further.

Pasta Dough (see Headnote)

2 cups all-purpose flour

1½ cups finely ground semolina

2 teaspoons salt

4 large eggs

2 tablespoons extra virgin olive oil

Mushroom Sauce

3 pounds assorted fresh wild or domesticated mushrooms (see Headnote) or 12 ounces dried wild mushrooms (see Note on page 120)

2 garlic cloves, peeled, trimmed, and thinly sliced

2 tablespoons extra virgin olive oil

Salt

Freshly ground black pepper

2 medium shallots, peeled, trimmed, and minced

2 cups dry red wine

3 cups chicken stock, mushroom rehydrating liquid, or vegetable stock

One 6-ounce can tomato paste

1 small bay leaf, fresh or dried

1 tablespoon chopped fresh thyme leaves or 1½ teaspoons dried

½ cup coarsely chopped Italian parsley leaves

1½ cups grated Parmesan cheese (6 ounces) and ¼ cup chopped Italian parsley for garnish

9   Roll to the second to last setting on the machine. Do not fold the dough after the initial kneading. It should roll into one long sheet. If the sheet gets too long, cut it in half and roll each piece separately. The dough may be very lightly dusted with flour if it seems that it is sticking in the machine. After all of the dough has been rolled cut the sheets into 12-inch lengths. Lightly dust the sheets with flour and roll the sheets up. Cut the rolls into 1-inch-wide pieces. Unroll the pieces to form ribbons. Dust the ribbons with flour and shake to coat each one and prevent them from sticking together.

10   Cook the papardelle as soon as possible after rolling or let the pasta air dry, uncovered, at room temperature. Do not cover, the condensation created will make the pasta soggy, causing it to stick together. It may also be frozen, uncovered, on a sheet pan and then wrapped tightly with plastic for use within a week. Be careful not to bang the pan once the pasta is frozen or it will break.

11   Reheat the sauce while the pasta is cooking. Cook the pasta al dente in a large pot of boiling, lightly salted water, 2 tablespoons of salt to 5 quarts of water. Fresh pasta will take only 2 to 3 minutes to cook.

12   Drain the pasta and quickly toss with one third of the hot sauce in a large pasta bowl. Ladle the remaining sauce over and sprinkle with ½ cup of the Parmesan cheese and the chopped parsley. Serve with the remaining Parmesan cheese on the side.

NOTE: If you are using dried mushrooms, place them in a large bowl. Add enough boiling water to cover the mushrooms by 2 inches. Let the mushrooms soak until the liquid has cooled. Strain the soaking liquid through cheesecloth to remove the dirt and use in place of or in conjunction with the chicken stock.

VARIATION: For a quick mushroom papardelle, sauté the mushrooms with the garlic and shallots, then add to the hot cooked pasta with a cup or two of pasta cooking water, 8 tablespoons of butter, and 1 cup Parmesan cheese. The papardelle won't be as saucy but the dish will still be loaded with flavor. Garnish with parsley leaves. Serve with additional Parmesan cheese on the side.

chocolate shortbread with vanilla cream filling

I loved Oreos as a child. Nowadays I prefer this homemade rendition. At first bite, the ever-so-slightly bittersweet chocolate shortbread crumbles and melts in your mouth as the vanilla cream filling rushes in, in a mouth-filling wave of sweet creaminess. Cut the shortbread into smaller rounds for bite-sized cookies or choose a cutter with a different shape. No matter what the dimension, these ethereal cookies will appeal to young and old alike. Serve them piled high on a plate with big glasses of cold milk.

SERVES 8; MAKES 16 SANDWICH COOKIES

1 To prepare the shortbread: In a standing mixer fitted with a paddle attachment or with an electric hand mixer, whip the butter until fluffy, about 2 to 3 minutes. Add the confectioners' sugar and beat until fluffy again. Add the vanilla extract to the mixture and then the cocoa powder; beat until they are combined. Scrape down the sides of the bowl.

2 Add the flour and salt and mix gently on low until incorporated. The dough will be very soft and slightly sticky. Turn the dough out of the bowl and onto a lightly floured board. Knead the dough lightly two to three times to incorporate the ingredients evenly.

3 Divide the dough in half and place each half between two sheets of parchment paper or plastic wrap. Roll ⅛ inch thick; make sure that both sides of the paper remain smooth. Wrap well and chill for 40 minutes.

Chocolate Shortbread

16 tablespoons (2 sticks) unsalted butter, at room temperature

1 cup confectioners' sugar, sifted

1 teaspoon pure vanilla extract

⅔ cup Dutch process or natural cocoa powder, sifted (see Note on page 122)

1½ cups all-purpose flour

1 teaspoon kosher salt

Vanilla Cream Filling

4 tablespoons unsalted butter, at room temperature

¼ teaspoon pure vanilla extract

Pinch of kosher salt

½ cup plus 2 tablespoons confectioners' sugar

4   Preheat the oven to 350 degrees F. Line a sheet pan with parchment paper.

5   Remove the dough from the refrigerator. Immediately peel off the top sheet of paper or plastic wrap and cut the dough into 2-inch rounds. Transfer to the parchment-lined sheet pan while the rounds are still firm. Let the cookies soften slightly and mark with a cookie stamp if you have one available or prick the rounds with a fork.

6   Bake for 12 to 15 minutes in the preheated oven. Turn the sheet pan once during baking. Cool before filling. The cookies may be stored in an airtight container for up to 2 days before filling.

7   Prepare the filling while the shortbreads are cooling. Combine all of the ingredients in the bowl of a standing mixer and beat with a paddle until very white and fluffy, 3 minutes. The beating time may be slightly longer if you use an electric hand mixer.

8   Spoon the filling into a pastry bag fitted with a number 6 plain tip or a plastic bag with the corner tip cut off so that the opening is ½ inch wide. Fill the cookies a few hours before serving to retain the crunch of the shortbread.

9   Line up sixteen cookies so that the side that was baked against the pan is facing up. Starting with one cookie, to get the technique down, pipe a thick ring ⅛ inch from the edge. Fill in the center of the ring with a dot of filling and place another cookie on top. Press lightly until the filling oozes almost to the edge of the cookie. Repeat with the remaining cookies. Any leftover filling may be chilled and reused. Wrap very tightly and store in the refrigerator. To reuse, bring to room temperature and then whip until fluffy again.

NOTE: Dutch process cocoa has been alkalinized, which allows the chocolate flavor and color to bloom. This creates a deeper chocolate flavor and also a richer dark color after the cookies are baked. It also reduces the acidity naturally found in cocoa powder. Natural cocoa powder can be used as a straight substitution for Dutch process powder. The cookies will be lighter in color and have a mellower chocolate flavor.

Winter Menu III

egg drop soup with pastini and swiss chard   124

grilled hanger steak with lemon and arugula   125

butterscotch crème brûlée   127

pecan shortbread fingers   129

WINES: It is difficult to pair soups with wine. Not because a good match is hard to find, but because serving a liquid with a liquid is a little odd. If you would like to serve a wine with the soup choose a simple white wine like an Italian Pinot Grigio or skip a wine for the soup and go right to the hanger steak. Either a fruity red Italian Rosso de Montalcino or a Chianti Classico is a good match for this dish. Choose a Malmsey Madeira or a sweet aged sherry for the brûlée.

egg drop soup with pastini and swiss chard

My mother would make this soup for us, minus the Swiss chard, every time we were sick and needed soothing. I loved scooping up the long ribbons of cooked egg with my spoon. The Parmesan rind, hardened cheese containing no wax or other unnatural ingredients, enriches the broth. Not all of it melts away leaving rich chewy chunks in the bottom of the pan to be scooped up and eaten. In Italy, Parmesan cooked in broth is often given to children and infants to settle their upset stomachs. Perhaps my mother's soup was just a folk remedy unknowingly passed down through the generations.

Since the chicken stock is such an integral part of this soup, it is important that it is rich and full flavored. Hold off from adding the egg until the very end of cooking, otherwise the delicate ribbons will disintegrate.

SERVES 8

1 Wash and drain the Swiss chard, trim ¼ inch off the bottom of the stems. Cut the leaves and stems into ½-inch ribbons and pieces. Reserve.

2 Bring the chicken stock with the Parmesan cheese rind to a boil in a large pot. Add the Swiss chard, reduce the heat, and simmer until the Swiss chard stems are tender, 30 to 40 minutes.

3 Whisk the eggs in a bowl until smooth, season with salt and pepper. Pour the beaten eggs quickly into the broth. Gently and slowly swirl them with a wooden spoon to form long thin ribbons. Do not boil the soup again. Add the cooked pastini and season with salt and pepper to taste.

4 Divide the soup among serving bowls and sprinkle with additional Parmesan.

1 pound Swiss chard

10 cups chicken stock

1 large piece of Parmesan cheese rind, plus 1 cup grated Parmesan cheese for sprinkling

4 large eggs

Salt

Freshly ground black pepper

2 cups pastini or other tiny pasta cooked al dente

grilled hanger steak
with lemon and arugula

Hanger steak, the popular *onglet* served in French bistros, used to be an overlooked cut of beef in the United States. Also known as a butcher's steak or hanging tender, it is an odd-shaped, oblong piece of meat that hangs inside the rear end of the rib cage, thus earning the name hanger steak. There being only one steak per steer made it difficult for a small neighborhood butcher to sell in quantity, so he would often take it home for his own use, hence the nickname butcher's steak.

Hanger steak is an extremely flavorful cut that does best cooked over high heat to medium-rare, undercooked it is chewy, overcooked it becomes tough and dry. This preparation is similar to that of a *bistecca alla fiorentina*, which is a thick-cut steak of Tuscan beef similar to a porterhouse that is prepared with lemon. The cut comes from Chianina breed of cattle and is known throughout the world for its significant tenderness and flavor. The *bistecca* is cooked on the coals to rare, then finished with a squeeze of lemon as it comes off the fire. The result is a crisp crust that holds in the juices of the flaming red interior. The lemon juice sizzles as it hits the crust of the meat, providing just enough acidity to balance its richness. It is often served with greens drizzled with very good olive oil. The hanger steak fares very well with this preparation and is quite delicious.

SERVES 8

½ pound arugula

8 hanger steaks or substitute 4 porterhouse steaks cut 2 inches thick

6 lemons

1 tablespoon extra virgin olive oil, plus more for rubbing the lemons

Salt

Freshly ground black pepper

1 cup shaved Parmesan

1   Trim the arugula, stem it, and wash well. Drain and spin dry. Reserve.

2   Hanger steaks are usually long, thick, and rectangular. If they are too thick they will take forever to cook. A good way to remedy this is to butterfly the steaks, which will greatly improve their proportions and their cooking time. To do this, make a cut down the center of the steak lengthwise stopping ¼ inch before cutting through the backside. Spread the steak along this cut like a pair of butterfly wings, hence the name. You will now have a thinner squarish steak versus a long thick chunky one.

3   Preheat the oven to 500 degrees F.

4   Cut four lemons in half, remove the pits, and rub them well with olive oil. Roast them in the preheated oven until they are caramelized, about 10 to 15 minutes. Cover them with foil to reserve their warmth until ready to serve.

5   Season both sides of the steaks well with salt and pepper. Heat a grill pan, indoor grill, or large sauté pan over high heat. Add a tablespoon of olive oil to the pan and then the steaks. Grill or pan fry them over high heat for 5 to 7 minutes on each side, depending on thickness, for medium-rare. If the pan smokes, reduce the heat to medium. The porterhouse steaks will take about 10 minutes per side. Squeeze the juice of two lemons over all just before removing from the pan. Let the steaks rest on a rack for 5 minutes before slicing.

6   Slice the steaks on the bias across the short width of the steak, or across both wings if the steaks are butterflied. If you are using a porterhouse, remove the meat from the bone and slice the steaks in the same manner. Placed the sliced meat on a large platter.

7   In a large bowl, toss the arugula with a little extra virgin olive oil to moisten, season with salt and pepper to taste. Top the sliced meat with the arugula. Sprinkle the shaved Parmesan cheese over the arugula and drizzle generously with olive oil. Garnish with the roasted lemon halves, one for each person, to squeeze over all after the steak is served.

butterscotch crème brûlée

Butterscotch Crème Brûlee warms the cockles of my heart. It reminds me of the comforting butterscotch puddings of my youth. If only my mother had had this recipe (if only I had known about crème brûlée), the consumption of a single butterscotch brûlée might have been turned into a life-defining moment. Crème brûlée is the refined city cousin of a pudding. Pudding relies on a thickener while crème brûlée relies on the alchemy of hot eggs and cream for its thick silky texture. The brûlées need to be baked at least 1 day before they are to be served to allow enough time for the custard to set.

The Pecan Shortbread Fingers (recipe follows) are a wonderful accompaniment for the crème brûlées. Serve the brûlées with or without them.

SERVES 8

1 cup whole milk

4 cups heavy cream

¼ cup granulated sugar, plus granulated or superfine sugar for caramelizing

12 large egg yolks

1 cup brown sugar

1   Place eight 6-ounce ramekins or custard cups in the bottom of a deep roasting pan.

2   Combine the milk and cream in a medium saucepan and bring it to a boil. Turn off the heat and cover to keep warm.

3   Place the ¼ cup of granulated sugar in a large heavy-bottomed saucepan. Heat over medium-high heat while stirring constantly with a wooden spoon. The sugar will begin to melt and lump. Continue stirring until the sugar starts to turn golden. Chop up large lumps of sugar into smaller pieces with the end of the spoon. They will dissolve as the sugar caramelizes. Stir until the caramel is a deep gold/brown color. If there are still a few lumps it is of no concern, they will be removed when the custard is strained.

4   When the sugar is golden brown in color remove the pan from the heat. Slowly pour in the cream and milk, a few tablespoons at a time at first, while stirring constantly to keep the sugar from seizing up and turning into hard ribbons. Note: Use caution when you pour the cream-milk mixture into the sugar. Do not place your face directly over the pan and be conscious of where your hands are. The steam rising from the pan can cause a serious burn.

5   After the cream mixture has been added place the pan back on the heat and stir until the sugar has dissolved and the mixture is smooth and caramel in color. Turn off the heat and cover the pan.

6   Place the oven rack on the lowest rung. Preheat the oven to 350 degrees F.

7   Whisk the yolks and brown sugar together lightly. Bring the cream mixture back to a boil. Pour it in thirds over the eggs while whisking constantly. Strain and skim off the air bubbles from the surface of the custard.

8   Pour the brûlée into your cups or ramekins to fill ¼ inch below the rim. Pour enough hot, not boiling, water, into the roasting pan to come three-quarters of the way up the sides of the ramekins. Bake the custards in the preheated oven on the low oven rack, covered with a flat piece of parchment paper until set, 30 to 40 minutes. To test to see if the custards are done, jiggle one gently with your hand. They are done if the custard is set in all but the very center, a circle about the size of a dime. Carefully remove the ramekins from the water bath. Cool the custards before placing in the refrigerator, uncovered, until they are completely cold. Then cover tightly with plastic until ready to serve.

9   To caramelize the brûlées, sprinkle the top of each with 1 tablespoon of granulated or superfine sugar. Roll and tap the ramekin to spread the sugar evenly on the surface of the custard. Use a blowtorch or a broiler to brûlée the sugar just until it has melted and turned golden. Be careful not to curdle the custards when using a broiler.

pecan shortbread fingers

While these shortbreads are amazing companions to Butterscotch Crème Brûlée they also handle themselves quite well served on their own with a cold glass of milk or a cup of hot tea. They can be baked ahead and stored in an airtight tin for up to a week.

MAKES THIRTY-SIX 3 BY ¾-INCH FINGERS

1   Preheat the oven to 350 degrees F.

2   In the bowl of a standing mixer fitted with the paddle attachment or with an electric hand mixer, beat the butter until it is light and fluffy. Add the confectioners' sugar, salt, and vanilla. Beat again until the mixture is light and fluffy. Add the ground pecans and mix until thoroughly combined. Mix in the flour until just combined.

8 tablespoons (1 stick) unsalted butter

½ cup confectioners' sugar

½ teaspoon salt

½ teaspoon pure vanilla extract

½ cup finely ground pecans

1 cup all-purpose flour

3   Turn the dough out of the bowl onto a lightly floured counter and knead it lightly to incorporate the ingredients evenly. Press the shortbread into an ungreased 9-inch square pan and prick all over with a fork. Bake for 30 to 35 minutes in the preheated oven until the edges are golden.

4   Cool to warm and then turn the shortbread out onto an odor-free cutting board (one that has not been used to cut onions or garlic or any other assertive food). Cut the shortbread twelve down and three across into long, thin, rectangular "fingers" while the shortbread is still warm from the oven. If the shortbread cools too much it will become brittle and break when it is cut. If this happens, slide the shortbread onto a sheet pan and place it back in the oven for 3 to 4 minutes to soften. Remove from the oven, slide back onto the board, and cut immediately.

Winter Menu IV

WINES: A medium-bodied American Pinot Noir or French red Burgundy will carry you through this meal. If you would like to serve a white wine with the first course, choose a crisp Chardonnay such as a French Pouilly-Fuissé. The tart would pair nicely with a tawny port.

herbed cheese beignets

Beignets are wonderful served warm from the fryer tucked inside a linen napkin lining a big wooden platter or willow basket. Have your guests gather around the kitchen table with a glass of wine and nibble away as they await the entrée. For a more formal presentation, make the beignets smaller and serve them with lightly dressed greens. Served either way they make a hearty winter appetizer.

SERVES 8; MAKES 36 SMALL BEIGNETS

1   Bring the milk, butter, cayenne, and salt to a boil in a heavy-bottomed saucepan. When the butter has completely melted, remove the pan from the heat and stir in the flour. Place the pan back on the heat and beat with a wooden spoon until the mixture is smooth and pulls away from the sides of the pan.

2   Place the batter in the bowl of a standing mixer fitted with a paddle attachment or beat the eggs in by hand. Add the eggs, one by one, beating well after each addition, about 15 seconds. Add the chopped herbs and then the cheeses. Reserve at room temperature for up to 4 hours until ready to fry.

3   Preheat the oven to 250 degrees F.

4   Pour the oil into a 4-quart saucepan. The oil should rise no higher than halfway up the side of the pan. If it is any higher you risk having the oil boil over the sides of the pan. Heat the oil to 375 degrees F. To test, drop a small piece of batter into the oil. It should dance merrily.

5   Drop the batter, one rounded tablespoon at a time, into the oil. Be careful not to let the temperature of the oil drop too low. Each addition of dough should elicit the same amount of sizzle as the first. Adjust the heat under the pan accordingly. A small ice cream scoop can be used to scoop the batter into the hot oil. Be careful not to drop the dough into the hot oil too abruptly or you risk being spattered.

1 cup whole milk

8 tablespoons (1 stick) unsalted butter

¼ teaspoon cayenne pepper

2½ teaspoons salt

1 cup all-purpose flour

4 large eggs

2 teaspoons chopped fresh thyme or
    1 teaspoon dried

½ teaspoon chopped fresh rosemary or
    ¼ teaspoon dried

½ cup grated Parmesan cheese

1 heaping cup grated Emmenthaler or
    Swiss Gruyère cheese

2 quarts expeller pressed vegetable oil for
    frying (see Note on page 16)

6   Fry the beignets until they are golden and puffed on one side, then turn them over with a slotted spoon and repeat on the other side. Remove them from the oil with a slotted spoon and drain on clean lint-free cloth or paper towels. Keep the beignets warm in a 250 degree F oven until all of the batter is cooked. Serve the beignets warm.

coq au vin

Coq au vin translates directly into cock in wine in English. This may not be considered polite in many circles, but those who enjoy food and have a working knowledge of French cuisine know that what we are talking about here is a male chicken cooked in wine, usually red. In the not so old days, a rooster, no longer able to serve his purpose, was eaten in order to make way for his successor. It was necessary to marinate and then stew the tough old bird in wine to break down the muscle fibers. Thus another dish born out of necessity. You'd be hard-pressed to find a rooster in your supermarket. The closest you could come would be to purchase a capon, which is a castrated rooster with large breasts. Enough said. So I think of this recipe as chicken rooster in red wine, which is a misnomer but has every intention of replicating the same procedure that you would use in preparing a rooster if you could find one. The breasts of the chicken tend to dry out in this preparation so it's good to remove them once they are cooked. You can add them back at the end. Should you wish to avoid this process, use only legs. They will turn out succulent, moist, and full of flavor every time.

SERVES 8

1   Ask your butcher to cut the chicken up into eight pieces on the bone. Each breast should be cut into two pieces, one piece with the wing and one without. The legs and thighs should be cut into two pieces.

2   Slice the stem of the mushrooms even with the cap. Quickly wash and drain the caps. Do not soak them in water. They are like sponges and will become water-logged in short order. Peel the onions and leave them whole. Wash and trim the celery. Slice the stalks thinly, about ⅛ inch thick. Slice the bacon into ¼-inch strips. Reserve each component separately.

3   Place the flour in a large shallow bowl or pan. Season the chicken pieces with salt and pepper. Dredge them in the flour and shake off the excess.

4   Heat 3 tablespoons of butter in the bottom of a deep sauté pan over medium heat. Have a large Dutch oven or roasting pan ready to receive the chicken after it is seared. Brown the chicken pieces until the skin is crisp and golden on all sides, about 5 to 10 minutes. Adjust the heat if the pan gets too hot and the flour starts to burn.

5   Remove the chicken from the pan and place it in the Dutch oven; drain off any grease and add half the red wine to the pan. Loosen any caramelized bits on the bottom of the pan with a wooden spoon. Simmer for 5 minutes and pour over the browned chicken. Scrape the pan well. Wipe the pan out with a paper towel or rinse and dry it. Add the bacon to the pan. Cook it until it is crisp. Remove it from the pan with a slotted spoon and add it to the chicken.

6   Preheat the oven to 400 degrees F.

7   Pour off the grease in the pan and add the remaining wine. Use the same deglazing procedure as for the chicken. Pour the wine over the chicken, wipe out the pan, and add 2 tablespoons of butter. Allow the butter to brown and then add the onions. When the onions start to brown, about 3 minutes, add the celery, and season with salt and pepper. When the vegetables are golden, about 4 to 5 minutes, add them to the chicken pan.

Two 4-pound roasting chickens, cut into 8 pieces each or 8 large whole legs and thighs

2 pounds small button mushrooms

24 small white boiling onions or pearl onions

2 celery stalks

1 pound of thick-cut smoked bacon

2 cups all-purpose flour

Salt

Freshly ground black pepper

6 tablespoons unsalted butter

One 750-ml bottle red wine

1 cup cold strong chicken stock

6 fresh thyme sprigs or 1½ teaspoons dried

6 Italian parsley sprigs, plus ¼ cup chopped Italian parsley leaves for garnish

1 large bay leaf, fresh or dried

8   Add the remaining tablespoon of butter to the pan and brown. Add the mushrooms and cook until their liquid has been exuded and they are golden. Season with salt and pepper.

9   Add them to the chicken. Whisk 2 tablespoons of the dredging flour into the cup of cold chicken stock. Add the mixture to the vegetable pan and bring it to a boil. Reduce the heat and simmer for 2 minutes until thickened. Strain the mixture over the chicken and stir to combine with the wine.

10   Add the herbs to the Dutch oven or roasting pan. Cover the pan with foil or a lid and place in the preheated oven. Cook for 20 minutes. Take the pan out of the oven and remove the breasts. Turn the oven down to 350 degrees F. Uncover the pan and place it back in the oven to braise for 40 more minutes. Keep the breasts covered with foil on a plate. Add them back to the pan for the last 15 minutes of cooking to reheat. Remove the bay leaf and taste the broth for seasoning. Add salt and pepper if necessary.

11   Serve one or two pieces of chicken per person; spoon the vegetables, bacon, and juices over. Garnish with the chopped parsley.

crisscross raspberry jam tart

This crisscross tart is my nod to the classic linzertorte. Every summer I make raspberry jam in anticipation of making this winter tart. I have to fight off my family to keep the last two pots of jam, reserved for the filling, from being eaten. The fight is worth it. The tartness of the jam is a wonderful foil to the rich crumbly, nut- and cinnamon-scented crust. Serve alone or with Vanilla Ice Cream (page 289) or softly whipped cream.

MAKES ONE 12-INCH TART

1   Preheat the oven to 350 degrees F.

2   Spread the almonds out evenly on a sheet pan. Toast them in the preheated oven for 10 minutes. Cool the nuts completely. Repeat the same process with the hazelnuts; increase the baking time to 12 minutes. After the hazelnuts have cooled, rub them together between your hands to remove any loose skin. Discard the skins. Mix the cooled nuts together and grind finely with ½ cup of the flour in a food processor. In a medium bowl, combine the ground nuts with the remaining flour, semolina, salt, and cinnamon. Reserve.

3   In the bowl of a standing mixer fitted with the paddle attachment or with an electric hand mixer, beat the butter for 2 to 3 minutes until light and fluffy. Add the sugar and vanilla and beat until fluffy, about 2 minutes. It will take longer if you are using a hand mixer.

4   Add the dry ingredients to the butter mixture and mix until uniform.

Hazelnut Almond Short Dough

½ cup whole almonds

¼ cup whole hazelnuts

1½ cups all-purpose flour

½ cup finely ground semolina

1 teaspoon salt

1 teaspoon ground cinnamon

16 tablespoons (2 sticks) unsalted butter, at room temperature

½ cup confectioners' sugar

½ teaspoon pure vanilla extract

Filling

1¼ cups raspberry jam, homemade or commercial

5   Turn the dough out of the bowl onto a lightly floured counter. Knead it lightly a couple of times to incorporate the ingredients evenly. Pat the dough into a flat round. Divide the round in half.

6   Roll half the dough ⅛ inch thick between two pieces of parchment paper. Make sure that the dough is large enough to fill a 12 by 1-inch tart pan. Use the upside down pan as a measure. Roll the other half ⅛ inch thick between two sheets of parchment for the strips. Place the parchment encased dough sheets on a sheet pan, wrap with plastic, and chill. Chill the dough for 1 hour before using it to line the tart pan. The dough may also be chilled as a 1-inch-thick patty, wrapped well in plastic, and refrigerated for up to 4 days before rolling or stored in the freezer for up to a month.

7   Remove one sheet of rolled dough from the refrigerator. Peel off the top sheet of parchment paper. Turn the tart pan over and place lightly on top of the dough. Use it as a guide to cut a circle 1 inch larger than the tart pan. Remove the excess dough. Let it warm up enough so that it is flexible and will not break if moved.

8   To transfer the dough to the tart pan, flip the dough upside down so that the dough circle is centered on the pan. Peel the remaining paper off. Don't worry if the dough crumbles, it can be pressed together with your fingers. No water is necessary to seal the broken dough; the high butter-to-flour ratio makes it self-sealing. Press the dough into the bottom and the sides of the tart pan. Trim the edges where it is necessary.

9   Chill the lined tart pan in the refrigerator for 20 minutes. Remove it from the refrigerator and spread the raspberry jam evenly across the dough about ¼ inch thick.

10   Preheat the oven to 350 degrees F.

11   Remove the remaining sheet of dough from the refrigerator. Remove the top sheet of parchment paper and cut the dough into ½-inch strips. Let the strips become slightly flexible, then use a long thin metal spatula to transfer the strips of dough to the tart. If the dough becomes too soft to handle, chill it in the refrigerator for 15 minutes to firm up.

12   Make a lattice pattern across the top of the jam. The strips do not have to be woven. They should lie one layer in one direction with the second layer of strips perpendicular to the first. Press the ends of the dough strips against the edge of the tart where they meet. Bake the tart in the preheated oven for 45 to 50 minutes or until the crust is golden. Cool to warm before slicing into wedges. Serve plain, with Vanilla Ice Cream, or softly whipped cream.

VARIATION: The tart can also be made into bite-sized cookies. I cut two circles, plain or fluted, of the same size and then cut a smaller circle or heart shape out of one of the circles. Once baked the circle with the cutout is heavily dusted with confectioners' sugar, while the other circle has raspberry jam lightly spread on it. The sugar-dusted circle is gently pressed on top of the jam-coated one, creating a beautiful and delicious cookie.

Winter Menu V

roasted beet and blood orange salad with spicy greens   142

braised lamb shanks with white beans
    and aromatic vegetables   145

lemon buttermilk pound cake with lemon glaze   147

WINES: Salads are challenging for wines because of vinegar. This salad contains the mellow acid of sherry vinegar and citrus. A crisp New Zealand Sauvignon Blanc or Italian Pinot Grigio will match the acidity of the salad if you wish to serve a wine with the first course. Serve a fruity Spanish Rioja or Italian Chianti Classico with the lamb shanks.

roasted beet and blood orange salad with spicy greens

Blood oranges parallel the flavor and color of beets. Both are sweet with an edge of bitterness and marked with red and gold. The lightness of the citrus balances the earthiness of the root. Perhaps that's what makes them the perfect match. The combination is tantalizing and delicious. The spice of arugula adds a nice spark of flavor to the salad. The salad can also be made without the greens or just a touch and served as a side dish. It makes a fabulous winter luncheon salad served with broiled goat cheese crostini.

The best blood oranges used to come Italy, which is long way to come if you're a freshly picked orange. The oranges were ruby red with a bittersweet intensity that held up well despite the long journey. Over the past 8 years, blood oranges have become increasing popular with American growers. They range in size from a small tangerine to a grapefruit. I always choose the smaller ones with a bit of blush on the skin. The oversized fruit always seems diluted and more grapefruit-like. If the larger size is your only option, slice the fruit into rounds and then halve or quarter them so that you don't have slices of platter-sized fruit in your salad.

SERVES 8

1 Preheat the oven to 400 degrees F.

2 Trim the tops and roots from the beets and wash well. Place the red beets on a piece of foil large enough to fold over and seal. Drizzle with olive oil and season with salt and pepper. Seal the foil and repeat with the gold beets. Place both foil pillows on a sheet tray and roast in the preheated oven for 1 to 1½ hours until the beets are tender when pierced with a knife. Allow the beets to cool and then peel.

3 While the beets are roasting, peel the oranges with a serrated knife and remove all of the white pith. Slice into rounds ¼ inch thick. Remove the pips and reserve the slices in the refrigerator unless you will be using them within 2 to 3 hours.

4 Prepare the Blood Orange Sherry Vinaigrette.

5 Wash the arugula and spinach well and spin dry. Mix the greens together and reserve covered with a damp towel in the refrigerator.

6 Cut each peeled beet into eight wedges. Keep the yellow and gold beets separate or their colors will bleed together. Toss each color with 2 tablespoons of sherry vinegar; season with salt and pepper. Allow the beets to marinate for at least 1 hour or overnight.

7 In a large bowl, toss the beets and their juices together with enough vinaigrette to coat; add the orange segments and toss gently so that they don't break up.

8 Drizzle the greens with vinaigrette to moisten and toss with the beets and blood oranges; season with salt and pepper to taste. Garnish with the chopped chives. You may also place the greens on a large platter and serve the beets and oranges on top.

1½ pounds medium gold beets

1½ pounds medium red beets

Extra virgin olive oil

Salt

Freshly ground black pepper

6 small blood oranges

Blood Orange Sherry Vinaigrette (recipe follows)

¼ pound baby arugula

¼ pound baby spinach

¼ cup sherry vinegar

¼ cup finely chopped chives

blood orange sherry vinaigrette

MAKES ½ TO ¾ CUP

1   Juice and strain the blood oranges.
    Measure ¼ cup of juice.

2   In a medium bowl, whisk the juice with
    the shallots and the sherry vinegar; season
    with salt and pepper to taste and let the
    mixture marinate for 10 minutes.

3   Whisk in the olive oil to taste. Add more
    olive oil if the vinaigrette is too acidic for
    your palate. Adjust the seasoning to taste.

2 small blood oranges

1 medium shallot, peeled,
  trimmed, and minced

2 tablespoons sherry vinegar

Salt

Freshly ground black pepper

¼ to ½ cup extra virgin olive oil

braised lamb shanks with white beans and aromatic vegetables

Long ago, mutton shanks, from full-grown sheep, were braised with vegetables and herbs to tenderize them and add flavor to balance their strong taste. Lamb shanks were a luxury consumed during the spring months, after the more expensive cuts of the lamb were sold. Nowadays in the United States, you would be hard-pressed to find any mutton to braise. Lamb-breeding programs last all year long and provide a constant supply of fresh meat. It is no longer a necessity to consume older sheep, unless you live on a sheep farm.

Lamb has become much more delicate in flavor so it is important to add just enough herbs to enhance its flavor without overpowering it. Too much rosemary will make it seem as though you are eating a plant instead of an animal. Request shanks from the hind legs; they are larger and meatier, unless you desire the smaller front ones. Ask your butcher to cut the lamb shanks in half crosswise almost all the way through. It makes the presentation of the shank a little more elegant and less prehistoric on the plate. Serve the shanks simply with a slice of good bread to soak up the juices.

SERVES 8

4 medium carrots

2 celery stalks

2 medium yellow onions

8 medium garlic cloves

5 tablespoons extra virgin olive oil

Salt

Freshly ground black pepper

1 cup canned peeled tomatoes, seeded and chopped with juice

2 bay leaves, fresh or dried

6 parsley sprigs plus ½ cup chopped Italian parsley for garnish

12 fresh thyme sprigs or 1 tablespoon dried

Two 2-inch fresh rosemary sprigs or 1½ teaspoons dried

1 pound (2½ cups) white cannellini or other large white beans, soaked overnight in cold water

8 meaty lamb shanks

One 750-ml bottle dry white wine

1   Preheat the oven to 450 degrees F.

2   Peel and trim the carrots. Cut into uniform ½-inch pieces or cubes. Wash and trim the ends off the celery and slice into ½-inch pieces. Peel and dice the onions into ¼-inch pieces. Peel the garlic cloves, trim off their tough ends, and cut them in half. Toss the vegetables in a bowl with 2 tablespoons of olive oil and season with salt and pepper.

3   Spread the vegetables out in the bottom of a roasting pan and roast in the preheated oven until golden, about 30 to 40 minutes. Stir occasionally. Remove the pan from the oven and leave on the stove top to receive the seared lamb shanks. Add the tomatoes, herbs, and beans to the vegetables and mix.

4   Heat a large sauté pan over medium-high heat and add 3 tablespoons of olive oil. Season the lamb shanks well with salt and pepper. Sear in olive oil and brown well on all sides, 10 to 15 minutes. Adjust the heat if the pan gets too hot and smokes. You don't want the bottom of the pan to burn. Remove the shanks from the sauté pan and place on top of the vegetables in the roasting pan. You may need to sear the shanks in two to three batches if your sauté pan is small.

5   Pour off the grease in the sauté pan and add the wine. Bring to a boil and simmer for 10 minutes to reduce by half. Loosen any caramelized bits on the bottom of the pan with a wooden spoon. Pour the wine over the lamb and vegetables. Add 2 cups of water and cover the pan with aluminum foil or a lid and place in the preheated oven for 30 minutes.

6   Reduce the oven heat to 350 degrees F and braise for 2½ hours until the shanks are tender and the meat pulls easily away from the bone. Turn the shanks over after 1½ hours. Uncover the pan for the last half hour of cooking.

7   To serve, remove the bay leaves and bare herb sprigs from the pan. Spoon the beans onto a large platter or into individual serving bowls and top with the lamb shanks. Ladle the juices over and sprinkle with chopped Italian parsley.

lemon buttermilk pound cake with lemon glaze

Meyer lemons add their distinct flavor to this versatile and delicious pound cake. I perfected this pound cake while working at an exclusive hotel in the Pacific Heights neighborhood of San Francisco. The owners had an affinity for lemon pound cake so I would bake it four or five times a week. It gave me a chance to test, adjust, and test again so that everything was in balance. Buttermilk adds tanginess, which enhances the lemon flavor. If Meyer lemons are unavailable another variety may be substituted.

This cake is best when prepared the day before it is served. Do not cover the glazed cake with plastic wrap because when you remove the wrap, you will take the glaze with it. The cake can be left unwrapped for 24 hours unsliced and still retain its moistness. After the cake has been sliced keep it in a sealed plastic container.

SERVES 8 TO 12

1 Preheat the oven to 350 degrees F. Butter and flour an 8-cup loaf pan. Reserve.

2 In the bowl of a standing mixer fitted with the paddle attachment or with an electric hand mixer, whip together the butter, zest, and sugar until fluffy, about 2 to 3 minutes. Scrape down the sides of the bowl. Add the eggs one by one, beating well after each addition.

Lemon Buttermilk Pound Cake

12 tablespoons (1½) sticks unsalted butter, at room temperature

2 teaspoons finely grated lemon zest

1½ cups granulated sugar

3 large eggs

2¼ cups all-purpose flour

2 teaspoons baking powder

¾ teaspoon salt

1 cup buttermilk

Lemon Glaze

½ cup lemon juice (use the zested lemons from the pound cake)

1 packed cup confectioners' sugar, sifted

3   Combine the dry ingredients in a small bowl. Add to the butter in thirds at slow speed alternating with the buttermilk. Spoon the batter into the prepared loaf pan. Bake in the preheated oven until a knife inserted into center comes out clean, 1 hour to 1 hour and 5 minutes. The very top of the cake will be a little moist. Cool the cake for 15 minutes in the pan.

4   Prepare the Lemon Glaze while the cake is cooling.

5   Pour the lemon juice into a small heavy-bottomed saucepan and whisk in the sifted sugar a little at a time. Stir over low heat until the powdered sugar is dissolved.

6   Bring the pan to a simmer and simmer for 2 minutes. Cool for 10 minutes before glazing the cake; the glaze will thicken slightly.

7   Remove the cake from the pan and place right side up on a cooling rack. Make copious amount of holes in cake with a skewer while the cake is still warm. Pour the warm lemon glaze over. The excess glaze that drips off the cake can be reheated and poured over the cake again. Cool the cake before serving.

VARIATIONS: Substitute orange zest for lemon or add a cup of chopped pecans or fresh blueberries to the batter. Sprinkle the crisp topping (page 303) over the batter before baking and omit the Lemon Glaze to create an excellent accompaniment for morning coffee or tea.

The cake also bakes well in a 9-cup Bundt pan.

Winter Menu VI

rapini with fresh mozzarella and hot peppers 150

red wine–braised short ribs with roasted root vegetables 152

fig spice cake with maple cream cheese frosting 154

WINES: Serve a crisp white Spanish Albariño or a juicy pink *rosado* to accompany the rapini. The fruitiness of the wine will work well with the spice in the dish. Complement the richness and earthiness of the short ribs with a young California Merlot or a fruity Italian Barbera d'Alba.

rapini with fresh mozzarella and hot peppers

As a child I always thought that rapini was an overly leafy bitter broccoli. My great-grandmother would drop it into a big pot of boiling water to tenderize the leaves and stems, then sauté it with huge cloves of toasted garlic and drowning amounts of olive oil to offset its bitterness. When I rediscovered broccoli rabe, the name by which rapini is more commonly known, it was taking the nation by storm and heralded as the hot "new" menu ingredient. It seemed too nouveau and expensive to be the vegetable of my youth, but it was indeed, under the guise of a different name.

The mozzarella and the toasted bread elevate this dish from a side vegetable to an appetizer. Similar to a bruschetta, the bread is used as a vehicle to soak up the juices thick with olive oil, rather than as a delivery system for the toppings. The bread is a moist savory treat at the end, reminiscent of olive oil, rapini, and the hot spice of chiles.

Calabrian chiles can be mail-ordered if you cannot find them at your local gourmet store. These special spicy peppers are cured with salt and herbs and preserved in olive oil. They pack not only heat but also an immense amount of flavor. For less heat remove the seeds and slice the chiles into fiery red rings.

SERVES 8

1   Wash and trim the tough ends off the rapini and cut the heads and tender stems into fork-sized pieces. Reserve.

2   Remove the stem and core from chiles and slice into rings. Discard the seeds if you prefer less heat. Reserve.

3   Preheat the oven to 400 degrees F, or a grill to medium, to toast the bread.

4   Bring a large pot of heavily salted water to a boil, 2 tablespoons per 2½ quarts of water. Blanch the rapini for 2 minutes to wilt and drain well. Reserve.

5   Slice the mozzarella balls into eight pieces each. Reserve at room temperature for up to 2 hours. Otherwise, refrigerate the slices and bring them up to room temperature before serving.

6   Drizzle the sliced bread generously with olive oil and season with salt and pepper. Toast in the preheated oven or on the grill until golden but still soft on the interior. Wrap with a cloth to keep warm.

7   Heat ½ cup of olive oil in a large sauté pan and add the sliced garlic cloves. Cook the cloves until they are golden and perfume the oil. Add the rapini and chile peppers. Be careful that the oil does not spatter. Sauté until the rapini is thoroughly heated and tender. Add the chicken stock and bring to a boil. Season to taste with salt.

8   Place the bread slices in flat bowls or deep plates. Place the mozzarella on top of the warm bread, three to four slices per piece. Divide the hot rapini evenly among the bowls over the top of the bread. Bring the pan juices to a boil and spoon over all. Drizzle with additional extra virgin olive oil.

---

2 pounds rapini

8 medium Calabrian chiles or other spicy red pepper salted and packed in oil

Four 4-ounce balls of fresh mozzarella

Eight 1-inch-thick slices of Italian or peasant bread

½ cup extra virgin olive oil, plus more for drizzling

Salt

Freshly ground black pepper

8 garlic cloves, peeled, trimmed, and thinly sliced

1 cup chicken stock

red wine–braised short ribs with roasted root vegetables

A bubbling roasting pan brimming with rich meat and hearty root vegetables is synonymous with the classic one-pot winter meal. The chopping of the vegetables can be tedious but once everything goes into the pot the dish can be all but forgotten for several hours until the cover is lifted releasing the savory perfume of the braise.

Short ribs should be cut into pieces so that there is one bone, about 3 inches in length, per piece.

SERVES 8

1   Preheat the oven to 450 degrees F.

2   Peel and trim the vegetables, dice into ½-inch pieces. The carrots may be sliced into rounds. Leave the garlic cloves whole. Reserve the diced potatoes in cold water to keep them from browning.

3   Toss the vegetables, except for the potatoes, together in a large bowl. Add 2 tablespoons of olive oil, season with salt and pepper, and toss again. Place the vegetables, except the reserved potatoes, in a roasting pan and roast in the preheated oven until the vegetables start to caramelize, about 30 minutes. Stir occasionally. Reserve the vegetables in the pan to await the arrival of the seared short ribs.

4   Season the ribs well on all sides with salt and pepper. Over medium-high heat, add 2 to 3 tablespoons of olive oil to a large sauté pan. Add the ribs and brown on all sides, about 10 to 15 minutes. Sear the ribs in batches if your pan is not large enough. If the pan gets too hot, adjust the heat. Place the ribs on top of the vegetables in the roasting pan.

5 Pour off the fat in the sauté pan and add the wine. Bring the wine to a boil and use a wooden spoon to loosen the caramelized juices and bits of meat on the bottom of the pan. Reduce the wine by half and pour it over the ribs.

6 Dissolve the tomato paste in 1 cup of water and add to the roasting pan. Add the thyme, bay leaf, and 1 cup parsley leaves. Cover the pan with a lid or aluminum foil.

7 Place the pan in the preheated oven and roast for 30 minutes. Reduce the oven heat to 350 degrees F and braise the ribs for 1½ hours. Check occasionally to make sure there is enough juice in the pan. Add a little water if necessary. Drain the reserved potatoes and add them to the pan. Continue to braise for 1 hour more. Remove the cover completely for the last half hour of cooking.

8 Using a slotted spoon, spoon the ribs with the vegetables onto a platter or individual plates and remove the bay leaf and thyme stems; reduce the pan juices if they are thin and season to taste with salt and pepper. Spoon the juices over the meat and vegetables. Garnish with Italian parsley leaves before serving.

2 large celery roots

4 medium carrots

2 medium yellow onions

3 medium turnips

3 medium rutabagas

4 large Yukon Gold or Yellow Finn potatoes

8 garlic cloves, peeled

4 to 5 tablespoons extra virgin olive oil

Salt

Freshly ground black pepper

24 pieces (8 pounds) short ribs

One 750-ml bottle red wine

4 tablespoons tomato paste

12 fresh thyme sprigs or 1 tablespoon dried

1 bay leaf, fresh or dried

1 cup loosely packed Italian parsley leaves, plus additional parsley leaves for garnish

fig spice cake with maple cream cheese frosting

Like many cakes that have added fruit this one is moist and rich—laced with figs and perfumed with spices. The Maple Cream Cheese Frosting is the delicious finishing touch.

MAKES TWO 9-INCH CAKE PANS OR 1 BUNDT PAN

1   Butter and flour two 9-inch cake pans or one 12-cup Bundt pan. Reserve.

2   Trim the stem off the figs and cut into quarters. Bring the rum to a boil and flame; be careful not to burn your face or hands. When the flames have died down add the figs and turn off the heat. Soak for 1 hour and then puree to a very thick smooth paste. Reserve.

3   Preheat the oven to 350 degrees F.

4   In the bowl of a standing mixer fitted with the paddle attachment or an electric hand mixer, beat the butter and sugars together until light and fluffy, 2 to 3 minutes. Turn off the mixer and scrape down the sides of the bowl. Add the eggs one by one, beating well after each addition, then add the vanilla and the fig puree. Mix at medium speed for 30 seconds. Scrape down the sides of the bowl.

5   Combine the dry ingredients, including the spices, in a bowl and mix well. Add the dry ingredients to the mixing bowl, half at a time, alternating with the buttermilk. Mix on low speed until moistened and smooth, 30 seconds.

6   Pour the batter into the prepared pans. Bake in the preheated oven 35 to 40 minutes for 9-inch pans, 50 minutes to 1 hour for a Bundt pan, until center of cake springs back when lightly pressed. Turn out of the pans and cool on a wire rack.

7   Prepare the frosting after the cake has cooled. It takes only 5 minutes.

8   In the bowl of a standing mixer with a paddle attachment or an electric hand mixer, beat the butter with the confectioners' sugar, salt, and vanilla until light and fluffy, about 2 to 3 minutes.

9   Add the cream cheese and beat until incorporated, about 20 seconds.

10 Turn off the mixer and scrape down the sides of the bowl. Drizzle in the maple syrup and beat until smooth, about 15 seconds. Sandwich the two layer cakes thickly with frosting and then frost the top and sides. For a Bundt cake, fill the hole with frosting and then frost the top and sides.

VARIATION: For simplicity the cake may be baked in a Bundt pan and the icing omitted. Top the cake instead with a sprinkle of confectioners' sugar.

Fig Spice Cake

12 ounces dried figs

2 cups dark rum

16 tablespoons (2 sticks) unsalted butter, at room temperature

1 cup granulated sugar

1 cup packed brown sugar

4 large eggs

1 teaspoon pure vanilla extract

3 cups all-purpose flour

1½ teaspoons baking powder

1 teaspoon baking soda

1 teaspoon salt

½ teaspoon ground nutmeg

2 teaspoons ground cinnamon

¼ teaspoon ground cloves

1½ cups buttermilk

Maple Cream Cheese Frosting

16 tablespoons (2 sticks) unsalted butter, at room temperature

2 cups confectioners' sugar, packed

¼ teaspoon salt

½ teaspoon pure vanilla extract

1 pound cream cheese, at room temperature

¼ cup pure maple syrup

Winter Menu VII

white bean and escarole soup with smoked ham   158

goose with roasted turnips and apples   160

fresh ginger gingerbread with soft cream   164

WINES: A fruity young California Pinot Noir or French red Burgundy can cover the soup and the goose. If you are not keen on serving wine with soup and you would like to serve wine only with the goose, choose an Alsatian Pinot Gris or a German Riesling Spätlese. The slight sweetness of these wines will complement the turnips and apples and their acidity will balance the richness of the goose.

white bean and escarole soup with smoked ham

I sigh when I think about how versatile and wonderfully tasty escarole is. I've used it as a wrapper for stuffing instead of cabbage leaves and I've braised it with bacon for a quick fill-in as a green vegetable. I save all of the outside leaves of the escarole from my winter salads in anticipation of this soup. There may be vegetable kings but escarole alone reigns beautifully as the queen of the bittersweet greens.

SERVES 8

1   Soak the beans overnight in 6 cups of cold water. Refrigerate them if your kitchen is warm.

2   Clean the escarole of any brown or damaged leaves. Wash well and cut into 1-inch-wide ribbons. Cut the ribbons in half if they are very long. Reserve.

3   Peel and dice the potatoes into ½-inch cubes. Store covered with cold water until ready to use.

4   Peel, trim, and slice the carrots thinly. Peel the onion; remove the root and its core and slice thinly from top to bottom, not across the diameter. Peel, trim, and slice the garlic thinly. Wash and trim the celery and slice thinly. Reserve the vegetables separately until you are ready to use them.

5   Add 2 tablespoons of olive oil to a large stockpot over medium-high heat. Add the ham hock and sauté until it browns and sizzles. Add the sliced garlic and sauté until it turns golden, about 2 to 3 minutes. Add the onion and celery and cook until they start to exude their juices. Add the carrots and season with salt and pepper. Drain and add the soaked beans, herbs, and enough water to cover the vegetables by 2 inches.

6   Bring the liquid to a boil and reduce the heat to a simmer. Simmer for 1 to 1½ hours until the beans are tender. Add additional liquid if necessary. Add the drained potatoes and escarole and cook for another ½ hour or until the potatoes are tender; season with salt and black pepper. Remove the bay and sage leaves, and parsely stems before serving.

7   To serve, spoon the soup into small bowls. Garnish with grated Parmesan and chopped Italian parsley and a drizzle of good extra virgin olive oil.

VARIATIONS: Use kale or cabbage instead of escarole for a heartier soup. Add them at the beginning of the soup preparation. For a vegetarian soup omit the ham hocks and add a medium piece of Parmesan rind. This will add richness and flavor to the broth.

1 pound cannellini beans, 2½ cups

1 pound escarole or 1 pound of the collected outer leaves of several heads

4 large Yellow Finn potatoes

2 medium carrots

1 medium yellow onion

4 garlic cloves

2 celery stalks

2 tablespoons extra virgin olive oil, plus more for drizzling

½ pound smoked ham hock or equal amount of smoked bacon

Salt

Freshly ground black pepper

1 sage leaf

1 bay leaf

6 sprigs Italian parsley

Grated Parmesan and chopped Italian parsley for garnish

goose with roasted turnips and apples

Goose is a fabulous eating bird, but it presents the same cooking challenge as a turkey. It is very difficult not to overcook the breast without undercooking the legs. Every time I cooked a goose, the bird always looked beautiful—the skin would be crisped and bronzed—but the legs would be tough and undercooked and the breast overcooked. Since I had tried this nearly impossible feat many times without success, I finally came to the realization that it was best to cook the breast and legs separately. Harmony has reigned ever since in the cooked goose department. Salting the skin side of the breast draws out some of the moisture from the fat, which makes the skin easier to crisp. The scored skin allows the fat to run out from the interior of the skin during rendering, leaving a thin crisp skin with little fat behind. I cook the breast mostly on the skin side until the skin is crisp and then turn it over and briefly roast it in the oven to finish cooking. The braised leg meat is succulent and moist and makes a beautiful companion to the roasted apples and turnips and a rosy slice of tender breast meat. I like to make goose stock with the bones after I marinate the breasts and legs because I hate to throw good bones away. It takes about 8 hours to make a really rich stock (the majority is simmering time). It's well worth it if you have the time. Start the preparation of this dish at least 1 day in advance.

SERVES 8

1   Ask the butcher to remove the breasts without bones and wings from the carcass and the legs and thighs as one piece with the bones intact. You can also do this at home if you know how. Reserve the carcass, wings, and neck for stock.

2   Trim the breasts of excess fat along the edges and remove the loose tenderloin strip on the inside of the breast. These will be cooked alongside the breast and used as a snack for the chef. Score the skin of the breasts in a crisscross pattern; take care not to drive the knife blade into the goose flesh.

3 To marinate the breasts and legs, sprinkle the skin side of each piece with 1 teaspoon of coarse sea salt. Press the salt into the skin. Press 2 sprigs of thyme into the meat side of each piece. Pepper both sides well and sprinkle ½ teaspoon of coarse salt on the meat side. Press the two halves of breasts and the two legs together with the skin side out. Marinate overnight or for a maximum of 3 days, turning the breasts and legs over each day.

4 Preheat the oven to 400 degrees F.

5 To cook the goose legs, brush off the thyme sprigs from the marinated legs. It is not necessary to season the legs further. Sear the legs in a dry heavy-bottomed ovenproof sauté pan over medium-high heat until both sides are golden, about 15 to 20 minutes. The fat will render and coat the pan as the legs begin to cook. As soon as the skin has formed a golden crust the legs will release from the pan, so don't worry about their sticking. Adjust the heat if the pan begins to smoke. Render as much fat off as possible. Pour off the fat as it accumulates into a heat-proof dish. Reserve the fat to sauté the apples and turnips.

6 Place the legs in a Dutch oven or a roasting pan and cover with 6 cups of stock. Bring the stock to a boil on the stove top, then place the pan in the preheated oven and braise the legs for 2 hours until the meat is tender and separates easily from the bone. Remove the pan from the oven and cool the legs in the stock until they are warm to the touch.

The Goose

One 11- to 12-pound goose

2 tablespoons coarse sea salt

8 fresh thyme sprigs or 2 teaspoons dried

Freshly ground black pepper

6 cups Goose Stock (recipe follows) or strong chicken stock

Roasted Turnips and Apples

1½ pounds medium turnips

1½ pounds medium apples

4 tablespoons (½ stick) unsalted butter or reserved goose fat

Salt

Freshly ground black pepper

½ cup granulated sugar

¼ cup cider vinegar

4 fresh thyme sprigs or ¾ teaspoon dried

2 cups goose stock or strong chicken stock

7   Remove the legs from the pan and place on a plate. Strain the braising juices and reserve. Pull the meat from the bone in large chunks, removing any fat, gristle, and veins; reserve the meat in the braising juices to keep it moist and discard the bones and debris. Reheat the leg meat in the braising juices to serve.

8   While the legs are braising prepare the turnips and apples. Peel the turnips and apples. Core the apples. Cut both into eight wedges each.

9   Heat the butter or goose fat, over high heat, in a large heavy-bottomed sauté pan until it begins to bubble. Add the turnips and apples. Sauté them until they are golden and caramelized, about 7 to 10 minutes; season with salt and pepper.

10   Reduce the heat to medium high and sprinkle the turnips and apples with the sugar and caramelize it to a dark gold. Add the vinegar and cook until it has evaporated, about 5 minutes. Add the thyme and the 2 cups of goose stock and place the pan in the oven with the braising legs. Roast the apple and turnips until the liquid has reduced and thickened, about 1 hour. Season to taste with salt and pepper and toss the apples and turnips to coat with the thickened juices. Cover to keep them warm. If they cool, reheat them in the oven while you cook the goose breasts.

11   After the legs are cooked and the turnips and apples are ready to go, it is time to cook the breasts. Your oven should be at 400 degrees F. Season the breasts lightly with salt. Remove the thyme sprigs. Render them skin side down in a dry pan over medium-low heat until most of the fat is gone and the skin is crisp and golden, about 15 to 20 minutes. Drain the fat into a clean dish as it accumulates in the pan so that you do not deep fry the breasts. Turn over and roast skin side up in the oven for 7 to 10 minutes. Let the breasts rest for 10 minutes before slicing. Strain and store the fat. It can be used to sauté very decadent side dish potatoes at another time.

12   To serve: Slice the breast at an angle across the muscle grain. If you see linear strings of muscle in the slices, cut at the opposite angle. Serve the sliced breast alongside the leg meat, apples, and turnips. Spoon the leg braising juices over.

goose stock

MAKES 8 CUPS

1 Preheat the oven to 400 degrees F.

2 To prepare the goose stock: Peel and trim the carrots and onions and cut into chunks. Wash, trim, and cut the celery stalks in half. Reserve.

3 Roast the carcass and assorted goose parts for 30 minutes in a large roasting pan in the preheated oven. Add the prepared vegetables and roast until the bones and vegetables are golden, about 45 minutes to 1 hour. Scrape the roasted vegetables and bones into a large stockpot.

4 Drain the oil in the roasting pan and discard. Add the white wine; simmer on the stove top and reduce by half, 5 minutes. Loosen any bits of caramelized juices and meat with a wooden spoon. Scrape all of this into the stockpot over the bones and vegetables.

5 Add the herbs and fill the pot with enough cold water to cover the bones by 2 inches. Bring the stock to a boil and skim off the fat. Reduce the heat and simmer for 6 hours, strain and reserve. Refrigerate if not using immediately. Reserve 2 cups of stock to cook the apples and turnips; use the remaining stock (6 cups) to cook the legs.

4 medium carrots

2 medium yellow onions

2 celery stalks

Carcass, wings and neck from an 11- to 12-pound goose

2 cups white wine

8 fresh thyme sprigs or 2 teaspoons dried

1 bay leaf, fresh or dried

6 Italian parsley sprigs with stems

fresh ginger gingerbread with soft cream

How often do we forget the joys of eating gingerbread warm from the oven as children? When I was a child the baking cake would fill the house with the scent of exotic spices and make us salivate. It was torture to have to wait long enough for it to cool so it wouldn't become a burning mass in our mouths. We couldn't get enough whipped cream and would pile dollop after dollop on top of our fragrant warm brown squares before my mother would pull it away. Fresh ginger adds a pungent note to this sweet bread much more so than using only powdered. Grate the ginger on the fine side of a grater and try to leave most of the fibers behind when taking away the juice and the pulp.

SERVES 8 TO 10

1   Preheat the oven to 350 degrees F. Butter and lightly flour an 8-cup loaf pan or a 9-inch square pan. Set it aside until ready to use.

2   In the bowl of a standing mixer fitted with the paddle attachment or with an electric hand mixer, whip together the butter and sugars until light and fluffy, 2 to 3 minutes. Turn off the mixer and scrape down the sides of the bowl. Add the grated fresh ginger and beat well for 15 seconds. Add the eggs one by one, beating well after each addition. Scrape down the sides of the bowl.

3   Combine the flour through salt in a small bowl. Whisk the molasses and buttermilk together in a small pitcher or measuring cup.

4   Add the flour mixture and the molasses mixture alternately in two parts to the butter mixture. Mix after each addition until the ingredients are uniformly combined.

5   Pour the batter into the prepared pan, scrape the bowl well, and bake in the preheated oven for 45 to 50 minutes or until a knife inserted in the center comes out clean. Cool in the pan to warm and then turn out onto a plate. Flip the cake over so the rounded top is up to serve.

6   In a medium bowl, whip the heavy cream to soft peaks with ½ teaspoon of vanilla and 1 tablespoon of sugar. Serve the gingerbread with the Soft Cream on top.

Gingerbread

12 tablespoons (1½ sticks) unsalted butter, at room temperature

½ cup granulated sugar

½ cup brown sugar

3 tablespoons grated fresh ginger with juice but without tough fibers

2 large eggs, at room temperature

2½ cups all-purpose flour

2 teaspoons baking powder

1 teaspoon baking soda

1 teaspoon ground cinnamon

1½ teaspoons ground ginger

¼ teaspoon ground cloves

1 teaspoon salt

¼ cup molasses

1 cup buttermilk

Soft Cream

1 cup heavy cream

½ teaspoon pure vanilla extract

1 tablespoon granulated sugar

Winter Menu VIII

parsnip soup with crispy parsnip chips   168

duck confit with french green lentils   170

chocolate soufflés with vanilla bean crème anglaise   174

WINES: If you would like to serve a wine with the soup a fragrant and spicy Alsatian Gewürztraminer would match the hint of spice in the parsnips. A German Riesling Spätlese with a bit of sweetness would also go quite well, particularly if the parsnips are mature and sweet. Otherwise head straight to the duck confit and pair it with a young French Burgundy or a California Pinot Noir. The acid of a young fruity Pinot Noir will balance the richness of the duck and go well with the earthiness and smokiness of the lentils.

parsnip soup with crispy parsnip chips

Parsnips are not funky white carrots. They have a haunting sweetness with a hint of spicy bitterness that is not easily forgotten. Parsnips make a terrific soup—earthy, sweet, and silken in texture; it needs little to prop up its flavors.

The parsnip chips are crisp ruffled rounds of sweet and salty delight. Their crunchiness plays off the smooth richness of the soup and adds yet another dimension. It is difficult not to eat them as you fry them, therefore the task always takes longer than necessary. They are wonderful warm and crisp from the fryer with a sprinkle of salt. I always make extra and put them in a bowl for my guests to nibble on. If you don't have time to make the chips, serve the soup with some good crusty bread.

SERVES 8

1   Peel and coarsely chop the parsnips. Peel the onion and cut it into a large dice. Reserve the vegetables in separate bowls.

2   Heat a large saucepan over medium-high heat. Add the fat; if you are using butter allow it to brown before adding the onion. Sauté the onion until it is golden, about 5 minutes. Add the parsnips and sauté until they are golden on the edges; season with salt and pepper. Drizzle the vegetables with the honey, if desired, and cook until the honey bubbles, a few minutes. Add the thyme leaves and the liquid. Bring the soup to a boil. Reduce the heat and simmer until the vegetables are very tender, about an hour.

3   Prepare the Parsnip Chips while the soup is cooking. Peel the parsnips and trim off the narrow tip at the point where the parsnip reaches ½ inch in diameter. Slice the root thinly, think potato chip, on the bias with a Japanese mandolin.

4   Pour the vegetable oil into a deep 4-quart pan. The oil should rise no higher than halfway up the side of the pan. Heat the oil to 375 degrees F until a chip bubbles when dropped in. Fry the Parsnip Chips a handful at a time to keep the heat of the oil consistent. Stir the oil once upon each addition of the sliced parsnips to separate the chips. Lower or raise the heat to adjust the temperature of the oil. When the chips are ruffled and golden remove them from the oil with a slotted spoon and drain on a towel; season them immediately and lightly with the salt.

5   Cool the soup slightly and puree in batches in a blender or food processor. Do not fill the blender more than two-thirds full or you risk having the contents of the blender explode. Allow the steam to escape by removing the center plug in the lid and covering the hole with a thick towel to protect your hand. Hold the lid securely down and lift the towel slightly to allow the pressurized air to escape as you blend. Add more liquid if the soup is too thick. Pass through a coarse strainer for a more refined soup. Return the soup to the pan and season with salt and pepper. Bring to a boil. Ladle the soup into bowls and garnish with a drizzle of Crème Fraîche and serve with a few Parsnip Chips on the side. The Crème Fraîche may also be folded in for a richer soup. Heat the soup gently after it has been added.

Soup

3 pounds parsnips

1 medium yellow onion

1 tablespoon unsalted butter or extra virgin olive oil

Salt

Freshly ground black pepper

2 teaspoons honey, optional

2 teaspoons chopped fresh thyme or ½ teaspoon dried

8 cups water or chicken stock

1 cup Crème Fraîche (page 39) for garnish

Parsnip Chips

2 large parsnips

2 quarts expeller pressed vegetable oil for frying (see Note, page 16)

Salt

duck confit with french green lentils

Long ago meat was made into a confit to preserve it for the winter ahead when there would be little fresh meat available. It was rubbed with salt, herbs, and spices, then cooked and stored in its fat. These vats of fatted meat were kept in the cool cellar for months with no adverse effect—the salt cured the meat and inhibited bacterial growth and the fat sealed out air. Pork and duck rillettes, duck leg confit, and whole goose livers in fat gave the farmers and village people the extra energy necessary to keep warm and go about their winter labor. A confit is flavorful and succulent no matter what type of meat is used.

There are few people today who need the calories provided by a meal of Duck Confit, but it's nice to indulge in it once in a while. The dish can be made a little lighter by substituting 2 cups of olive oil for 2 cups of the duck fat. Serve the duck legs whole with the skin crisped or remove the meat from the bone and serve in chunks on top of the lentils. The duck legs need to be marinated for 3 days before cooking, so plan your meal accordingly.

Tiny green lentils from Le Puy, France, are my favorite. Unlike the widely known brown lentil in America, green lentils don't lose their shape or their texture unless they are badly overcooked. Be sure to wash the lentils and pick through them to remove stones and debris to avoid any unpleasant surprises.

SERVES 8

1   With a small sharp knife, remove the thigh bone from the duck legs. Make a cut on either side of the bone, using the bone as a guide, and scrape the meat away from the bone. Slide the knife underneath the bone to loosen it from the meat. Cut the bone at the leg joint. Use your hand and with the aid of a dishcloth grasp the slippery bone and pull and twist it away from the meat. Leave the drumstick bone intact.

2. Lay the duck legs on a flat surface so that the meatier side is facing up. Sprinkle the exposed meat evenly with ½ teaspoon of coarse salt per leg. Distribute the garlic, thyme, black pepper, and cloves evenly over the legs, pressing into the meat well.

3. Press the two legs, meat side against meat side, together. You will have four pairs of legs. Sprinkle the skin side of each leg with 1 teaspoon of coarse salt. Rub it into the skin well. Place the legs in a shallow pan. Cover with plastic wrap and press the legs lightly with a weighted pan and refrigerate.

4. Turn the legs over the next day. Drain off any juice in the bottom of the pan, reweight and marinate overnight. The following day turn again, drain off the excess juice in the pan, reweight, and marinate 1 day more. Keep the legs under refrigeration while they marinate.

5. To prepare the confit, unpair the legs and clean off the excess salt, garlic, and cloves.

6. Preheat the oven to 350 degrees F.

Duck Confit

Eight 12-ounce duck legs

¼ cup coarse sea salt

6 garlic cloves, peeled and thinly sliced

2 tablespoons fresh chopped thyme leaves or 1 tablespoon dried

1 tablespoon cracked black pepper

8 whole cloves

6 cups rendered duck fat

Lentils

1 pound (2¼ cups) dry Le Puy lentils

4 garlic cloves

2 medium carrots

1 medium yellow onion

4 whole cloves

2 celery stalks

2 strips applewood-smoked bacon

Salt

Freshly ground black pepper

1 bay leaf, fresh or dried

6 cups water or chicken stock

7   In a large sauté pan over medium-high heat, sear the legs until golden, about 5 to 10 minutes on each side. It is not necessary to add fat to the pan; the rendered fat from the searing legs will provide enough. This may have to be done in two batches if your pan is not large enough. Adjust the heat if the pan gets too hot. Remove the seared legs to a pan large and deep enough to contain all of the legs when covered with the duck fat. Pair the legs together as they were when they were marinated. Pour any duck fat that has accumulated in the pan over the legs.

8   Heat 4 cups of the rendered duck fat until it is melted and hot and pour over the seared legs. Melt more fat to cover the legs if necessary. Place in the preheated oven and cook for 2 hours until the meat is tender and is easily removed from the bone. Cool to the touch and strain off the fat. Store the legs in the fat if you will not be using them immediately. The Duck Confit may be prepared a week in advance of serving. The legs can be stored in their fat under refrigeration for 1 week and will develop more flavor as they sit.

9   Prepare the lentils while the legs are cooking. Clean the lentils (see Headnote above).

10   Peel and trim the garlic cloves; leave whole. Peel, trim, and dice the carrots into ¼-inch cubes. Peel and halve the onion. Dice one half of the onion finely. Stick the cloves into the remaining onion half. Wash, trim, and dice the celery into ¼-inch cubes. Cut the bacon strips into thirds.

11   Heat a 4-quart pot over medium heat. Add the bacon and render it until it exudes fat and starts to brown. Turn up the heat and add the diced onion, celery, carrot, and garlic. Sauté the vegetables until they start to brown, about 5 minutes; season with salt and pepper.

12   Add the lentils to the pot and sauté until the lentils are warm to the touch. Add the bay leaf and the onion half studded with cloves. Add the liquid and bring the pan to a boil. Reduce the heat to a gentle simmer. Taste the broth for seasoning and add more salt and pepper if necessary. Cook until the lentils and vegetables are tender, 30 to 40 minutes.

13   Drain the lentils (reserve some of the cooking liquid for reheating) and cool. Remove the bay leaf, bacon, and the onion half stuck with the cloves. Reheat the lentils with a little of the reserved cooking liquid when you are ready to serve them. The lentils can be made up to 4 days ahead of time. Store them in their cooking liquid under refrigeration until ready to use.

14   To serve the legs, heat a large nonstick pan over medium heat and place the duck legs skin side down with the meatier side up. Cook until the skin is crisp and duck is hot, about 15 minutes. Turn the legs once during cooking to brown the other side. Serve the crisped leg over the lentils.

NOTE: For a heart healthier dish the duck legs can be braised in duck stock for 1½ to 2 hours or until the leg meat is tender. The legs will be packed with flavor but will have less richness and a softer texture.

VARIATION: To make wonderful duck rillettes, remove the skin from the leg and discard, shred and chop the meat finely, and mix it with some of the strained flavored fat. Season the mixture to taste and place the chopped meat in a crock or Mason jar. Seal with some melted fat to keep the air out and store in the refrigerator for a month. Serve on a toasted sliced baguette for a flavorful appetizer.

chocolate soufflés with vanilla bean crème anglaise

Soufflés are a dessert rarely served at home. It's a shame since they are easy to prepare.

The last minute whipping of the egg whites is what usually throws people into a tailspin along with the fear that the soufflés will not rise, or they will rise and then fall before reaching the table, deflating the expectations of the guests as well as the cook. This soufflé recipe takes away a lot of the pain. The base can be mixed with the egg whites ahead of time and the soufflé cups can be filled and left to stand at room temperature before their trip into a hot oven. The chocolate acts as a stabilizer, which makes these soufflés more like a warm flourless chocolate cake rather than a true soufflé. No matter, these soufflés are delicious and chocolaty and will make you a soufflé hero to your guests. Be sure to instruct your guests to break the center of the soufflé with their spoons and fill the cavity with crème anglaise before their first bite. The crème anglaise is so good that people have been known to drink it directly from the pitcher. When that happens you know your dessert is a success.

It is very important to whip the egg yolks and the sugar by hand; do not use an electric mixer for this task or your soufflés will be flat. The egg whites, however, should be beaten with a mixer to avoid tiring out your arm.

SERVES 8

1   To prepare the crème anglaise: In a medium-sized, heavy-bottomed saucepan, heat the milk and cream to boiling with the vanilla seeds and scraped pod. Remove the pan from the heat and let the mixture steep for 20 minutes.

2   In a large bowl, whisk together the yolks and sugar to a thick ribbon.

3   Return the milk and cream to a boil and slowly pour it over the egg yolks while whisking constantly; strain and cool. Store under refrigeration in a tightly sealed container for up to 4 days.

4   Butter and sugar the soufflé molds.

5   Melt the chocolate, butter, and cream together in a double boiler or in a metal bowl placed over a pot of water that has been brought to a boil and turned off. The chocolate will melt by the residual heat. Stir the mixture occasionally as it melts to prevent hot spots from forming. Remove the bowl from the pot and reserve in a warm place next to the stove.

6   In a large bowl, whisk the yolks and ¼ cup of sugar together, by hand, to a thick ribbon. Stir the warm chocolate mixture into the yolk mixture. Reserve in a warm spot next to the stove.

7   Preheat the oven to 425 degrees F.

8   Place the egg whites in a mixing bowl. Whip them with an electric hand mixer or in a standing mixer fitted with the whisk attachment until they are foamy. Add the cream of tartar, the remaining ¼ cup of sugar, and a pinch of salt. Whip to stiff peaks.

Vanilla Bean Crème Anglaise

1 cup whole milk

1½ cups heavy cream

1 vanilla bean, split and scraped

4 large egg yolks

¼ cup granulated sugar

Chocolate Soufflés

6 ounces chopped bittersweet chocolate (70 percent cocoa solids works best)

2 tablespoons unsalted butter

2 tablespoons heavy cream

3 large egg yolks

½ cup granulated sugar

5 large egg whites

Pinch of cream of tartar

Pinch of salt

Confectioners' sugar for dusting

9   Fold the whipped egg whites into the chocolate-egg mixture one-third at a time. Fill the prepared ramekins or soufflé cups three-quarters full.

10 Bake in a the preheated oven for 20 to 30 minutes until the soufflés have risen 1½ to 2 inches over the sides of the ramekins. Serve immediately, dusted with powdered sugar and with the crème anglaise in a pitcher on the side.

NOTE: The soufflés may be prepared up to 4 hours in advance and left covered at room temperature. Remove the cover before baking.

Winter Menu IX

celery root galettes with crème fraîche and caviar   178

bouillabaisse with a spicy red pepper rouille   180

sweet ricotta pie with grated bittersweet chocolate   183

WINES: French Champagne or a crisp French Chablis would go nicely with the celery root and caviar. A French Bandol rosé or a juicy Spanish *rosado* would pair well with the rich shellfish and fish flavors of the bouillabaisse and the hint of spiciness in the rouille.

celery root galettes with crème fraîche and caviar

Purists prefer their caviar with a spoon or with buckwheat blinis and no other garnish save for a squeeze of lemon. Others prefer their caviar loaded down with chopped egg, onions, and capers. Caviar served with celery root galettes and Crème Fraîche lands somewhere in between these two extremes. It is not necessary to serve the finest beluga in this preparation. Its delicate flavor would be lost. Osetra is very fine caviar preferred by many for its large eggs, nuttiness, and rich flavor. Sevruga suits this preparation well for those who prefer smaller eggs with sturdier flavors. The more caviar you pile on top of these galettes the more showy the presentation will be, especially if your guests appreciate caviar whatever way it is served. If you're not into caviar at all, these galettes can be served alone with Crème Fraîche or with thinly sliced smoked fish.

SERVES 8; MAKES TWENTY-FOUR 2-INCH PANCAKES

1 Peel the celery root and shred in a food processor or by hand. Place them in a large bowl and sprinkle with 1¼ teaspoons of salt. Let it stand for 20 minutes. Squeeze out the excess water so that the celery root is dry. Reserve.

2 Preheat the oven to 400 degrees F.

3 In a large bowl, combine the flours, 1 teaspoon of salt, and the baking powder.

4 In a small bowl, beat the eggs lightly and whisk in the milk and cooled melted butter. Add to the flour mixture a little bit at a time and mix until smooth. Add the celery root and mix together until well incorporated. Let the batter rest, covered, for 20 minutes.

5   Brush a large nonstick pan lightly with soft butter. Heat the pan until the butter starts to bubble. Add 1 rounded tablespoon of celery root batter to the pan to form a thin 2-inch pancake. Fill the pan with the galettes but do not crowd. Cook over medium heat until golden on one side, about 2 to 3 minutes. Turn over and finish cooking in the preheated oven for 5 minutes. The galettes will puff and the celery root will become tender. Remove the galettes from the pan and repeat the process until all of the batter is finished. Wrap the cooked galettes with a towel to keep warm while you make the remainder.

2 medium celery root

2¼ teaspoons salt

1 cup all-purpose flour

4 tablespoons whole-wheat flour

½ teaspoon baking powder

2 eggs

½ cup milk plus 2 tablespoons

4 tablespoons (½ stick) unsalted butter, melted and cooled

1 cup Crème Fraîche (page 39)

4 to 8 ounces osetra or sevruga caviar

2 tablespoons chopped chives, optional, and 8 lemon wedges for garnish

6   Place a dollop of Crème Fraîche on top of each galette and then a spoonful of caviar on top of that. Sprinkle with chopped chives. Serve with wedges of lemon. Enjoy.

bouillabaisse with a spicy red pepper rouille

Traditionally, bouillabaisse was a Mediterranean fish soup prepared by fishermen on the shores of the sea with fish left over from the day's catch. It consisted of whatever fish or shellfish was available at the time that the pot was put on the fire. Today's versions are much more luxurious, incorporating lobsters and scallops and a host of other seafood items. While this version does allow some creative license with ingredients, the basic framework of the recipe is true to the original. Olive oil is added to the broth to enrich it. Add a dollop of Spicy Red Pepper Rouille directly

to the soup or spread it on thick slices of toasted bread to be dipped into the broth. The spicy note that it adds balances the definitive seafood flavor of the soup.

For a variety of texture use a mix of flaky white fish such as snapper or cod and a firmer fish such as monkfish. Monkfish, also known as poor man's lobster, has a sweet flesh and will add some of the same flavors and texture as lobster.

Shellfish should be added with their shells on so that when they open their precious liquid is incorporated into the broth. Prawns that are cooked in the shell stay moist and flavorful. Your guests might grumble at using their hands to peel them so be sure to supply them with finger bowls of lemon water to cleanse their hands after enjoying your wonderful meal.

SERVES 8

1 Preheat the oven to 400 degrees F.

2 Drizzle the slices of bread with olive oil, place on a sheet pan, and toast in the preheated oven until golden and crisp, about 10 minutes.

3 Clean the fish of skin and bones and cut into 4-inch pieces. Split the backs of the prawns and remove the vein. Leave the shell intact. Scrub the shells of the clams and mussels and remove the beard from the mussels. Reserve.

4 Peel, trim, and thinly slice the onions and garlic. Reserve separately.

5 Heat a large deep pot over medium heat and add ¼ cup of olive oil. Add the sliced garlic and toast until golden, about 2 to 3 minutes. Add the onions and sauté until golden, about 5 minutes. Add the white wine, bring to a boil, lower the heat, and simmer for 5 minutes.

6 Add the herbs, saffron, tomatoes, another ¼ cup of olive oil, and the liquid to the pot and bring to a boil. Reduce the heat and simmer for 10 minutes; season to taste with salt. The aromatic broth can be held in the pan until you are ready to cook and finish the bouillabaisse or refrigerated for later use.

Spicy Red Pepper Rouille (recipe follows) (see Note on page 182)

8 slices of bâtarde or other wide/long loaf cut 1 inch thick

½ cup extra virgin olive oil, plus more for drizzling

3-pound mix of red snapper, halibut, cod, or monkfish

16 prawns or shrimp, 16/20 count, unpeeled

2 dozen cherrystone clams

2 dozen black mussels

2 medium yellow onions

8 medium garlic cloves

2 cups dry white wine

1 tablespoon packed chopped fresh thyme leaves or 1½ teaspoons dried

½ cup coarsely chopped Italian parsley leaves

1 bay leaf, fresh or dried

1 teaspoon saffron

2 cups canned whole peeled tomatoes, seeded and chopped with juice

10 cups water or fish stock

Salt

½ cup coarsely chopped Italian parsley for garnish

7   When you are ready to finish the bouillabaisse add the fish, prawns, mussels, and clams. Simmer, covered, for 10 to 15 minutes, season to taste with salt. Remove the bay leaf and divide the seafood and broth among large flat bowls. Serve with the toasted bread and a generous dollop of the rouille. Garnish with coarsely chopped Italian parsley and a hearty drizzle of olive oil.

NOTE: Prepare the rouille a day in advance to allow its flavors to marry. Store well wrapped in the refrigerator.

spicy red pepper rouille

Rouille is not just for bouillabaisse; use it for soups, purees, and crostini, whenever a spicy accent is desired.

MAKES 2 CUPS

1   Char the skin of the sweet and hot peppers over an open flame or grill. Place the sweet peppers in a sealed paper bag to cool. Peel, core, and seed the sweet peppers. Core and seed the hot peppers; it is not necessary to peel them. Coarsely chop both types of peppers.

2   In a medium sauté pan over medium-high heat, sauté the garlic in 2 tablespoons of olive oil until it is golden, about 2 to 3 minutes. Add the cleaned peppers and sauté until heated through.

3   Puree the peppers in a food processor with the parsley and lemon juice; season with salt to taste. Add the bread crumbs and process while drizzling in ½ cup of olive oil. Drizzle in enough broth or hot water to make the rouille a thin spreadable paste and season with salt to taste.

2 medium red bell peppers

Four 3-inch hot red chiles

4 medium garlic cloves, peeled, trimmed, and thinly sliced

2 tablespoons plus ½ cup extra virgin olive oil

2 tablespoons chopped Italian parsley

1 tablespoon lemon juice

Salt

½ cup bread crumbs

Hot broth from bouillabaisse or water

sweet ricotta pie with grated bittersweet chocolate

Some people might call this a cheesecake but my family has always called it a pie. My grandmother would often bake it in a rectangular pan or deep pie plate with a few buttered bread crumbs for a crust if any. She never had anything as newfangled as a springform pan. This is almost the same recipe that my great-grandmother used but I have added mascarpone for extra smoothness and a chocolate crust for easier service. Freezing the grated chocolate assures you that it won't melt and streak as you fold it in. For the best texture and flavor, make the pie the day before you need it and chill it overnight. Leave it out for an hour or two before serving so that the flavors can be appreciated.

SERVES 8 TO 12

1   Prepare the Chocolate Crust. In the bowl of a standing mixer fitted with the paddle attachment or with an electric hand mixer, beat the butter and sugar until fluffy, 2 to 3 minutes. Beat in the salt, vanilla, and cocoa powder. Turn off the mixer and scrape down the sides of the bowl.

2   Combine the flour and semolina in a small bowl and add to the butter-sugar mixture. Mix until the dough is uniform, scraping down the sides of the bowl if necessary.

Chocolate Crust

8 tablespoons (1 stick) unsalted butter, at room temperature

½ cup packed confectioners' sugar

½ teaspoon salt

½ teaspoon pure vanilla extract

3 tablespoons unsweetened cocoa powder

½ cup all-purpose flour

½ cup semolina

Ricotta Filling

1 pound fresh cow's milk ricotta

4 large eggs

2 pounds mascarpone

1 cup granulated sugar

1 tablespoon Marsala wine

1 teaspoon pure vanilla extract

1 teaspoon finely grated orange peel

2 ounces grated bittersweet chocolate (70 percent cocoa solids), frozen

3   Gather the dough into a ball with lightly floured hands and place in the center of an ungreased springform pan. Keep your hands floured and press the dough to the edges and halfway up the sides of the pan. Make sure the crust is of uniform thickness throughout. Chill in the refrigerator until very firm, about 1 hour.

4   Preheat the oven to 350 degrees F.

5   Cut a square of aluminum foil large enough to line the pan and press snugly into the chilled dough. Weight with pie weights or baking beans and bake in the preheated oven for 25 minutes. Remove from the oven and cool to warm.

6   Remove the pie weights and carefully remove the foil. It's fine if some of the crust crumbles, it doesn't have to be perfect. It may be prepared a day or two ahead of time and stored well wrapped at room temperature.

7   Preheat the oven to 325 degrees F, or lower the oven to 325 degrees F if you will be baking the pie immediately after baking the crust.

8   Sieve the ricotta through a fine strainer into a small bowl.

9   In another small bowl, beat the eggs lightly to incorporate the yolks with the whites.

10 In a large bowl, mix together the ricotta, mascarpone, and sugar until smooth. Add the Marsala, vanilla, orange peel, and then the eggs. Fold in the frozen chocolate and fill the prepared crust.

11 Bake the pie in the preheated oven for 45 minutes or until the filling is set on the outside and loose at the center. Turn off the oven and leave the pie in the oven for 1 hour with the door closed. It will continue to cook by the residual heat.

12 Remove the pie from the oven and chill overnight. Leave at room temperature 1 hour before slicing and serving.

Winter Menu X

watercress and endive salad with blue cheese, toasted
  walnuts, and walnut vinaigrette

salt and herb—crusted prime rib with horseradish cream

potato gratin

meyer lemon meringue tart

WINES: As always it is challenging to pair salad with wine because of the vinegar. A crisp, young, fruity California Chardonnay would pair well with the blue cheese and walnuts in the salad and be able to handle the vinegar. The prime rib screams for a Cabernet Sauvignon—based Bordeaux such as a Pauillac or St. Estèphe or a California blend of Cabernet Sauvignon, Merlot, and Cabernet Franc.

watercress and endive salad with blue cheese, toasted walnuts, and walnut vinaigrette

A beautiful, simple salad of slightly bitter, juicy yellow endive and spicy green watercress makes a wonderful start to a meal. The toasted walnuts, blue cheese, and tangy dressing complement the greens without overpowering them.

SERVES 8

Walnut Vinaigrette (recipe follows)

1 cup walnut pieces

1 pound watercress, standard or upland

1½ pounds Belgian endive

Salt

Freshly ground black pepper

4 ounces blue cheese such as Roquefort, Point Reyes Original Blue, or Maytag blue

1   Prepare the Walnut Vinaigrette according to the recipe that follows. Reserve at room temperature until ready to use or refrigerate overnight. Bring to room temperature and whisk before using.

2   Preheat the oven to 350 degrees F.

3   Spread the walnuts on a sheet pan and toast for 8 to 10 minutes in the preheated oven. Cool and rub the toasted walnuts between your hands to remove any loose skin. Reserve.

4   Pick through the watercress and remove the thick stems and damaged leaves. Tear into fork-sized pieces. If you are using upland cress, cut off the root ends and trim the stems into a manageable length. Wash and spin dry if the watercress seems gritty.

5   Cut the endive heads in half lengthwise and remove the core in a long triangular wedge. Cut the endive across its width into ½-inch pieces.

6   In a large bowl, toss the watercress and endive together. Mix with a little
    vinaigrette to moisten, season with salt and pepper. Add more vinaigrette if you
    desire. Sprinkle with walnuts that have been tossed with a little of the vinaigrette.
    Crumble the blue cheese on top. Serve immediately.

VARIATION: Omit the walnuts and blue cheese for a simple before or after dinner salad.

walnut vinaigrette

MAKES I CUP

1   In a medium-sized bowl, mix together the minced
    shallot, mustard, sugar, and vinegar; season to taste
    with salt and pepper. Let the mixture sit for 10 minutes
    and then taste for seasoning; adjust if necessary.

2   Whisk in the walnut oil and then the olive oil, a little
    at a time. Add more or less olive oil, depending on
    whether or not you desire a more or less tangy
    vinaigrette.

1 medium shallot, peeled,
    trimmed, and minced

2 teaspoons Dijon mustard

1 teaspoon sugar

¼ cup sherry vinegar

Salt

Freshly ground black pepper

3 tablespoons walnut oil

¼ to ½ cup extra virgin olive
    oil

salt and herb–crusted prime rib with horseradish cream

Meat lovers will be salivating when this roast comes out of the oven. It is magnificent, as an 8-pound roast should be. The meat is salty and crusty on the outside and tender and juicy on the inside. The excess salt should be removed before slicing to prevent the slices from becoming overly salted. Save some of the salt should people request extra. Ask your butcher to trim off any excess fat and leave a ¼ inch of it all around. If you desire, he can remove the roast from the bone and then tie the bone back on for easier slicing. You can also carve the meat off the bone just before serving in order to make it easier to slice. Serve the ribs to whoever would like to

chew on one. Ask the butcher to include some of those frilly white things to put on the end of the bones for presentation after roasting. They're not necessary but it's one of the few times you'll actually be able to use them. Because of the salty nature of this roast you will not be able to use the pan juices to make a jus for the prime rib. Veal stock can be made ahead for this purpose or you can serve the Horseradish Cream instead. Serve the prime rib with the Potato Gratin or a good baked potato.

The Horseradish Cream is very potent. You need to be careful when you are pureeing the fresh horseradish. Do not place your face over the vent or top of the food processor when you are running it or when you remove the top. The fumes from the horseradish are very sharp and can cause quite a shock to your system. I have had several prep cooks fall over. I don't think they believed my warning and had to see for themselves. Substitute ¼ to ½ cup of prepared horseradish for the fresh root and vinegar. Gradually add the horseradish to the Crème Fraîche until it reaches the spiciness you want. Start the preparation of this dish a day in advance of serving for maximum flavor.

SERVES 8 TO 10

1   Prepare the Horseradish Cream: Peel the horseradish root with a vegetable peeler and trim off the ends. Grate or chop in a food processor until very fine. Add the vinegar and season with salt and pepper.

2   Whisk the Crème Fraîche in a bowl until it thickens slightly. Fold in the horseradish and chopped parsley; season with salt and pepper to taste. Prepare 1 day in advance to allow the flavors to develop. Store tightly sealed in the refrigerator.

3   For the roast: In a small bowl, combine the herbs, ½ cup of olive oil, and the cracked pepper.

4   Peel, trim, and cut the garlic cloves in half. Make a small slit in the meat with a small sharp knife. Stick a piece of garlic in the cut before it disappears. Continue to make small slits all over the prime rib and fill them with garlic slices as you go, until the garlic is finished.

Horseradish Cream

¼ pound fresh horseradish root

2 tablespoons white wine vinegar

Salt

Freshly ground black pepper

1½ cups Crème Fraîche (page 39)

3 tablespoons chopped Italian parsley

Prime Rib

¼ cup chopped fresh rosemary
    or 2 tablespoons dried

¼ cup chopped fresh thyme
    or 2 tablespoons dried

½ cup extra virgin olive oil

3 tablespoons cracked black pepper

8 garlic cloves

One 4- to 5-rib prime rib roast,
    8 to 10 pounds

1 cup coarse sea salt

5   Rub the herb mixture all over the roast and let it marinate, well wrapped, in the refrigerator, overnight.

6   Remove the roast from the refrigerator 1 hour before roasting.

7   Preheat the oven to 450 degrees F.

8   Moisten the salt with 2 tablespoons of cold water and press it into the fat side and ends of the roast. Place the roast in a large roasting pan and then in the preheated oven. Roast for 25 minutes.

9   Turn the oven down to 350 degrees F and roast for 1½ to 2 hours. The internal temperature should read 120 degrees F for medium / medium-rare when you remove it from the oven. The meat will continue to cook as it rests. The gratin can be placed in the oven to cook after the heat has been reduced.

10   If you like your rib roast rare, remove it from the oven when the thermometer hits 118 degrees F. Let the meat rest for 20 minutes before slicing to allow the juices to redistribute evenly.

11   Scrape the excess salt off of the roast. Using the bones as a guide, slide your knife down the ribs, keeping the blade flat against the ribs. When you reach the bottom of the ribs, run your knife under the boneless eye of meat. The cut should be parallel to the cutting board and closely follow the bone. You may have to raise and lower your cut slightly to accommodate ridges in the bones. Place the meat on a cutting board.

12   Slice the boneless roast into medium-thick slices. Cut the bones apart and serve them on the side for those who relish chewing on them. Serve with the Horseradish Cream on the side. Accompany with the Potato Gratin, or mashed or baked potatoes.

potato gratin

potato gratin This is a wonderfully creamy and surprisingly delicate gratin. Lack of heavy cheese, the scent of thyme, and paper-thin slices of potato make it just short of ethereal. It is important to slice the potatoes at the last minute to keep them from turning pink and then black. For ease they can be sliced into a bowl and then deposited, all at once, into the hot cream.

Prepare the potato gratin 1 hour before roasting the prime rib. Finish cooking it in the oven with the prime rib after the heat has been reduced. To prepare the Potato Gratin in advance, follow the recipe up to step 7. Chill it overnight in a well-wrapped baking dish. Remove the gratin from the refrigerator 1 hour before baking and bake until it is golden and bubbling. It will take 20 to 30 minutes longer to bake than a gratin that is hot when it is placed in the oven.

SERVES 8 TO 10

1   Butter a 13 by 9 by 2-inch pan well.

2   Peel the potatoes and reserve them whole, covered with cold water. Thin-skinned potatoes such as Yukon Gold and Yellow Finn may be used unpeeled if their skin has been well scrubbed. If you use unpeeled potatoes trim both ends off before slicing so that you do not end up with pieces that are mostly skin.

3   Peel, trim, and finely dice the onions.

4   In a large pot over medium-high heat, sauté the onions in 2 tablespoons of butter until golden, about 5 minutes. Add the garlic and cook until tender. Add the thyme and cream and bring to a boil. Remove the pot from the heat and place on top of a thick towel on the counter to insulate the counter from the heat.

6 large Russet or Yukon Gold potatoes

2 medium yellow onions

2 tablespoons unsalted butter

4 garlic cloves, peeled, trimmed, and minced

2 tablespoons chopped fresh thyme leaves or 1 tablespoon dried

4 cups heavy cream

Salt

Freshly ground black pepper

5   Use a Japanese mandolin (see Resources, page 380) to slice the potatoes as thinly as possible directly into the hot cream. The potatoes can also be sliced thinly by hand. To do this, slice a small amount of potato off one side to make a flat surface so that the potato can be sliced without rolling dangerously. Hand-sliced potatoes should be transferred to the pot of cream as they accumulate.

6   Preheat the oven to 350 degrees F.

7   Bring the potatoes and cream to a simmer over medium heat. Fold the potatoes gently with a heatproof rubber spatula to keep them from sticking to the bottom and scorching. Cook until the cream has been thickened by the release of starch from the potatoes; season with salt and pepper to taste. Pour into the prepared baking dish. The gratin may be refrigerated or baked to finish at this point.

8   Bake in the preheated oven for one and half hours until the gratin is bubbling and golden on top and the potatoes are tender. Spoon out to serve.

meyer lemon meringue tart

Meyer lemons again! Once you've experienced them you'll never go back to the standard variety. When I first moved to San Francisco I lived in the Mission District, which had the perfect microclimate for growing citrus of all kinds. Tree branches loaded with ripe lemons and oranges would hang over back fences above the street. Being from upstate New York I had never experienced a bounty of that kind. I would pick one or two on my way to work and then more on my way home. Of course, I wasn't the only one picking the fruit and the branches would soon be stripped bare. I would peek longingly over the fence at the remaining out-of-reach branches heavy with fruit. Sadly most of the fruit ended up on the ground and I vowed that if I was ever lucky enough to have a tree like that I would make sure that none of the fruit would ever go to waste. I keep that promise most of the time. I've realized it takes quite a bit of effort to keep up with several lemon trees.

During their season, early winter to late spring with a small crop at the end of summer, it's sometimes difficult to give them away as it seems everyone knows someone with a tree eager to share.

This spectacular lemon meringue tart shows off Meyer lemons at their best. Because they are sweeter I use less sugar in the curd than when I use regular lemons. Bear this in mind if you have no Meyers on hand and increase the sugar by half a cup. Regular lemons may be substituted for Meyer lemons, but they are not as juicy so you might need more.

SERVES 8 TO 10

Meyer Lemon Curd

¾ cup Meyer lemon juice (4 to 5 lemons) with zest—grate the zest before juicing the lemons

1 teaspoon cornstarch

3 large eggs, lightly beaten

¾ cup sugar

6 tablespoons (¾ stick) unsalted butter

½ recipe Pâte Brisée (page 55)

Meringue

2 large egg whites, at room temperature

⅛ teaspoon salt

¼ cup sugar

1   Prepare the Meyer Lemon Curd, which may be done up to a week in advance and stored well covered in the refrigerator. In a medium-sized heavy-bottomed saucepan, whisk together the lemon juice, zest, cornstarch, eggs, and sugar. Add the butter.

2   Heat the pan over medium heat, stirring constantly, until the butter melts, the mixture thickens, and bubbles form around the edge of the pan. Stir for 3 to 4 minutes more and strain into a bowl. Cool before using.

3   Prepare the tart shell. Roll the brisée dough ⅛ inch thick. Cut it into a circle to fit the tart pan and trim the edges. Chill the lined tart pan until the dough is very firm, about 1 hour.

4   Preheat the oven to 400 degrees F.

5   Remove the lined tart pan from the refrigerator. Quickly prick the dough well with a fork and line the dough with foil. Press the foil into the corners of the chilled dough firmly.

6   Fill the foil-lined shell with dried beans or pie weights. Blind bake the tart in the preheated oven for 20 minutes. Remove the beans and the foil with an oven mitt and continue to bake the shell for another 10 minutes or until it is golden. Cool the tart shell before filling.

7   Fill the cooled tart shell with lemon curd almost to the top edge, about ⅛ inch under.

8   Preheat the oven to 350 degrees F.

9   Prepare the meringue. Place the whites and the salt in a large bowl. Whisk together until foamy. Gradually add the sugar and beat to stiff peaks. Place the meringue in a piping bag with a plain or fluted tip or use a Ziploc bag that has the corner cut off. Make the cut ½ inch wide. Pipe the top of the curd-filled tart with a swirl of meringue starting at the outside edge and working toward a peak at the center. Bake in the preheated oven for 15 to 20 minutes until the meringue is golden.

10   Chill for 1 hour before serving. The longer the tart shell sits with the curd filling the softer it becomes, so if you enjoy a crisp shell serve sooner rather than later.

spring

Spring forth from winter's icy grasp!

Watch, as tender shoots, lithe and hesitant, poke their

Curled heads from beneath their earthy cover.

Behold, all that rises anew.

For spring hath come and wrapped us

in her warm green cape.

—MARIA HELM SINSKEY, 1989

After a long, cold rainy winter we begin to search for any sign of spring: the first warm breeze carrying the rich damp smell of earth; tender shoots poking through the brown sodden felt of last year's greenery; the first robin pulling a worm from the ground. It's a difficult time. It teases us with warm days and torments us with cooler ones. Gardens are eagerly planted, perhaps too soon, and then beaten back by a late frost. We struggle to control our energy, pent up by the short days and long nights of winter, which cling to us unwilling to let go.

Suddenly yet tentatively, spring arrives in her full glory. Her great green cape flung open to reveal the earthly bounties of spring. Lambs lie quietly in the fields. Cows, sheep, and goats produce milk of exquisite sweetness and richness brought on by the abundance of tender grass. Asparagus shoots from the ground overnight while artichokes weigh heavily in their spiky cradles.

From the wilds come coiled fiddleheads, morels, porcini, and ramps. We infuse our meals with the aromatics of green garlic and spring onions. Fava beans, swaddled in their luxurious pods, come in with a rush and challenge us to consume them. Begrudgingly we do, for their tedious cleaning makes them all the more precious to spin into purees and toss into salads.

Spring rewards us with a burst of vegetables in all shades of green, a just one for tolerating months of root vegetables, cabbages, and kale. We longingly look at apples and pears, but do not buy, knowing that their last contact with the branch that sustained them was more than half a year ago or half a world away. When we cannot bear another day without a fruit to eat out of hand, the first strawberries arrive, a slash of vivid red in the market, seductively mocking us to come hither and eat just one. And we do eat one and then another and another until our stomachs ache. Rhubarb's scarlet partner has arrived, ready for pies tarts and crumbles.

Spring forms the bridge that will gently lead us from winter to summer; it is a time of rebirth and regeneration for plants, animals, and ourselves. Take stock of your gardening shed, clean out your pantry, prune your fruit trees, and appreciate all that is tender, green, and bright. Spring allows us but a short time of warm rain-soaked and sun-spotted days to prepare for the intense explosion of summer.

spring menus

Spring Menu I

WINES: The cheese and onions in the soufflé would pair elegantly with a dry German or Alsatian Riesling or a young, crisp California Chardonnay. The fragrant spring lamb stew calls for a fruity American Cabernet Franc or French Côtes du Rhone.

sweet vidalia onion and gruyère soufflé

Sweet Vidalia onions arrive midspring. It is an important arrival since sweet onions do not store well. Their high sugar content causes them to become spongy and soft late in the year. Uncured, the spring incarnation of these onions have yet to develop their papery skins and are much easier to use—just trim and slice. Onions that have been cured on racks in cool drying barns arrive midsummer, enrobed in their papery skins, which are the dried outer layer of the onion. Cured onions, protected by their outer skin, have a longer shelf life. If you can't find sweet Vidalias, substitute another sweet spring onion or a sweet cured onion. There are many varieties to choose from.

The final steps of this soufflé make you live in the present. The base can be made ahead but the egg whites need to be whipped and added just before baking. Prepare your soufflé cups ahead of time and it will take a minimal amount of time to get the soufflés into the oven. I like to make this soufflé in two big soufflé dishes with paper collars. It makes a spectacular presentation.

MAKES TWO 1-QUART SOUFFLÉS
SERVES 8 AS AN APPETIZER;
4 AS A LIGHT SUPPER

1   Butter the bottom and sides of two 1-quart soufflé dishes well with the room temperature butter. Cut a strip of parchment paper 5 inches wide and long enough to wrap around the inside of the soufflé mold. Use the outside of the mold to measure the length. The ends should overlap on the inside. Butter both sides of the parchment and press it against the inside of the soufflé cup to line. The paper should stick over the edge of the mold by 2 inches. Place ¼ cup of Parmesan cheese into each of the paper-lined molds and roll it about until all the sides are coated. It is unnecessary to coat the paper that sticks out above the soufflé dish. Dump out the excess cheese.

Unsalted butter, at room temperature, and ½ cup finely grated Parmesan cheese for lining the soufflé molds

¾ pound Vidalia onions or other sweet onions, spring or cured (see Headnote)

9 tablespoons unsalted butter

2 teaspoons packed chopped fresh thyme or 1 teaspoon dried

Salt

Freshly ground black pepper

½ cup all-purpose flour

2½ cups whole milk

6 large eggs, separated

1½ cups grated Gruyère cheese

½ cup finely grated Parmesan cheese

2   Trim and dice the spring onions finely. Peel and trim cured onions before dicing.

3   Heat 1 tablespoon of the butter in a sauté pan over medium-high heat and brown lightly. Add the diced onions and cook until lightly caramelized, 5 to 6 minutes, stirring occasionally. Add the chopped thyme and season with salt and pepper. Cool and reserve at room temperature if you will be using it within a few hours. The onions may be prepared a day in advance. Store well wrapped in the refrigerator.

4   Melt the remaining 8 tablespoons butter in a heavy-bottomed saucepan over medium heat. Add the flour and continue to cook over medium heat while stirring constantly until well combined and thoroughly heated. Remove the pan from the heat and gradually add the milk, stirring constantly. Each time you add a little milk mix the batter until it is very smooth before adding more. Add 1 teaspoon of

salt and a few grinds of black pepper. Place the pan back on the heat and stir until the mixture is smooth and pulls away from the sides of the pan. It will look shiny, and the texture will be thick and smooth. Turn the base into a mixing bowl.

5   Mix the base on medium speed in a standing mixer fitted with the paddle attachment. The egg yolks can also be beaten in by hand with a large wooden spoon. Add the egg yolks one at a time. After each egg yolk is added increase the mixer speed to high for 10 seconds to thoroughly incorporate the yolk. Return to medium speed and add the next yolk; repeat until all of the yolks are incorporated. After the last yolk is added beat for 20 seconds on high speed. Scrape down the sides of the bowl. Return to medium speed and stir in the cheese and the onion. Mix until well combined.

6   Turn the batter out into a large mixing bowl and press plastic wrap against its surface. Store at room temperature for up to 4 hours until ready to use. If you refrigerate the soufflé batter it must be brought up to room temperature before incorporating the egg whites, otherwise your soufflés will be flat. To speed the warming process along, beat the chilled batter with the paddle attachment on high speed in your mixer for 2 minutes.

7   To finish the soufflés: Preheat the oven to 400 degrees F.

8   In the bowl of a standing mixer fitted with the whisk attachment or in a mixing bowl with an electric hand mixer, whip the egg whites to stiff peaks with ½ teaspoon of salt on high speed. Fold in thirds into the prepared soufflé base and mix lightly until the whites are incorporated into the batter. A few streaks of whites are acceptable. Spoon the soufflé batter into the prepared molds, almost to the top of the dish (not the collar) and bake in the preheated oven until the soufflés are well puffed and golden, 35 to 40 minutes.

9   Serve on plates lined with a folded napkin or paper doilies.

VARIATION: For smaller soufflés, line 10 small molds in the same manner as the large molds but without the collar. Bake for 20 to 30 minutes at 400 degrees F.

spring lamb stew

Years ago people would look forward to spring lamb, by far the best lamb of the year. Its tender, delicate meat was sweet from the rich spring milk of its grass-fed mother. During the spring, ask your butcher to find a source for milk-fed lamb or order directly from a local farm. There are many small lamb producers around the country that would be happy to put their lamb on your table. You will be amazed at the flavor difference. It might persuade you to eat lamb during only one season or at least revere it during spring.

I prefer lamb shoulder to lamb leg for stew. It is the most flavorful of cuts and remains moist when cooked because of the fat distribution. Cubed boneless lamb shoulder can be more difficult to acquire because oftentimes it is cut into shoulder chops. Talk to your butcher about the availability of lamb shoulder and preorder it when necessary.

Do not be horrified by frozen peas, they are often sweeter and fresher then fresh peas. The sweetness and texture of a fresh pea decline rapidly after picking. The best peas are ones that you pick yourself in the morning and eat that night. Frozen peas are picked and flash frozen at their peak of flavor and therefore can be much sweeter then fresh. Even a fresh pea snob like me can be lured to the organic frozen vegetable section if the fresh pea pickings are slim.

SERVES 8

8 medium carrots

16 waxy creamer-sized potatoes

24 white boiling onions or other small onion

6 garlic cloves

2 cups English peas, about 2 pounds in the shell (frozen organic may be substituted)

Salt

Freshly ground black pepper

4 pounds lamb shoulder or leg, cut into 2-inch cubes

2 to 4 tablespoons extra virgin olive oil

2 cups red wine

1 tablespoon lightly chopped fresh thyme leaves or 2 teaspoons dried

1 bay leaf, fresh or dried

¼ cup packed chopped Italian parsley

Slurry, optional (recipe follows)

1   Peel, trim, and cut the carrots into 1-inch lengths on the bias. Scrub the potatoes clean. Cut them in half and reserve them in cold water to prevent them from turning brown.

2   Trim the root end of the onions so that a small amount of root remains. This will hold the onion together while it cooks. Trim off the other end. Peel the onions and leave whole. Peel the garlic cloves, trim off the ends, and leave them whole. Clean the fresh peas or, if you are using frozen, measure out 2 cups and keep the peas frozen until ready to add to the stew.

3   Season the lamb well with salt and pepper. It is important to salt the lamb well at this point to lock in the flavor when it is seared. Underseasoned meat will be bland when cooked. Heat a large sauté pan over high heat and add 2 tablespoons of olive oil. Add enough lamb just to cover the bottom of the pan. Do not pile it into the pan or the lamb will not brown but instead steam in its juices. Sear until well browned on all sides, about 10 minutes per batch. Add more olive oil to the pan between batches if necessary. Remove the lamb from the sauté pan and place in a large stew or stockpot.

4   After all the lamb has been seared, pour off any grease left in the pan into a heatproof container to be discarded later. Add the wine to the pan and bring to a boil. Reduce the heat to a simmer and simmer for 5 minutes to reduce the wine by half. Scrape any bits of browned meat and juices from the pan while the wine is reducing. Pour the reduced wine over the lamb in the stew pot.

5   Add the carrots, garlic, and onions to the stew pot. The potatoes and peas will be added at the end. Add enough water to the stew pot to barely cover the browned meat and vegetables and bring to a boil then reduce the heat to a simmer. Add the chopped thyme leaves, bay leaf, and chopped parsley.

6 After the stew comes to a boil and the heat is reduced, prepare the slurry if you prefer a stew with thickened juices. Whisk 3 cups of hot stew liquid gradually into the slurry until smooth and well combined. Strain the mixture back into the stew and simmer for 1 hour. Skim off any grease that rises to the surface of the stew and discard. Add the potatoes and cook for an additional half hour until the potatoes and meat are tender. Add the peas and simmer for 5 minutes; if you are using frozen peas, simmer for 7 minutes. Remove the bay leaf and season to taste with salt and freshly ground pepper. Serve with buttered egg noodles or alone with some warm crusty bread.

slurry

Slurry is defined as a liquid mixture of water and an insoluble material, in this case flour. The water is a vehicle in which to deliver the thickening ability of the flour, so that the flour stays smooth and does not lump up. This ratio of flour to water will create a stew that is slightly thickened but still light. The juices will cling gently to the meat and vegetables. It is essential to add the slurry to the stew shortly after the first boil as it takes some time for the raw flour taste to cook out. If you want vegetables and meat with unthickened juices omit the slurry altogether.

Put the flour in a medium bowl. Whisk the water slowly into the flour until smooth.

2 cups cold water

8 tablespoons flour

almond madeleines

Marcel Proust changed the way we look at madeleines with his beautiful and simple tale of his emotions evoked by a cup of tea and a small cake. I feel the same way every time I bite into one of these warm madeleines. They are wonderful not only for dessert but in the afternoon with tea or in the morning with a big bowl of steaming café au lait. Close your eyes; you will feel as though you are in Paris, if only for a moment.

SERVES 8; MAKES 24 MADELEINES

1   Butter a madeleine pan well with a brush or your fingers. Sprinkle the pan liberally with flour and then shake the pan side to side to thoroughly coat the cookie indentations with flour. Turn the pan upside down over your sink and tap out the excess flour.

2   In a small sauté pan over medium heat, cook the butter until it starts to brown. Pour into a small bowl to cool. Fold in the orange zest if you are using it.

3   In the bowl of a standing mixer fitted with the paddle attachment or with an electric hand mixer, beat the almond paste and the sugar at medium speed until smooth. Add the eggs one by one, beating well after each addition.

4   Mix the flour, salt, and baking powder together in a small bowl and fold in. Remove the mixing bowl from the stand and fold in the melted cooled butter and the orange zest by hand. Use immediately or let the batter rest overnight in the refrigerator.

5   Preheat the oven to 350 degrees F.

6   Spoon 1 heaping tablespoon of batter into each mold. Bake in the preheated oven for 12 minutes until the edges are golden and the centers have risen and

8 tablespoons (1 stick) unsalted butter

½ teaspoon grated orange zest, optional

6 ounces almond paste, commercial or homemade (recipe follows)

⅓ cup sugar

3 large eggs

½ cup all-purpose flour

½ teaspoon salt

½ teaspoon baking powder

spring back when lightly pressed. Turn out of the pan immediately and cool to warm on a wire rack.

7   Serve the madeleines on a plate or in a cloth-lined basket. Your guests can help themselves. For a more substantial dessert accompany the madeleines with strawberries and cream (recipe follows).

NOTE: These madeleines can be baked immediately after the batter is made and they will be delicious. However, if you would like the characteristic bump found on the backside of a madeleine much like the hump on a camel, the batter must be chilled overnight. It sounds mysterious but it's true.

almond paste

Substitute this homemade almond paste for expensive store-bought almond paste and avoid all the fillers and artificial flavors. Blanch the almonds for a more traditional paste. The skins of the unblanched almonds will cause your finished baked goods to be more rustic in appearance because of the brown flecks they provide; use blanched almonds if the flecks are undesirable.

MAKES 1 POUND

1   Preheat the oven to 350 degrees F.

½ cup granulated sugar

16 ounces whole almonds

½ cup confectioners' sugar

2   In a small saucepan, combine the ½ cup of granulated sugar with ½ cup of water. Heat over medium heat and stir to dissolve the sugar. Once the sugar has dissolved bring the mixture to a boil, turn the heat down, and simmer for 5 minutes. Cool and reserve.

3   Spread the almonds, blanched (page 345) or unblanched, in a single layer on a sheet pan and toast for 10 minutes. Cool and reserve.

4   Puree the cooled toasted almonds with the confectioners' sugar to a fine meal in a food processor. Add ½ cup of the cooled syrup and puree to a smooth paste. Use as a direct substitute, by weight, for store-bought almond paste.

strawberries and cream

SERVES 8

2 pints small strawberries

3 tablespoons sugar

1 cup heavy cream

¼ teaspoon pure vanilla extract

1   Place the berries in a bowl of cold water and gently swish around. Lift from the bowl to avoid pouring all of the sediment in the bottom over the cleaned strawberries. Drain in a colander and remove the tops with a sharp knife. Slice the larger berries in half. Leave the smaller ones whole. Sprinkle the berries with 2 tablespoons of the sugar and marinate for 20 minutes at room temperature.

2   Pour the cream into a chilled bowl and add the vanilla. Whisk by hand or with a mixer until the cream begins to thicken. Sprinkle in the remaining 1 tablespoon of sugar and whip to soft peaks. Store well wrapped in the refrigerator.

3   Serve the strawberries in small bowls topped with a nice-sized dollop of whipped cream.

Spring Menu II

WINES: Artichokes are challenging for wine. The roasting of the artichokes combined with the cheese takes away most of the challenge. A crisp Pinot Blanc or Sauvignon Blanc/Sémillon blend will pair well with the bruschetta. A Chinon will pair well with the skirt steak. A fruity California Cabernet Sauvignon would also do well.

teleme cheese and roasted baby artichoke bruschetta

I served these bruschetta to my father-in-law and he loved them so much he asked for the recipe. He made the recipe so often for his friends that I feared he had gone insane. He finally stopped when artichokes went out of season.

Soft, creamy, mild, and slightly tangy Teleme supports the nutty sweet flavor of the roasted artichokes in this dish. Double the recipe and serve the bruschetta as a wonderful light supper accompanied by a bowl of soup or a green salad.

SERVES 8

1   Peel, trim, and dice the shallots into small ¼-inch pieces. Reserve.

2   Fill a bowl with 4 cups of water and squeeze in the juice of one lemon. This is the acidulated water for the turned artichokes. Clean or turn the baby artichokes by peeling off the outer leaves until you reach the leaves that are pale green on the bottom with dark green tips. Slice off the dark green tips and use a paring knife to trim the base of any tough green outer layers. The artichokes should be entirely pale yellow-green in color. Place the cleaned artichokes in the acidulated water. Just before cooking drain the artichokes well, pat them dry, and cut them in half.

3   Preheat the oven to 400 degrees F.

4   Heat 2 tablespoons of extra virgin olive oil in a medium ovenproof sauté pan over medium-high heat. Add the artichokes and shake the pan. When the artichokes begin to brown, 3 to 4 minutes, add the shallots and chopped thyme. Season well with salt and pepper and place the pan in the preheated oven and roast until the artichokes are tender, about 20 to 25 minutes. Remove the pan from the oven, squeeze half a lemon over, and taste for seasoning. Add more salt and pepper if necessary. Cover to reserve their warmth until ready to serve.

5   Preheat the broiler and/or grill.

6   Peel the garlic and leave the cloves whole. Cut eight 1-inch-thick slices of bread and rub them with the garlic cloves (agitate the cloves and get the juices flowing by rubbing on the rough crust of the bread and then rubbing the juices on the soft

2 medium shallots

1½ lemons

40 baby artichokes (see Note and Substitutions on page 216)

2 tablespoons extra virgin olive oil, plus more for drizzling

1 tablespoon chopped fresh thyme leaves or 1½ teaspoons dried

Salt

Freshly ground black pepper

2 large garlic cloves

1 loaf of pugliese or Italian bread

½ pound Teleme cheese (see Note and Substitutions on page 216)

sides of the bread). Drizzle the slices liberally with extra virgin olive oil. Toast under the broiler or grill the bread until golden on both sides but still soft in the center, about 5 minutes. Place the bread on a sheet pan.

7   Divide the artichokes evenly among the toasted bread. Slice the Teleme into eight pieces and place it on top of the artichokes. Place the bruschetta under a broiler until the cheese melts and bubbles, 2 to 5 minutes, depending on the heat of your broiler. Drizzle with extra virgin olive oil before serving. Serve on a platter or individual plates.

NOTE: The artichokes may be prepared up to two days in advance. Store well wrapped in the refrigerator. Reheat to serve.

Greek immigrants in California created Teleme in the early 1900s. Their hope was to produce cheeses that were similar to ones found in the old country. The name Teleme was derived from the old world Greek goat's milk cheese called Touloumi. Teleme is a very soft cow's milk cheese whose exterior is sometimes dusted with rice flour early in the ripening stage. The flour creates a pale, thick leathery rind that encases the soft cheese, holding its shape to a square and preventing the interior from running out. Teleme has a tangy delicate flavor that gains intensity as it ages. Very ripe Teleme is runny and is best doled out with a spoon. Young Teleme is sold without the rice flour rind and should be consumed within a short time of purchase.

SUBSTITUTIONS: Eight large artichokes may be substituted for the baby-sized. They can be trimmed the same way but the inedible choke must be removed with a spoon or melon baller. Slice the artichokes into thin wedges and continue preparing as indicated by the recipe.

Fontina or Taleggio cheese may be substituted for the Teleme if it is unavailable.

VARIATION: These bruschettas make wonderful hors d'oeuvres. Use a thin baguette and slice it into ¼-inch-thick pieces; top in the same manner as the large bruschetta. Reserve at room temperature and broil just before serving.

marinated skirt steak

Skirt steaks look ugly when they are uncooked, but those long, fatty, stringy-looking pieces of meat are flavor magnets for marinades. The fat gives them an incredibly flavorful juiciness not found in many other cuts. The skirt is found hanging inside the ribs of the steer and helps to hold the organs of the animal in place. It sees action when the animal moves so it isn't a fork-tender cut like a filet. The generous fat content helps to tenderize the meat and hold flavor. Overcooking the steak and leaching out all of the fat will make the steaks dry and tough. Medium/medium-rare is the perfect temperature.

SERVES 8

12 large garlic cloves

Four 5-inch fresh rosemary sprigs or 2 tablespoons dried

16 fresh thyme sprigs or 1½ tablespoons dried

4 skirt steaks, about 4 pounds

1 tablespoon cracked black pepper

Extra virgin olive oil

Salt

1   Smash the garlic cloves with a heavy knife. Crush and tear the rosemary and thyme sprigs to release their perfume. Toss the steaks with the thyme, rosemary, garlic, cracked pepper, and enough olive oil to coat all its surfaces. Marinate for 1 to 2 days. The longer the steaks are marinated the greater the transference of flavor from the herbs to the meat.

2   Preheat the grill (see Note below).

3   Remove the steaks from the refrigerator 30 minutes before grilling and brush off the herbs and garlic and season with salt. There is plenty of cracked pepper on the steaks so no additional pepper is necessary.

4   Grill the steaks over medium-high heat for 6 minutes on each side for medium-rare. Let the steaks rest for 10 minutes.

5   To serve: Cut each steak in half and serve on a platter with accompaniments on the side. Buttered Peas (recipe follows), Roasted Garlic Fingerling Potatoes (page 236), or a good baked potato will complement the steak.

NOTE: The skirt steak may also be cooked on the stove top. Heat a large sauté pan over medium-high heat. When the pan is hot, add enough olive oil to coat the bottom lightly. Cook the steaks 5 to 6 minutes per side for medium-rare. Adjust the heat to the pan to prevent it from smoking. The skirt steaks can be cut in half crosswise to accommodate smaller pans.

VARIATION: After you brush the marinade off the steaks, tightly roll the steaks into rounds starting with the thick end of the skirt. Cut the rolled steak in half across its diameter so that you have two round steaks. Secure the loose end of the steak with a toothpick so that it holds its shape. Season both sides with salt and grill as you would a regular steak. It will take 7 minutes per side for medium-rare. Remove the toothpick before serving. This type of cooking will produce a steak that is slightly more fatty in texture because less of the fat is exposed to the heat and it therefore does not have a chance to melt and drip off. I learned this trick from the butcher at my local meat market.

buttered peas

Sweet spring peas—nothing tastes better fresh from the vine.

Quickly cooked buttered peas make a homey accompaniment to this homely steak. The perkiness of the peas offsets the richness and flavor of the steak. What makes spring peas even more precious is that tasty ones are available for only a short time in most regions. Fresh peas need very little cooking. They are sweet enough and tender enough to eat raw. However, sautéing them quickly with a little butter brings out their most charming characteristics.

Buy peas from the farmer who grew them whenever possible, or grow them yourself—this is the best assurance of knowing when they've been picked. Their sweetness deteriorates rapidly as their sugars turn to starch so it is best to use them soon after purchase. Nothing is more disappointing than to buy fresh peas, shuck them, and cook them only to find out that they are hard and starchy. Break open one pod and taste the peas at the market before you purchase them to avoid this hardship.

SERVES 8

1 Shuck the peas and reserve. This may be done up to a day in advance and the peas reserved in the refrigerator.

2 Cook the peas while the steaks are resting. Bring 1 cup of water and the butter to a boil in a large sauté pan. Season the liquid with salt and pepper. Add the peas and simmer for 4 minutes, stirring frequently. Turn off the heat and serve immediately.

4 cups English peas (4½ pounds in the pod)

4 tablespoons unsalted butter

Salt

Freshly ground black pepper

orange-scented fallen chocolate soufflé cake

I created this cake from a soufflé recipe that had gone awry one day. It is rich without being dense and heavy and possesses a wonderful melt-in-your-mouth quality. The orange and brandy add a taste reminiscent of a famous orange liquor, but with much more intensity. The cake must be cooled to barely warm if you're using one large pan, or it will be too delicate to slice. It can be served hot out of the oven if you're baking it in individual soufflé cups.

SERVES 10 TO 12

1   Line the bottom of a 10-inch springform pan with a parchment paper circle; grease the bottom and sides well with a little soft butter. Reserve.

2   Melt the chocolate, butter, brandy, cream, and orange zest together in a bowl over water that has been brought to a boil and turned off. Stir frequently to prevent hot spots from forming. Remove from the heat and cool slightly.

3   Preheat the oven to 350 degrees F.

4   Separate the eggs. In a large bowl, whip the egg yolks and the sugar to a thick ribbon by hand. Fold the chocolate mixture into the whipped yolks. Fold in the cocoa powder. Reserve.

5   In a standing mixer fitted with the whisk attachment, or with an electric hand mixer, whip together the egg whites, salt, and cream of tartar to stiff peaks. Fold the whites into the chocolate mixture by first incorporating one-third of the whites thoroughly and then gently folding the remaining two-thirds into the mixture until they are just combined.

6   Pour the batter into the prepared pan and bake in the preheated oven for 30 minutes. Let the cake cool to warm before slicing. Serve with barely sweetened softly whipped cream.

NOTE: The cake may be prepared a day in advance and stored well wrapped at room temperature.

VARIATION: To make individual cakes, divide the batter among 10 buttered and sugared soufflé cups. Bake at the same temperature for 20 minutes and serve warm in the cups or cool and turn out on a plate.

8 ounces bittersweet chocolate, chopped

½ pound (2 sticks) unsalted butter

2 tablespoons good brandy

2 tablespoons heavy cream

2 teaspoons finely grated orange zest

6 large eggs

½ cup sugar

3 tablespoons cocoa powder, sifted

¼ teaspoon salt

¼ teaspoon cream of tartar

Spring Menu III

WINES: The poached artichokes are challenging for most wines. The aioli will help with a pairing. A crisp American or Alsatian Pinot Blanc will rise to the occasion. The artichoke will bring out their fruit. The veal breast can either go with a red or white wine because of the lightness of the meat and the raisins in the stuffing. The soft tannins of a fruity red Italian Chianti or a white German Riesling Spätlese with a hint of sweetness will pair beautifully with the veal breast. Choose a Muscat de Beaumes-de-Venise for the crème caramel.

poached artichokes with lemon aioli

These artichokes retain so many flavors from the poaching liquid that no sauce is necessary. Nonetheless, most people expect to dip their artichoke leaves into one sauce or another.

Lemon Aioli is a slightly different take on a traditional aioli that is garlic-enhanced mayonnaise. This version of aioli is an admirable partner to the subtle flavors of the artichoke. The tang of extra lemon and the spiciness of cayenne make it zippy. Do not do your final seasoning of the aioli with salt until you have balanced the acid or you might end up with an overly salted sauce. Acid magnifies salt so proceed with caution.

SERVES 8

1 Preheat the oven to 400 degrees F.

2 Cut the whole garlic bulb across the diameter and place the two halves back together. Wrap the garlic tightly in foil and roast in the preheated oven for 45 minutes or until soft and caramelized. Cool and squeeze the garlic from its paper. Press through a strainer to remove any hard or tough pieces. Reserve at room temperature.

3 To poach the artichokes: Peel, trim, and cut the onions into 6 wedges. Smash and peel the garlic cloves. Fill a large stockpot with 10 quarts of cold water. Add the onions and garlic. Cut the lemons in half and squeeze their juices into the water. Throw in the squeezed lemon halves and the bay leaves.

4 Use a serrated knife to trim the stem off the artichokes and make an "X" in the bottom. Trim 2 inches off the top of the artichokes so that they are flat. Using scissors, cut ¼ inch off the top of each leaf to remove the spike. Add the trimmed artichokes to the pot.

5 Weight the artichokes down with two small heatproof plates that fit within the diameter of the pot, otherwise the artichokes will float and cook unevenly. Bring the pot to a boil and add the salt. Reduce the heat and simmer until the artichokes

are tender, about 45 minutes from cold water start to finish. To test for doneness, stick a small knife into the base of an artichoke. If it slides in easily it is done.

6   To finish the aioli: Place the eggs in a food processor fitted with the blade attachment; add the roasted garlic, cayenne, ½ teaspoon of salt, and lemon juice. Pulse until smooth.

7   Slowly drizzle in the olive oil in a thin stream with the machine running until the mixture becomes thick and glossy. If necessary, adjust the acidity with a few more drops of lemon juice. Taste the aioli and season with salt to taste.

8   Remove the artichokes from the cooking liquid and cool upside down on a plate to allow the poaching liquid to drain off. Store the artichokes in the refrigerator if you will not be using them within an hour or two.

9   Serve the artichokes on a platter with the aioli on the side. Set large empty bowls on the table to collect the leaves.

Lemon Aioli (see Notes below)

1 large garlic bulb

2 large eggs

¼ teaspoon cayenne pepper

Salt

3 tablespoons lemon juice

1¼ to 1½ cups extra virgin olive oil

Poached Artichokes

2 medium yellow onions

8 large garlic cloves

10 quarts cold water

4 lemons

2 bay leaves

8 large artichokes, 24 to 36 count

½ cup salt

NOTES: The aioli may be prepared up to 2 days in advance; refrigerate well wrapped. The artichokes may be prepared up to a day in advance; refrigerate well wrapped.

If by chance you add too much olive oil or add it too quickly, and the aioli separates, add a teaspoon of warm water to ¼ cup of the broken aioli and slowly whisk in the remainder by hand or in the food processor. If this doesn't work place an egg yolk in the bottom of a bowl and gradually whisk in the broken aioli.

The aioli contains raw eggs so it is not recommended for pregnant women, the very young, the very old, and people with compromised immune systems.

VARIATIONS: If you prefer the heat of raw garlic, substitute 1 large minced clove for the roasted garlic bulb. Other sauces you might consider to dip your leaves: Dijon Vinaigrette (page 50) or a salted drawn butter flavored with chopped tarragon, chives, and chervil. The aioli can also be served as a dip for poached asparagus, slathered on sliced tomatoes and BLTs to give them extra zip, or used as a binder for potato salad instead of plain old mayonnaise. Its use is bounded only by your imagination.

breast of veal with pine nut, golden raisin, and spinach stuffing

A majestic roast emerges from this recipe. The breast is the vessel that holds the aromatic stuffing. There is not that much meat on a breast—just a few flaps with seven or so rib bones. The bones add flavor and can be eaten like spareribs after the stuffing is consumed. The stuffing perfumes the meat and keeps it moist while roasting. The sweetness of the golden raisins and the earthiness of the pine nuts complement each other as well as the spinach and the herbs in the stuffing. The veal is really a full-flavored meal in itself but if you need to serve an accompaniment small potatoes roasted in olive oil with sea salt and black pepper or an unadorned Simple Soft Polenta (recipe follows) are very nice.

SERVES 8

1   Cut the large stems from the spinach leaves. Wash the leaves until they are free of grit.

2   Place 2 tablespoons of butter in a large sauté pan and brown lightly over medium-high heat. Add the spinach and cook until all its liquid evaporates; season with salt and pepper. Drain in a strainer and squeeze dry. Chop finely and chill.

3   Cut a pocket in the veal breast or ask your butcher to do it. It is important to note that when you make the pocket in the breast you should always know where your

fingers are at all times. Do not bury your knife in the breast without knowing where your other hand is located.

4   At either end of the breast are boneless flaps of meat. These are your starting points and the technique is the same for both ends. Push your knife through the center of the flap and cut a slit 3 inches long across the width of the breast, the width being the top to the bottom of the bone. Head toward the first rib with the tip of your knife and when you hit the rib run the edge of the blade along the length of the bone from top to bottom, loosening the meat on top of the bones to form a pocket. Take care not to make a hole in the edge of the top or the bottom of the breast. Make the pocket as deep into the length of the breast as you can; use the rib bones as a guide. Then repeat on the other end so that the pocket meets in the center. The pocket will expand as it is stuffed.

3 pounds spinach

2 tablespoons unsalted butter

Salt

Freshly ground black pepper

One 2½- to 3-pound breast of veal

2 pounds coarsely ground veal (see Note below)

1 pound chopped or coarsely ground or lightly smoked bacon (see Note on page 228)

½ cup golden raisins, coarsely chopped

½ cup pine nuts, lightly toasted and coarsely chopped

1 large garlic clove, peeled, trimmed, and minced

1 tablespoon chopped fresh sage or 1 teaspoon dried ground sage

2 teaspoons chopped fresh rosemary or 1 teaspoon dried

¼ cup chopped Italian parsley

Extra virgin olive oil

5   Mix together the ground veal, bacon, raisins, pine nuts, spinach, garlic, and herbs. Season the stuffing well with 2 teaspoons of salt and some black pepper. Test the seasoning by making a small patty and sautéing it in a little olive oil until it is well cooked. Add more salt to taste if necessary.

6   Preheat the oven to 475 degrees F.

7   Stuff the pocket with your hands, packing the stuffing in well. Secure the slits with toothpicks. It's fine if some of the stuffing spills out while the meat is roasting.

8   Season the breast well with salt and pepper and place it in a large roasting pan. Roast in the preheated oven for 20 minutes.

9   Add ½ cup of water to the pan and reduce the heat to 325 degrees F. Roast for 1½ to 2 hours until a meat thermometer reads 130 degrees F.

10   Prepare your accompaniments while the breast is roasting.

11   When the breast is cooked, let it rest covered with foil for 15 to 20 minutes so that the juices have a chance to settle. Remove the breast to a serving plate and drizzle the pan juices over the top. Slice in between the bones to make 1-inch-thick chops. One person will not get a bone. This will probably be the cook. Serve with your choice of accompaniments.

NOTES: The breast can be stuffed a day ahead of time to allow the flavors to marry. Store in the refrigerator well wrapped.

I like to grind my own veal and bacon with a hand grinder. I place the assembled grinder in the freezer for a few hours before using so that the meat will stay cool while grinding. I also stick the meats that I will be grinding in the freezer for an hour so they will stay well chilled while grinding. It is important that your hands and all surfaces are impeccably clean and that all meat stays chilled. Chill the filling in the refrigerator before stuffing the breast. Your butcher might also grind your veal and bacon together for you if he has the equipment.

simple soft polenta

This polenta serves as a wonderful backdrop for richly spiced meats, fishes, and vegetables.

SERVES 8

1 Bring the milk, 2 cups water, and the butter to a boil in a large pot; season with 1½ teaspoons of salt.

2 Remove the pan from the heat and whisk in the polenta. Place the pan back over low heat and stir the polenta with a wooden spoon until it is smooth, tender, and creamy, about 30 minutes. Season to taste with salt and pepper, remove from the heat, and cover until ready to serve. Reheat if necessary; add a little water to thin if the polenta has stiffened.

3 cups whole milk

4 tablespoons unsalted butter

Salt

1 cup coarse polenta

Freshly ground black pepper

vanilla bean crème caramel

Crème caramel, the cousin of crème brûlée, is perfect when you're in the mood for something creamy but not too rich. Instead of caramelizing the sugar at the end, the custard is baked with it, making a delicious, slightly bitter caramel sauce to contrast with the sweet vanilla-scented custard. Egg whites are added to the crème caramel to make the custard firmer, allowing it to be unmolded. I have changed the recipe slightly from most classical ones, by adding a little cream and substituting egg yolks for whole eggs. It makes the crème caramel a little richer than most, but still allows it to be light.

When caramelizing sugar it is very important always to have a bowl of ice water at hand. This is in case any sugar comes in contact with your skin. If this happens plunge the affected area immediately into the ice water to prevent severe burning. Do not stick your caramelized finger in your mouth as we are prone to automatically do or it will also result in a mouth burn.

SERVES 8

1   Place eight ramekins in a roasting pan with enough room to accommodate all of the ramekins with an inch of space around each.

2   Put 1½ cups of sugar in a heavy-bottomed saucepan. Heat over medium heat while stirring constantly with a wooden spoon. If lumps occur break them apart with the spoon and continue to stir. When the sugar has melted and is dark gold in color, quickly pour or ladle it equally among the ramekins. Roll each ramekin around to coat the bottom evenly with sugar. Let the sugar harden and cool.

3   In a medium saucepan, bring the milk, cream, and scraped vanilla beans, seeds and pods, to a boil over medium-high heat. Turn off the heat and let the mixture steep for 20 minutes.

4   Place an oven rack on the lowest rung. Preheat the oven to 350 degrees F.

5   In a large bowl, beat the eggs, egg yolks, and remaining ½ cup of sugar lightly. Return the liquid to a boil and add to the eggs in a steady stream while whisking constantly.

6   Strain and pour the custard into the prepared ramekins. Pour enough hot, not boiling, water into the roasting pan to come three-quarters of the way up the sides of the ramekins. Bake on the low oven rack covered with a flat piece of parchment paper or foil in the preheated oven until set, 30 to 40 minutes. To test, jiggle one gently with your hand. They are done if the custard is set. Carefully remove the ramekins from the water bath. Cool the crème caramels before placing in the refrigerator, uncovered, until they are completely cold. Then cover tightly with plastic until ready to serve.

7   To release the crème caramels from the ramekins, run a knife around the edge. Take care not to cut into the custard. Bring a cup of water to a boil in a small sauté pan. Dip the bottom of the ramekin in the water for 20 seconds. Remove the ramekin from the water and place a small serving plate over the top of the crème caramel. Hold the ramekin tight to the plate and flip the plate over gently. Jiggle the ramekin until the custard slides out onto the plate. Allow the caramel to spill over the custard.

2 cups sugar

2½ cups whole milk

½ cup heavy cream

2 vanilla beans, split and scraped

5 large eggs

2 large egg yolks

Spring Menu IV

grilled asparagus with prosciutto
and a meyer lemon vinaigrette 234

herb-marinated rack of lamb
with roasted garlic fingerling potatoes 236

strawberry ice cream profiteroles
with bittersweet chocolate sauce 238

WINES: The grilling and prosciutto take away a lot of the challenge of pairing the asparagus with wine. The vinaigrette adds a little challenge back but nothing insurmountable. A crisp New Zealand Sauvignon Blanc or a Sancerre will pair well with the vinaigrette and any grassy notes remaining in the asparagus after it is cooked. The simple preparation of the rack of lamb calls for a fruity California Cabernet Sauvignon or Merlot.

grilled asparagus with prosciutto and a meyer lemon vinaigrette

When poached asparagus just won't do anymore, it's time to grill. The flames caramelize the naturally occurring sugars in the stalk, giving more dimension to the asparagus taste. This also makes the asparagus more wine-friendly. The addition of thinly sliced prosciutto and Meyer Lemon Vinaigrette doesn't hurt either. Order your prosciutto by the slice not the pound. The person who is ever so carefully slicing and laying your prosciutto on paper is counting each and every slice, grateful that it is only sixteen slices. Ask to see the first slice to make sure the thickness is correct. It shouldn't be so thin as to shred upon removal from its wrapper nor so thick that it is chewy. I use jumbo asparagus because they're sweeter and meatier than other sizes. If jumbo asparagus are not available extra large or standard size may be substituted.

SERVES 8

1   Prepare the Meyer Lemon Vinaigrette
    according to the recipe below.

2   Preheat the grill.

3   Snap off the ends of the asparagus stems
    by holding the spear at both ends and
    bending gently. The end will naturally
    break off at the point where the spear
    becomes tender. You may also trim the
    ends off for a neater look. Toss the
    asparagus with enough olive oil to lightly coat and season with salt and pepper.
    Grill over medium heat until they are caramelized and tender, about 8 to 10
    minutes. Remove from the grill and cool to warm.

4   Toss with a little of the vinaigrette in a bowl and arrange on a platter, drizzling
    extra vinaigrette over the top. Place ruffles of prosciutto across the center of
    the asparagus like a belt. This dish can also be plated in single servings using
    the same method.

Meyer Lemon Vinaigrette (recipe
  follows)

3 pounds jumbo green asparagus

Extra virgin olive oil

Salt

Freshly ground black pepper

16 slices thinly sliced prosciutto, more if
  you like to snack

meyer lemon vinaigrette

This is a simple nonemulsified vinaigrette. It speaks purely of its ingredients when
it is tossed with vegetables of any kind. It should be stored in the refrigerator
between uses as the lemon juice has a tendency to ferment when left at room
temperature for more than a few hours.

MAKES ¾ CUP

1   In a small bowl, combine the minced shallot and the
    lemon juice; season with salt and pepper and let the
    mixture rest for 10 minutes.

2   Drizzle the olive oil into the lemon juice while
    whisking constantly. Reserve at room temperature
    until ready to use.

1 medium shallot, peeled,
  trimmed, and minced

3 tablespoons Meyer lemon
  juice

Salt

Freshly ground black pepper

½ cup extra virgin olive oil

herb-marinated rack of lamb with roasted garlic fingerling potatoes

Rack of lamb is simple to prepare and quite elegant for a proper dinner party. Racks have become so popular and expensive in the United States that chefs have turned to overseas sources to supply their restaurants at a much cheaper price. There are many New Zealand producers selling lamb with no added hormones or antibiotics. Small organic and free-range producers in the United States sell their animals whole, so you not only get two racks, you get everything else: legs, shoulders, shanks, etc. Lambs are very small, 35 to 40 pounds, so if you split a whole one with a friend it is easy to use all the cuts.

The herb marinade for the rack really perfumes the meat when it is done a day or two ahead of time. The same marinade can be used for many other cuts as well. It is best to remove as many of the herbs and garlic before roasting as they will burn and create off flavors.

The unpeeled garlic cloves add a beautiful rusticity to the potatoes. The garlic perfumes the potatoes as they roast and can be eaten by those who love garlic. Fingerling potatoes do indeed look like fingers. Select potatoes that are similar in size for even roasting. Large potatoes should be cut in half lengthwise to show off their unique shape. Smaller-sized potatoes can be roasted whole.

SERVES 8

1   Clean the rib bones well by scraping off the meat and sinew with a small sharp knife. Cut the racks in half so that each has four ribs. In a large bowl, combine ¼ cup olive oil and the crushed garlic. Crush 4 rosemary sprigs and the thyme sprigs with your hands and add. Add the lamb and coat well. Grind some coarse black pepper over all. Wrap well and marinate the racks overnight.

2   Preheat the oven to 400 degrees F.

3   Wash and scrub the potatoes under running water to remove all traces of dirt. Drain well. If the potatoes are large cut them in half lengthwise.

4   In a big bowl, toss the potatoes, 16 whole unpeeled garlic cloves, 3 tablespoons coarse sea salt, and ¼ cup olive oil together; season with freshly ground black pepper.

5   Spread the potatoes out in one layer on a sheet or roasting pan and place them in the oven 15 minutes before you begin cooking the lamb racks. The potatoes need to roast 45 minutes to 1 hour until they are tender and golden.

6   Remove the lamb from the marinade and scrape off as many herbs as possible. Heat a large ovenproof sauté pan over medium-high heat and add the remaining 2 tablespoons of olive oil.

4 lamb racks, 8 to 9 ribs each (see Note below)

½ cup plus 2 tablespoons extra virgin olive oil

8 large whole garlic cloves, unpeeled and crushed, plus 16 large whole garlic cloves

Twelve 4-inch fresh rosemary sprigs or 4 tablespoons dried

12 fresh thyme sprigs or 1 tablespoon dried

Freshly ground black pepper

3 pounds fingerling potatoes (see Headnote)

3 tablespoons coarse sea salt

Salt

7   Season the lamb well with salt—no additional pepper should be necessary—and sear fat side down until golden, about 7 minutes. Turn the racks over so that the fat side is up and roast in the oven for 20 to 30 minutes. Remove the lamb from the oven and let it rest on a platter or cutting board for 10 minutes before cutting each piece of rack in half. The potatoes can continue to roast while the lamb is resting if they need more time. Otherwise, remove them from the oven and cover them with foil to keep them warm until ready to serve.

8   Serve the lamb on a platter surrounded with the roasted potatoes.

NOTE: Marinate the lamb racks the day before they are to be served.

strawberry ice cream profiteroles with bittersweet chocolate sauce

Presentation of this dessert is impressive, eliciting gasps and exclamations of praise from most everyone, except perhaps for the most severely jaded, and even they might have cause to break down. How can you go wrong with fresh strawberry ice cream, light as air choux puffs, and sinfully decadent Bittersweet Chocolate Sauce? Premium store-bought ice cream can be substituted for the homemade.

SERVES 8

1   Prepare the profiteroles: Bring 1½ cups water, the butter, sugar, and salt to a boil in a heavy-bottomed saucepan. Remove the pan from the heat and stir in the flour, using a wooden spoon. Place it back over medium heat and stir until the mixture pulls cleanly away from the sides of the pan. Transfer to a mixing bowl.

2   Use a standing mixer fitted with the paddle attachment, beat in six eggs, one at a time. This may also be done by hand. Incorporate the egg fully each time one is added. After all six of the eggs have been added, beat well for 30 seconds. Spoon into a piping bag and pipe into 1½-inch-diameter mounds on a parchment-lined sheet pan. They should resemble a Ping-Pong ball that has been cut in half, or use a spoon to drop by rounded tablespoons.

3   Place the puffs in the freezer for 30 minutes to an hour. They may also be frozen and wrapped with plastic to be baked at a later date.

4   Preheat the oven to 425 degrees F.

5   In a small bowl, whisk together the remaining egg with 2 teaspoons of cold water.

6   Remove the puffs from the freezer, brush with the egg wash, and bake immediately in the preheated oven for 20 minutes. (You should have twenty-four profiteroles.)

7   Turn the oven down to 350 degrees F and bake until golden and dry, 20 to 25 minutes. Test by breaking one open. Cool before using.

8   Extra puffs can be frozen when completely cool. To use the frozen puffs: Thaw them at room temperature then warm in a 400 degree F oven for 10 to 15 minutes. The puffs will crisp as they cool.

9   Split 24 profiteroles in half; there should be three for each person (six halves). Prepare one or two profiteroles for more delicate appetites. Fill with one scoop of ice cream each. Place the filled profiteroles on a platter. Top with the cap of the profiteroles and dust with confectioners' sugar. Serve the chocolate sauce on the side to pour over.

Profiteroles (see Note Below)

12 tablespoons (1½ sticks) unsalted butter

1 tablespoon granulated sugar

1½ teaspoons salt

1½ cups all-purpose flour

7 large eggs

Strawberry Ice Cream (recipe follows) or high-quality store-bought ice cream (see Note below)

Bittersweet Chocolate Sauce (recipe follows) (see Note below)

Confectioners' sugar for dusting

NOTE: The Strawberry Ice Cream and Chocolate Sauce may be made a day or two in advance. The profiteroles may be made a week in advance. Pipe and freeze them well wrapped until you are ready to bake them.

strawberry ice cream

This is a custard-based ice cream, which is much richer than one using only milk and cream. The strawberries need to be macerated to draw out some of their water, otherwise they will become hard and crystallized when frozen. Because the strawberries are not cooked the ice cream tastes like fresh strawberries and cream.

MAKES 2 QUARTS

1   Place the strawberries in a large bowl of cold water. Swish them around, then lift them out of the water and drain them. Do not dump them into a strainer or all of the debris that will have sunk to the bottom of the bowl will end up on top of them. Core and dice into ¼-inch pieces. Place the diced strawberries and ½ cup of the sugar in a bowl; mix and let macerate for at least 1 hour. The sugar will draw out some of the strawberry juices.

3 cups strawberries

1¼ cups sugar

8 large egg yolks

3 cups whole milk

2 cups heavy cream

¼ teaspoon pure vanilla extract

2   In a large bowl, whisk the remaining ¾ cup of sugar with the egg yolks to a thick ribbon.

3   In a heavy-bottomed pot, bring the milk and cream to a boil. Add the hot cream mixture to the egg yolks while whisking vigorously. Add the vanilla. Strain and cool.

4   Add the strawberries and their liquid just before turning the ice cream. Turn according to ice cream maker's instructions.

bittersweet chocolate sauce

This sauce truly is a bittersweet chocolate sauce. Because there is no additional
sugar, the recipe relies on the sugar added to the chocolate when it was made.
If it is too intense for you, add up to 2 tablespoons of sugar.

MAKES 2 CUPS

1   Chop the chocolate finely and place in a 2-quart bowl.

2   Bring the cream, milk, and rum to a boil in a
    heavy-bottomed saucepan. Turn off the heat and
    cool slightly.

3   Slowly pour the milk-cream mixture into the chopped
    chocolate, stirring rapidly. Stir until well combined.

4   Stir in the butter until it is completely incorporated.
    Store at room temperature for 1 day, otherwise refrigerate
    for up to a month. Warm slightly to a pourable consistency to serve.

8 ounces bittersweet chocolate
    (70 percent cocoa solids)

1 cup heavy cream

¼ cup whole milk

1 ounce good rum, optional

4 tablespoons unsalted butter,
    at room temperature

Spring Menu V

WINES: Green vegetables always present a challenge when pairing wines. A grassy crisp French Sauvignon Blanc/Sémillon blend from Bordeaux or a New Zealand Sauvignon Blanc would pair well with the fava beans and mint. These wines will also pair well with the asparagus risotto so drink either one or both throughout the meal.

fava and mint crostini with spring greens

What was this strange green kidney–shaped bean on my plate? Its taste was brighter and grassier in flavor than a lima bean and lacked the starchy texture of its diffident cousin. What a curious bean made all the more so when its shiny green pod was produced for my inspection. I marveled at its smoothness and weight. Upon popping the pod open, the beans were presented, wrapped in their pale moist slip of a cover and tucked into a bed of spun silk. I marveled at the care nature took to ensure the comfort of these marvelous beans and wondered what prompted such precious care to be taken to shield them from consumption.

I was enchanted by my first brush with favas, yet to truly appreciate a fava you must first cook with them and learn the amount of effort it takes to prepare them. You will never again take them for granted and you will find yourself chiding people for not cleaning their plates. You will need a copious amount of favas for this dish. Cleaning them may try your patience but it is worth the effort. Enlist the help of friends and family and the job will go much faster. Or clean the favas the night before and make the puree the next day. Buy favas whose pods are shiny and bright green. They should feel crisp in your hand. Dull, limp, and blackened pods are a sign of old age.

SERVES 8

1 Preheat the oven to 375 degrees F.

2 In a small bowl, toss the garlic cloves with 2 teaspoons of olive oil and season with the sugar, a pinch of salt, and a few grinds of black pepper.

3 Place the cloves in the center of a square of aluminum foil, fold it in half, and roll up the edges to seal on all sides.

4 Roast in the preheated oven for 45 to 50 minutes until soft and golden. Shake the foil after 20 minutes to keep the garlic from burning. Cool and reserve at room temperature.

5   While the garlic is roasting, spread the sliced bread on a sheet pan, drizzle with olive oil, and bake in the oven until golden and crisp, about 15 minutes. Cool and reserve.

6   Wash the mixed greens and dry them well. Store covered with a damp cloth in the refrigerator until ready to use.

7   Shuck, blanch, and peel the favas (see Note below).

8   Place the mint, fava beans, and roasted garlic into a food processor fitted with the steel blade and pulse until they are finely chopped. Drizzle in ¾ to 1 cup of olive oil slowly until you have a thick smooth puree. Season the puree with salt and pepper to taste.

¼ cup garlic cloves, peeled and trimmed

2 teaspoons plus ¾ to 1 cup extra virgin olive oil, plus more for drizzling

¼ teaspoon granulated sugar

Salt

Freshly ground black pepper

Twenty-four ¼-inch-thick slices of baguette (see Note below)

½ pound mixed spring greens

5 pounds unshelled fava beans, nice plump shiny pods (yield about 3 cups) (see Note below)

14 large mint leaves

Shaved Pecorino cheese to garnish, about 1 cup

Meyer Lemon Vinaigrette (page 235)

9   To serve, spread the fava bean puree on top of the crostini, then top the puree with the shaved Pecorino and a drizzle of olive oil. Toss the greens lightly with the Meyer Lemon Vinaigrette and serve alongside the crostini.

NOTE: Toast the bread a day in advance; cool and store in a Ziploc bag at room temperature. The fava bean puree and the lemon vinaigrette can be made the day before and refrigerated well covered overnight. Bring to room temperature before serving.

Fava beans are cleaned in a two-step process. First the beans must be removed from their luxurious pod and blanched in heavily salted boiling water for 4 minutes and then immediately plunged into an ice bath. Second, the pale green outer covering of the cooked bean must be peeled off to reveal the bright green bean within.

asparagus and lemon risotto with shaved reggiano

Thinking about this dish during the winter makes me pine for spring. I love to use big fat juicy jumbo asparagus for this risotto. I believe they are much sweeter and have more flavor than the smaller ones. I usually do not precook my asparagus but allow the heat of the rice to cook them and release their juices during the last 10 minutes of stirring. The delicate flavor of the chervil intensifies the taste of spring. If you cannot find chervil you may substitute Italian parsley. Be sure to fold the herbs in at the very end so that their perfume is not lost. Cut the recipe in half for a second course or light entrée.

SERVES 8 AS A MAIN COURSE; 12 AS AN APPETIZER

1   Break off the tough ends of the asparagus by holding the spear at the base of the tip and the root end and bending downward. Allow the asparagus to break naturally at the most tender point. Cut the tips off on the diagonal and slice in half. Slice the remaining stem on the diagonal ¼ inch thick. Reserve with tips.

2   Peel, trim, and dice the onion finely.

3   Bring the chicken stock to a boil in a pot large enough to accommodate it. Reduce the heat and keep it at a simmer.

4   Over medium heat, melt the butter in a heavy-bottomed stockpot until it bubbles and starts to turn golden. Add the onions and sauté them until they are translucent and tender, about 5 minutes; season with salt and pepper. Add the rice and sauté until it is hot.

5   Add the white wine and simmer, stirring constantly, until the rice has absorbed the wine. Start to add the simmering chicken stock to the rice one ladleful at a time. Wait until the rice absorbs the stock before adding more; keep adding the stock and stirring constantly for 14 minutes.

6   Add the lemon juice and zest, then add the asparagus and cook 4 to 6 minutes more, adding stock as necessary, until the rice is tender but not mushy or soupy. The rice should be creamy and silky with the individual grains holding their shape. Fold in the grated cheese and chervil; season to taste with salt and pepper. Spoon the risotto into bowls and garnish with shaved Reggiano Parmesan.

2 pounds asparagus, jumbo, extra large, or standard size

1 medium yellow onion

3 to 3½ quarts chicken stock

2 tablespoons unsalted butter

Salt

Freshly ground black pepper

2 pounds (4⅔ cups) Carnaroli rice (see Headnote on page 20)

1 cup white wine

1 lemon, juice and grated zest

1 cup grated Reggiano Parmesan cheese

2 tablespoons chopped chervil or Italian parsley

Reggiano Parmesan cheese to shave for garnish

grapefruit sorbet with opal basil and a citrus salad

The pairing of pink grapefruit and purple opal basil is as refreshing as it is heavenly. This satisfying dessert is light and full of exotic flavors. The sorbet should be turned the day before it is needed to allow the proper amount of freezing time. Remove from the freezer 20 minutes before serving for ease in scooping. Serve alone or with lemon-scented sugar cookies (recipe follows) for a more substantial dessert.

SERVES 8

1 cup sugar

12 large opal basil leaves, julienned and then cut crosswise to form small pieces

3 cups freshly squeezed pink grapefruit juice, about 5 large grapefruits

5 large pink grapefruit

1 Make a syrup: Combine 1 cup water and the sugar in a small saucepan; stir and bring to a boil. Reduce the heat and simmer for 5 minutes. Add the chopped basil and cool.

2 Reserve ¼ cup of the basil-infused syrup to marinate the grapefruit sections.

3 Combine the grapefruit juice and the remaining 1¾ cups of syrup. Turn in an ice cream freezer according to the manufacturer's directions. Place in a resealable container and freeze overnight well sealed.

4 An hour or two before serving the sorbet, peel and section the grapefruit. Drain the juice from the segments and macerate the segments in a bowl with the reserved ¼ cup of simple syrup.

5 To serve: Place the grapefruit sections in the bottom of glass bowls or wineglasses and scoop the sorbet on top. Serve the cookies on the side.

lemon-scented sugar cookies

Crunchy, buttery, and lightly scented with lemon, enough said. They should be baked the day they're served though you can prepare the dough a day in advance.

MAKES 4 DOZEN 2-INCH COOKIES

1 In the bowl of a standing mixer fitted with the paddle attachment or with an electric hand mixer, beat the butter, lemon zest, and sugar until fluffy, about 3 minutes.

2 Add the egg yolks one at a time and beat well after each addition.

3 Mix together the dry ingredients and add to the butter-egg mixture. Mix until combined and roll into 1½-inch-diameter logs on a lightly floured surface. Flour your hands if necessary to keep the dough from sticking to them. Chill the logs on a sheet pan, wrapped with plastic, until they are firm, 2 hours or overnight.

4 Preheat the oven to 375 degrees F.

5 Remove the logs from the refrigerator and unwrap. Slice the cookies ¼ inch thick and roll in granulated or baker's sugar. Bake in the preheated oven on a parchment-lined sheet pan until golden on the edges, about 12 minutes. Unused dough logs may be individually wrapped and frozen for up to 1 month.

1 pound (4 sticks) unsalted butter

2 tablespoons finely grated lemon zest

2 cups granulated sugar

2 large egg yolks

4 cups all-purpose flour

1 teaspoon salt

½ teaspoon baking powder

Granulated sugar or baker's sugar (see Note below) for rolling

NOTE: Baker's sugar is a large crystal sugar that doesn't lose its crunch when baked. It is available at specialty food stores and baking supply stores. (See Resources, page 380.)

Spring Menu VI

WINES: The leeks are a complicated dish for wine. You have the sweetness of the cooked leeks, the fat and flavor of the eggs, and the sharpness of mustard in the vinaigrette. All these components call for a simple, crisp, fruity wine. An American or Alsatian Pinot Blanc would pair well. The olives and fennel in the pork call for a fruity American Cabernet Sauvignon or Cabernet Franc.

baby leeks vinaigrette

This recipe is a French classic. I look forward to visiting France in the spring just to savor leeks vinaigrette. Poached artichokes and asparagus as well as haricots vert and larger green beans can be served in the same manner.

SERVES 8

1   Place the eggs in cold water with 1 tablespoon of vinegar and bring to a boil. Reduce the heat and simmer for 8 minutes. Drain and cool in cold water. Peel the eggs and separate the whites from the yolks. Sieve the yolks though a coarse strainer. Reserve in a small bowl. Repeat with the whites and reserve separately from the sieved yolks. The yolks and the whites may also be chopped by hand.

4 large eggs

1 tablespoon white wine vinegar

24 baby leeks, ½- to ¾-inch diameter

Salt

Dijon Vinaigrette (page 50)

Freshly ground black pepper

2 tablespoons chopped Italian parsley

Fleur de Sel (see Note page 49)

2   Trim the root end from the leeks so that there is still a small amount of root to hold the leek together. Cut the green tops so that the leeks are 6 inches in length. Bring a large pot of water to a boil and salt well. Cook the leeks until tender, 6 to 7 minutes. Test by piercing a leek with a pointed knife. If the knife penetrates the leek easily the leeks are cooked. Remove them from the boiling water with a slotted spoon and cool in an ice bath. Drain the leeks well on a rack or towels.

3   Cut the drained leeks in half lengthwise. In a large bowl, gently toss the leeks with a little of the Dijon Vinaigrette and let them marinate at room temperature for 1 hour. Toss again and season with salt and pepper to taste.

4   Arrange the leeks on one large platter or divide among several small plates. Sprinkle the leeks with a belt of sieved egg white topped by a line of sieved egg yolk across the middle. Sprinkle the chopped parsley and Fleur de Sel over the egg along with a few grinds of black pepper. Serve with additional vinaigrette on the side.

slow-roasted pork with fennel, tomatoes, and olives with flat bread

This dish can be thrown together in a pot and then forgotten about for a few hours. You can use that time to make the Flat Bread or use store-bought flat bread. Wrap the fragrant tender chunks of pork in the Flat Bread and top with the olives and vegetables. The juices will dribble down hands and chins as they are eaten so provide plenty of napkins. Good flat breads can be purchased at most Indian and Middle Eastern grocery stores.

SERVES 8

1   Preheat the oven to 400 degrees F.

2   Spread the fennel seeds in a small ovenproof pan and toast in the preheated oven until their perfume is released, about 6 minutes. Cool and reserve.

3   Reduce the oven temperature to 325 degrees F.

4   Peel the onions and remove the root core. Slice the onions into thin ¼-inch wedges. Reserve.

5   Wash and trim the fennel bulbs. Cut them in half and remove the core in a triangular wedge. Slice into thin ¼-inch wedges. Reserve.

1 tablespoon fennel seed

2 medium yellow onions

2 large fennel bulbs

5 pounds pork shoulder, cut into 2-inch cubes

Salt

Freshly ground black pepper

5 to 8 tablespoons extra virgin olive oil plus more for drizzling

6 large garlic cloves, peeled and trimmed

1 cup white wine

1½ cups canned whole peeled tomatoes, seeded and chopped

2 cups pitted mixed olives (Picholine, Niçoise, Kalamata)

2 bay leaves, fresh or dried

2 tablespoons chopped Italian parsley

12 Flat Breads (recipe follows) or store-bought flat bread

6   Season the meat well with salt and pepper. Heat a large braising pan over medium-high heat and add 3 tablespoons of olive oil to cover the bottom. Add one layer of pork to the pan. It should sizzle instantly when it hits the pan. Add more olive oil if necessary. You might have to sear the meat in two or three batches depending on the size of your pan. Sear the meat until it is golden and crisp on all sides. This will take about 15 minutes for each batch of pork. Reduce the heat in the pan if it begins to smoke or burn. Remove the pork from the pan and let it rest on a plate. Drain the fat from the pan.

7   Add 2 tablespoons of olive oil to the pan. Add the onions, garlic, and fennel and sauté until they are wilted, about 15 minutes. Add the white wine and reduce by half, 5 minutes. Add the tomatoes, olives, bay leaves, and fennel seed and stir. Add the meat back to the pan and place in the oven, uncovered.

8   Roast until the juices are thick and meat is tender, 2 to 3 hours. Turn the meat over after 1 hour. Add water, 1 cup at a time, if the juices evaporate before the meat is tender. Salt and pepper to taste.

9   Prepare the Flat Bread according to the recipe while the pork is roasting.

10   To serve, remove the bay leaves and spoon the pork and vegetables into flat bowls with some of the olives and juice. Garnish with the chopped parsley and a drizzle of extra virgin olive oil. Serve the Flat Breads on the side.

flat bread

You must have patience when you make these Flat Breads. The small amount of yeast in the dough causes them to rise ever so slowly. This slow rising develops the taste and texture of the bread, so your efforts will be duly rewarded. Allow 2½ hours for the flat breads to rise.

MAKES TWELVE 10-INCH FLAT BREADS

1   Combine the flour and salt in a mixing bowl. Make a well in the center. Whisk together the yeast and water in small bowl to dissolve. Pour it into the well in the flour and let it sit for 10 minutes.

2   Add the olive oil and thyme leaves to the well. Mix everything together and knead until you have a soft pliable dough, about 5 minutes. Add more water if necessary.

> 4 cups all-purpose flour
>
> 1 tablespoon salt
>
> 1 teaspoon yeast
>
> 1¼ cups warm water
>
> ¼ cup extra virgin olive oil
>
> 1 tablespoon chopped fresh thyme leaves

3   Let the dough rise, covered with a damp towel or plastic wrap until doubled, about 2 hours, depending on how warm your kitchen is. If you have a cool kitchen it might take even longer.

4   After the dough has doubled, punch down and divide into twelve equal pieces. Roll each piece out as thinly as possible and place the rounds on parchment-lined sheet pans. Let the Flat Breads rise covered with a towel for 20 minutes.

5   Heat a 12-inch cast-iron or heavy-bottomed sauté pan over medium-high heat. Place a Flat Bread in the pan and let it brown and puff on one side, turn it over and let the other side brown and puff. The Flat Breads may also be cooked directly on a hot grill.

6   Remove the Flat Bread from the pan and wrap in a towel to keep warm. Repeat with the remaining dough. Adjust the heat as necessary to prevent the pan from smoking and the Flat Breads from burning. Serve warm.

NOTE: You will think you have ruined your pan after you have cooked all of the Flat Breads. Clean it by gently scraping off the blackened bits with a knife and scrubbing it with Bon Ami cleanser (do not scrape a nonstick pan; do not use Bon Ami on a cast-iron pan or you will ruin the seasoning—just scrape it lightly). Your pan will be shinier than new with a little elbow grease.

chocolate-glazed butter cake

Imagine a rich, moist, buttery golden cake with a decadent bittersweet chocolate glaze. It's simple, elegant, and delicious, great for birthdays, and decorates very well. Serve it with fresh strawberries or Vanilla Ice Cream (page 289). The cake can be made and glazed a day ahead of time. Do not attempt to wrap the glazed cake or you will have a mess—the glaze will stick to the plastic wrap upon removal. Leave the cake uncovered and uncut at room temperature for up to 24 hours.

SERVES 8 TO 10

1   Preheat the oven to 350 degrees F. Butter and flour a 10 by 3-inch cake pan.

2   In the bowl of a standing mixer fitted with the paddle attachment or with an electric hand mixer, whip together the butter and sugar until light and fluffy, about 2 to 3 minutes. Scrape down the sides of the bowl. Add the vanilla and then egg yolks one by one. Beat well for 10 seconds after each yolk is added. Scrape down the sides of the bowl.

3   In a small bowl, combine the flour, salt, and baking powder.

4   Add the dry ingredients in thirds to the butter-egg mixture alternating each time with the milk. Mix until combined. Pour into the prepared pan and level the batter.

5   Bake in the preheated oven for 40 to 50 minutes until a toothpick inserted into the center comes out clean. Cool the cake to warm in the pan then turn it out onto a rack and remove the pan. Flip the cake over so that the rounded surface is on the top for glazing.

6   Prepare the glaze while the cake is baking. Chop the chocolate finely and place it in a medium bowl.

7   In a medium pot, heat the cream, milk, and sugar to a boil and let it rest for 2 minutes. Pour it over the chopped chocolate and stir until well combined.

8   Add the butter and stir until it is fully incorporated. Cool to warm before using.

9   Glaze the cake on the rack to allow the excess glaze to drip through. Place the cake over a sheet pan lined with wax or parchment paper. Spoon the warm glaze over the top of the cake starting in the center and smoothing out toward the edges with the back of the spoon or a metal spatula. Spoon more glaze around the edge of the cake so that it runs down the sides and completely covers them. Let the glaze set for an hour.

10   Run a hot wet thin metal spatula around the base of the cake to release it from the wire rack. Use a large flat metal spatula to lift and slide the cake from the rack onto a serving plate. Scrape off the excess glaze on the liner paper into a bowl and gently warm, strain it and add to the leftover glaze to be used again. The leftover glaze may be stored, tightly covered, in the refrigerator for up to 1 month. To reuse the glaze, rewarm it gently in a metal bowl over a pan of hot water. Stir it as it melts.

11   Serve the cake on its own or with ice cream or fresh fruit.

NOTE: Egg whites can be stored in an airtight container for up to 3 months in the refrigerator. Use them to make Pine Nut Macaroons (page 344).

Butter Cake

½ pound (2 sticks) unsalted butter, at room temperature

1½ cups sugar

1 teaspoon pure vanilla extract

8 large egg yolks (see Note below)

2 cups all-purpose flour

1 teaspoon salt

1½ teaspoons baking powder

1 cup whole milk

Chocolate Glaze

8 ounces bittersweet chocolate (70 percent cocoa solids)

¾ cup heavy cream

¼ cup whole milk

¼ cup sugar

4 tablespoons unsalted butter

Spring Menu VII

minted sweet pea soup

soft-shell crab with lemon-caper brown butter

marble pound cake

WINES: The sweet pea soup will pair well with a white Bordeaux or a Sauvignon Blanc from New Zealand. Either of these wines will carry through the appetizer and move on to pair well with the crab.

minted sweet pea soup

Wonderful hot or cold, this soup plays off a traditional French dish of peas, butter, and a chiffonade of mint. The peas should be as fresh as possible. Open a pod and taste the peas for sweetness and tenderness before buying them. Good peas are delicious enough to eat raw. Reject them if they are starchy and hard. Frozen organic peas can be substituted for fresh. As much as I hate to say it, these oftentimes can be better than ones sold at the market. If you really love peas make an effort to grow your own or locate a farmer at the market and have him keep you up to date on his growing schedule. It is your best bet to get peas fresh off the vine.

The Crème Fraîche provides richness and a touch of tanginess to the soup. It can also be used as a garnish by drizzling it into the soup just before serving.

SERVES 8

1   Peel and dice the onions coarsely.

2   Heat the butter in a large saucepan over medium-high heat until it starts to brown. Add the onions and sauté them until they are golden and tender, about 5 minutes. Drizzle the onions with honey and cook until the honey bubbles, about 3 minutes.

3   Add the peas and stir until they start popping, about 5 minutes. Add 2 teaspoons of salt to the peas. Add enough water or light chicken stock to the pan to cover the vegetables by 1 inch and bring to a boil. Reduce the heat and simmer until the peas are tender, 5 to 10 minutes.

4   Add the mint leaves and turn off the heat. Let the soup sit for 10 minutes.

5   Puree the soup in a blender in batches. Do not fill the blender more than two-thirds full or you risk having the contents of the blender explode. Allow the steam to escape by removing the center plug in the lid and covering the hole with a thick towel to protect your hand. Hold the lid securely down and lift the towel slightly to allow the pressurized air to escape as you blend.

2 tablespoons unsalted butter

2 medium yellow onions

2 teaspoons honey—omit if your peas are candy sweet

6 cups shelled peas (about 6 pounds in the pod)

2 teaspoons salt

20 large mint leaves

1 cup Crème Fraîche (page 39) (see Headnote)

Freshly ground black pepper

6   Strain the pureed soup through a coarse strainer back into the pan. If the soup is too thick add more water. Return the soup to a boil, turn off the heat, and fold in the Crème Fraîche; season the soup with salt and pepper to taste. Whisk lightly and serve immediately.

soft-shell crab with
lemon-caper brown butter

For crab lovers, soft-shells are nirvana; others wonder what all the fuss is about. I favor soft-shell crabs from the shores of Chesapeake Bay, where they are trapped right before they are about to shed and kept in saltwater tanks until they do. Farmed soft shells are available most of the year but the wild spring and early summer crabs are the ones to buy.

Cleaning live soft-shell crabs is a barbaric yet necessary act. You can ask your fishmonger to do it but you should use the crabs as quickly as possible. Crabs deteriorate quickly once they are dead. The crabs are wonderful served on their own or with Golden Potato Coins (page 352).

SERVES 8

1   To clean the crabs: Snip off the eyes with scissors and squeeze out the brain sack. Lift the shell from each side and gently pull out the lungs, they look like feathery fingers. Pull the tail flap out and cut it off. Reserve the cleaned crabs in the refrigerator until ready to cook, the sooner the better.

2   Preheat the oven to 250 degrees F.

3   Place the flour in a shallow bowl or pan; season with salt and pepper. Dredge the cleaned crabs in it and shake off the excess.

4   Heat 4 tablespoons of butter (1 tablespoon per crab) over medium-high heat in a 12-inch nonstick pan. Add four of the crabs, shell side down. Fry the crabs until they are golden on both sides, about 3 to 4 minutes per side. You can cook more than four at a time if the size of pan will allow it. Remove the crabs from the pan and drain on a paper towel; repeat until all the crabs are cooked. Keep the cooked crabs warm in the preheated oven.

16 soft-shell crabs, prime or jumbo size

2 cups all-purpose flour

Salt

Freshly ground black pepper

¾ pound (3 sticks) unsalted butter

¼ cup chopped capers

Juice of 1 large lemon

½ pound watercress, washed and dried, for garnish

5   Melt the remaining 8 tablespoons of butter in the same pan and brown it. Add the capers and lemon juice and bring to a boil; season with salt and pepper to taste. Serve the crabs immediately with the sauce drizzled over and with Golden Potato Coins, if desired. Garnish with watercress.

marble pound cake

A pound cake was first named a pound cake because it required 1 pound each of four ingredients, butter, sugar, flour, and eggs. This is just a spiffed-up version of the original recipe. It is a simple satisfying cake that gets better each day, until the last crumb is eaten. When I was a child we would cut pieces of pound cake to fit in the toaster, toast them, slather them with butter, and eat them for breakfast. In our eyes, it was a breakfast fit for a king.

SERVES 8 TO 10

½ pound (2 sticks) unsalted butter, at room temperature

1¼ cups sugar

4 large eggs

1 teaspoon pure vanilla extract

1¾ cups all-purpose flour

1 teaspoon salt

1½ teaspoons baking powder

¾ cup whole milk

2 tablespoons dark cocoa powder, sifted

1   Preheat the oven to 350 degrees F. Butter and flour an 8-cup loaf pan.

2   In the bowl of a standing mixer fitted with the paddle attachment or with an electric hand mixer, beat the butter and the sugar together until fluffy, 2 to 3 minutes. Scrape down the sides of the bowl. Add the eggs one by one; beat for 15 seconds after each addition. Add the vanilla and beat for 30 seconds.

3   In a medium bowl, combine the flour, salt, and baking powder and slowly fold into the egg mixture, alternating with the milk.

4   Pour two-thirds of the batter into the prepared loaf pan. Fold the sifted cocoa powder into the remaining third of the batter and combine well. Pour the chocolate batter down the center of the yellow batter in the pan. Run a knife down the center swirling it as you go.

5   Place the pan in the oven and bake in the preheated oven for 1 hour to 1 hour and 5 minutes or until a toothpick inserted into the center comes out clean. Cool in the pan for 15 minutes before turning out onto a rack.

Spring Menu VIII

peppered chicken livers with two endives
  and a sherry-mustard vinaigrette   266

rock cornish game hens with lemon
  and roasted baby artichokes   268

tapioca pudding with tahitian vanilla   270

WINES: This menu flips the order of red and white. If the salad were without livers I would pair it with a white wine. The livers are the twist. They call for a red wine with light or soft tannins and lots of fruit. This is necessary to carry the acid of the salad and earthy flavors of the liver. Beaujolais would be the best pairing with this salad with Chianti as a backup. The roasted birds with the lemon and difficult artichokes call for a Sauvignon Blanc such as a Sancerre or a crisp New Zealand Sauvignon Blanc. Either will pair beautifully.

peppered chicken livers with two endives and a sherry-mustard vinaigrette

I love the contrast between the crunchy, salty, peppery, tangy exterior of these chicken livers and their creamy interiors. Buy the freshest organic chicken livers that you can find. Livers are filters so you want to be sure they are filtering the very best and purest feed. Have the greens dressed and ready to go on the plates, then quickly sauté the livers right before serving to preserve their crunchy exterior. Curly endive, also called chicory, is sturdier than frisée and has much more texture and flavor; frisée may be substituted if chicory is unavailable.

SERVES 8

1   Remove the outer brown or wilted leaves from both endives. Cut the Belgian endive in half and remove the core in a triangular wedge. Cut into long strips ¼ inch thick, the length of the endive. Trim the root end off the curly endive and remove the tough outer leaves. Wash and dry the leaves well. Tear off the dark green ends if they are tough. Tear the remaining leaves into bite-sized pieces. Do not cut them with a knife or they will look like trimmed hair. Combine the endives and reserve in a large bowl covered with a damp cloth in the refrigerator.

2   Clean any visible veins and fat from the livers with a small sharp knife. Refrigerate the livers until ready to use.

3   Just before sautéing the livers, remove the greens from the refrigerator and toss lightly with the Sherry Mustard Vinaigrette; season with salt and pepper to taste. Divide among eight salad plates.

4   Remove the livers from the refrigerator and place on a plate. Pat them dry with a paper towel. Season them well with salt and freshly ground black pepper.

5   Heat a large heavy sauté pan over high heat. Add 2 tablespoons olive oil and sauté the livers until golden and crisp on each side, 3 to 4 minutes. If your pan is not large enough to accommodate all of the chicken livers in one loose layer, use two pans or sauté them in batches.

6 Remove the livers from the pan and place on a plate. Add ½ cup of sherry vinegar to the pan to deglaze all of the crunchy bits. Simmer until the vinegar has reduced by two-thirds, about 4 minutes. Pour it over the cooked livers and divide the livers among the plates on top of the dressed endive. Serve with crostini or a crusty baguette on the side.

NOTE: For Crostini: Slice an old baguette into ¼-inch-thick pieces, drizzle with olive oil, and toast in a 400 degree F oven until golden, 15 minutes.

1 pound Belgian endive

¾ pound curly endive (chicory) or frisée

2 pounds very fresh chicken livers (2 livers per person) (see Headnote)

¾ cup Sherry Mustard Vinaigrette (recipe follows)

Salt

Freshly ground black pepper

2 tablespoons extra virgin olive oil, plus more for drizzling, optional

½ cup sherry vinegar

16 crostini (see Note) or a crusty baguette

sherry-mustard vinaigrette

MAKES ¾ CUP

1 Place the minced shallot, vinegar, and mustard in a bowl and season with ½ teaspoon of salt and freshly ground black pepper. Let the mixture macerate for 10 minutes.

2 Slowly drizzle in the olive oil while whisking constantly. Let the vinaigrette sit for 20 minutes then season to taste. This vinaigrette can be made up to 2 weeks ahead of time and refrigerated.

1 medium shallot, peeled, trimmed, and minced

3 tablespoons sherry vinegar

2 teaspoons Dijon mustard

Salt

Freshly ground black pepper

½ cup extra virgin olive oil or more depending on the tanginess you desire

rock cornish game hens with lemon and roasted baby artichokes

I have had major debates on whether or not a Rock Cornish game hen is the same bird as a *poussin*. After much research I have discovered that they are one and the same bird—merely a small underage chicken about 5 weeks old. A Rock Cornish game hen is a cross between a Cornish game hen, slow-growing and prized for its plump breasts, and a fast-growing white Rock chicken. The birds were originally marketed in the 1960s for the upscale gourmet.

Game hens usually come frozen, but more and more frequently they are being sold fresh. The fresh ones cook up moist and succulent. You will find yourself licking your fingers and sucking on the bones long after the last shred of meat is gone. The frozen ones benefit from this method of cooking: the lemon and bay leaves perfume the meat and the pan searing seals in the juices. Take care not to overcook the birds or the breasts will become dry.

SERVES 8

1   Remove the outer leaves from the baby artichokes until you reach the leaves that are a light bright green. Trim the exterior of the artichoke base to a pale green. Cut dark green tips off straight across at the point where they turn light bright yellow/green. Toss lightly with the juice of one lemon, or if you will not be roasting the artichokes immediately, hold them in 4 cups of water mixed with the juice of one lemon to prevent the artichokes from turning black. Drain them well and cut them in half before sautéing.

2   Peel and slice the onions into ¼-inch-thick wedges. If you are using cipollini or pearl onions, peel off the skin, trim the root end, and leave them whole. Reserve.

3   Trim the wing tips and tail from the hens. Season the inside of each hen well with salt and black pepper. Cut the four lemons in half and squeeze one half into each cavity. Stuff one squeezed lemon half and one bay leaf into each bird. Truss with a string (see method, page 96). Rub the skin with olive oil and season well with salt and pepper.

4   Preheat the oven to 400 degrees F.

5   Heat a large sauté pan over medium-high heat; add enough olive oil to just cover the bottom of the pan. Sauté the birds two to three at a time until they are golden brown, about 15 minutes. Turn the birds as they sear to brown all sides. Reduce the heat if the pan smokes too much. Remove to a plate until all of the birds are seared.

6   When all of the birds have been seared, drain the pan of grease. Heat the pan over medium-high heat and add 2 tablespoons of olive oil. Add the onions and artichokes to the pan and sauté until slightly golden, about 3 to 5 minutes. This can be done in two or three batches depending on the size of your pan. Season the vegetables well with salt and pepper. Place them in the bottom of a heavy roasting pan with the seared birds on top.

7   Add 1 cup of white wine to the sauté pan to deglaze the pan. Scrape off any caramelized bits; simmer for 5 minutes to reduce by half and pour over the birds and vegetables.

8   Place the pan in the preheated oven and roast for 30 minutes then add 1 cup of water. Continue roasting for 30 minutes. The juice on the leg should run clear when pierced with a knife. Cut into the leg if you're not sure if the hens are done. Eat that bird yourself. Serve one bird per person with the artichokes and onions on the side. Roasted potatoes may also be served as an accompaniment.

SUBSTITUTIONS: If game hens are unavailable, two good-sized roasting chickens may be substituted. Substitute larger artichokes for baby artichokes if they are unavailable. If artichokes fail you altogether, substitute creamer-sized potatoes that have been washed well and cut in half.

---

48 baby artichokes

1 lemon plus 4 lemons for stuffing the birds

2 medium yellow onions or 24 small cipollini or pearl onions

8 Rock Cornish game hens

Salt

Freshly ground black pepper

8 bay leaves, fresh or dried

Extra virgin olive oil

1 cup dry white wine

tapioca pudding
with tahitian vanilla

Late one night after eating this pudding my father-in-law exclaimed, "Gosh, I haven't had tapioca pudding since I was in the Navy." I didn't know what to say; was it a knock or a compliment? He then followed with, "But yours is much better." I breathed a sigh of relief.

Using the larger pearl tapioca rather than the chopped-up minute tapioca makes this pudding a textural sensation. It is a must to soak the pearls overnight in cold water to soften them. The cooking method and timing are the same whether you use the large pearl or small pearls. The addition of cream to pudding that traditionally uses only milk makes it extra rich. Tahitian vanilla beans are much more aromatic than Mexican or Madagascar vanilla beans. The pods are much larger, heavier, and flatter than the two latter vanilla beans and burst with seeds. Their flavor makes this twist on a plebeian pudding all the more special. If you cannot locate Tahitian vanilla beans substitute another variety.

SERVES 8

1 Soak the tapioca overnight in 4 cups of water at room temperature. Drain well.

2 In a large heavy-bottomed saucepan, combine the milk, 2 cups heavy cream, and vanilla beans and bring to a boil. Turn down the heat, add the tapioca, and cook for 30 minutes at barely a simmer. Stir frequently to prevent the bottom from scorching.

3 Whisk the yolks and ¾ cup sugar in a bowl until fluffy. Stir the hot tapioca into the eggs and mix thoroughly to incorporate. Return everything to the pan. Over low heat, stirring constantly, cook until mixture has thickened, about 3 to 5 minutes; pour the pudding into a bowl. Continue stirring for 5 minutes to make sure everything is well incorporated. Remove the vanilla bean pod. Leave the pudding in the bowl to cool or pour into individual dishes.

4   Serve slightly warm or chilled with soft whipped cream. The puddings may be served as a brûlée by sprinkling 1 tablespoon of sugar evenly over the surface and caramelizing them with a blowtorch or under a very hot broiler.

SUBSTITUTIONS: For a less heart-stopping pudding all whole milk may be used instead of cream. If vanilla beans are not available, substitute 2 teaspoons of pure vanilla extract. Commonly available coarse-textured, long-cooking tapioca may be substituted for either size pearl tapioca; quick-cooking tapioca, however, may not.

1 cup large or small pearl tapioca

3 cups whole milk

2 cups heavy cream, plus 1 cup heavy cream, whipped to soft peaks, optional

2 Tahitian vanilla beans, split and scraped

6 large egg yolks

¾ cup sugar, plus ½ cup sugar for brûlée, optional

Spring Menu IX

spring onion and green garlic tart   274

pan-fried halibut with a ragout of sweet peas
    and morels   276

grand marnier soufflés   279

WINES: A crisp white Burgundy such as a Chablis or a Pouilly-Fuissé will pair well with the tart. You can carry either wine through to the halibut. They wines will complement the fish and provide balance to the earthy notes of the leeks and morels.

spring onion and green garlic tart

Spring onions are onions that are uprooted before they form a bulb. Some of them might have a small bulb but they all have yet to form their papery skin. The skin develops when they are harvested at maturity and left to dry or cure on racks.

Spring garlic is also called green garlic. It is also pulled before the bulb forms. Chefs love this form of onion and garlic because the shoots are young, tender, and full of flavor. The lack of skin dispenses with the troublesome and tedious task of peeling. The flavors of these vegetables are both intense and delicate at the same time. The custard base of this tart carries the flavors well and heightens their youthful sweetness.

SERVES 8 TO 10

1   Roll the Pâte Brisée ⅛ inch thick. Cut it into a circle to fit a 12 by 1-inch tart pan. Trim the edges of excess dough. Chill the lined tart pan until the dough is very firm, about 1 hour.

2   Position an oven rack on the top rung and preheat oven to 400 degrees F.

3   Quickly prick the dough well with a fork and line the tart shell with foil. Press the foil into the corners of the chilled dough firmly.

4   Fill the foil-lined shell with dried beans or pie weights. Blind bake in the preheated oven for 25 minutes. Remove the beans and the foil with an oven mitt and continue to bake the shell for another 10 to 15 minutes. Cool.

5   Trim off the roots and tough tops of the spring onions and green garlic. The trimmed length will be about 7 to 8 inches. Wash well in a large bowl of cold water and slice thinly.

6   Heat the butter over medium-high heat in a large sauté pan until it turns golden, about 3 minutes. Add the vegetables and sauté until tender, about 5 to 7 minutes.

Season them well with salt and pepper. Turn out onto a sheet pan to cool. Reserve.

7 In a large bowl, whisk the eggs and the milk together. Whisk in the Crème Fraîche until smooth; season with 1 teaspoon of salt, a pinch of nutmeg, and a grind of black pepper. Whisk in the flour. Place the onions and garlic in the bottom of the tart shell and pour the custard over. Mix lightly with a fork to distribute the custard and vegetables evenly. Bake on the top rack in the preheated oven for 30 to 40 minutes until the top is golden and custard is set.

½ recipe Pâte Brisée (page 55)

1½ pounds red or white spring onions, untrimmed

¼ pound green garlic shoots, untrimmed

2 tablespoons unsalted butter

Salt

Freshly ground black pepper

2 large eggs

½ cup whole milk

1 cup Crème Fraîche (page 39)

Pinch of ground nutmeg

1 tablespoon all-purpose flour

8 If the custard is well set before the top becomes golden the tart may be broiled for 1 to 2 minutes to add color. Do not leave the tart under the broiler without your rapt attention, otherwise you risk burning it. Serve the tart warm, cut into wedges.

SUBSTITUTIONS: Substitute 3 medium (1 pound) sweet onions for spring onions. Substitute ½ pound of baby leeks for the spring garlic.

pan-fried halibut with a ragout of sweet peas and morels

Halibut, both Pacific and Alaskan, is abundant in the spring and throughout the summer. The vegetable sidekicks for the halibut scream spring.

The curious-looking morel comes on strong in the beginning of spring as the soggy earth begins to warm. It is earthy and pungent, eagerly awaited by mushroom lovers around the country. The sweetness of the peas is juxtaposed against the morels' earthiness. This ragout is symbolic of springtime in a bowl.

SERVES 8

1   Trim the dark green ends and the root ends off the leeks. Wash them if they are dirty and slice them thinly. Reserve.

2   Shell the peas.

3   Cut any dirty stems off the morels. If the mushrooms are gritty, fill a bowl with cold water, dip them in and swish them around, then lift them out of the water

and drain them. This will allow any dirt to sink to the bottom of the bowl and keep the mushrooms from absorbing a lot of water. Drain the mushrooms well. Cut the larger mushrooms into ¼-inch rings; small mushrooms can be left whole.

4   Heat a large sauté pan over medium-high heat. Add 2 tablespoons of butter. When the butter begins to brown add the well-drained morels. Sauté until they are golden and the liquid they have exuded is almost dry, about 10 minutes; season with salt and pepper.

5 Add the sliced leeks to the mushrooms and continue to cook until they are wilted and tender, about 4 minutes; pearl onions will take longer. Add the stock and 2 tablespoons of butter and bring to a boil. Reserve the mixture covered in the pan off the heat until you are ready to add the peas. They will be added at the last minute before the ragout is served.

6 Preheat the oven to 400 degrees F.

7 Season the halibut fillets with salt and pepper. Heat the remaining 2 tablespoons of the butter in a nonstick ovenproof pan over medium-high heat. When the butter begins to brown, add the halibut fillets to the pan. Wait until the fish is golden on one side, about 4 to 5 minutes, before turning over. Complete the cooking in the preheated oven for 10 minutes or on the stove top for 5 to 7 minutes more. Lower the heat if the pan gets too hot.

8 While the halibut is cooking bring the morel and spring onion ragout to a boil. Add the peas and cook for 3 minutes. Season the ragout with salt and pepper to taste and finish with more butter if desired.

9 To serve, place the fish in flat bowls and spoon the ragout over the top. Garnish with chopped chervil.

1 pound baby leeks or 32 pearl onions, peeled and trimmed

3 cups shelled peas (3 pounds in the pod)

1 pound morel mushrooms (see Notes on page 278)

6 tablespoons unsalted butter, more if desired

Salt

Freshly ground black pepper

1 cup chicken or vegetable stock

Eight 6-ounce halibut fillets, cut 1 to 2 inches thick, or eight 8-ounce steaks cut 1¼ inches thick (see Notes and Substitutions on page 278)

Chopped chervil or Italian parsley for garnish

NOTES: You can use two pans to cook the halibut, or pan sear the fillets on each side until golden and then place them on a sheet pan and complete the cooking in a 400 degree F oven for 10 to 15 minutes. This way the fillets will all finish cooking at the same time.

A note on buying morels: Morels contain worm eggs, most wild mushrooms do. Poorly handled mushrooms will have worms crawling on them. Choose morels that are dry, plump, and free of worms. Always store your mushrooms loosely wrapped in cloth in the refrigerator so that they have air circulating around them. Do not let them sit at room temperature and become warm and moist or the worms will hatch. If the thought of eating a worm repulses you, you may substitute white button mushrooms. They will not contain any worms.

SUBSTITUTIONS: This recipe can be prepared with halibut steaks instead of fillets. Increase the cooking time 1 to 2 minutes more for each side.

grand marnier soufflés

May I present the grand dame of classic soufflés—light, airy, sweet with a hint of orange-scented liqueur and totally decadent. No one serves soufflés nowadays in this heart-healthy world. I am not sure why they're so expensive in restaurants, they are certainly easier to make than most desserts—whip some egg whites with sugar, pop them in the oven, and forget about them for 30 minutes or so while you entertain your guests. Pouring the cold crème anglaise into the hot center of the soufflé sends this dessert over the top.

SERVES 8 TO 10

1   Butter and sugar ten 6-ounce or two 1-quart soufflé dishes.

2   For large soufflés it is important to use a paper collar to help support the edges of the soufflé. To do this, cut a strip of parchment long enough to fit around the outside of the soufflé dish plus 3 inches. It should be wide enough to rise 2 inches over the top edge of the soufflé dish with the bottom edge of the paper at the bottom of the soufflé dish. Butter the soufflé dish and line the inside of the dish with the paper collar. The ends should overlap by at least 3 inches. Butter and sugar the ramekin and paper collar.

4 tablespoons unsalted butter

¾ cup all-purpose flour

1½ cups whole milk

1 teaspoon salt

6 large eggs, separated

½ cup Grand Marnier

½ cup granulated sugar

Confectioners' sugar for dusting

Vanilla Bean Crème Anglaise (page 174)

3   Heat 4 tablespoons of butter in a heavy-bottomed pan over medium heat until melted. Add the flour and stir with a wooden spoon until the mixture is combined and crumbly.

4   Remove the pan from the heat and add the milk gradually, stirring with a wooden spoon after each addition until the paste is smooth. After all of the milk has been added, put the pan back onto the heat and stir until the mixture is completely smooth and thick and bubbles in the center. Add the salt.

5   Place the batter in the bowl of a standing mixer or a large mixing bowl. With the paddle attachment or by hand with a wooden spoon, beat in the egg yolks one by one. Add the Grand Marnier and beat until smooth. Store at room temperature for up to 4 hours, until ready to use (the mixture may be stored overnight in refrigerator, but it needs to be brought up to room temperature before use).

6   To assemble the soufflés: Preheat the oven to 425 degrees F.

7   Place the egg whites in a mixing bowl or the bowl of a standing mixer. With a whisk attachment or by hand, beat the egg whites with ½ cup of sugar to stiff peaks. Temper the whites into the soufflé batter one-third at a time until the mixture is almost completely mixed. It is fine if there are some streaks of egg whites. The key thing is not to overmix. Spoon the batter into the prepared small ramekins and fill to the top. Large ramekins will be filled almost to the top.

8   Bake the soufflés well spaced on a sheet pan in the preheated oven 20 minutes for small soufflés and 30 minutes for large soufflés. They will be puffed, golden, and magnificent.

9   Remove from the oven and dust with confectioners' sugar. Place the hot soufflés on a doily- or napkin-lined plate to serve. Serve the crème anglaise on the side in a pitcher.

Spring Menu X

gathered greens with a red wine vinaigrette 282

manicotti with sheep's milk ricotta 283

caramelized rum-scented bananas
   with vanilla ice cream 288

WINES: Skip a wine with the salad or serve a crisp fruity white wine such as a Spanish Albariño beforehand as an aperitif. The acid of the tomatoes and the richness of the ricotta cheese will pair wonderfully with a Chianti Classico or Barbera d'Alba.

gathered greens with a red wine vinaigrette

This recipe isn't a recipe at all, merely a guideline for throwing together the simplest of salads. You'll need to trust your taste buds and culinary instincts on this one. After a few times you will have perfected your technique. My mother has made this salad for years and my father always commented, and still does, that as far as salads were concerned, when my mother was "on" there was none better. So there you have it.

SERVES 8

1½ pounds mixed leaf lettuces

Extra virgin olive oil for drizzling

Salt

Freshly ground black pepper

¼ to ½ teaspoon sugar

2 to 3 teaspoons red wine vinegar

1   Wash the greens well. Spin dry and place in bowl.

2   Drizzle olive oil lightly over the greens and toss to coat. Season with salt and pepper and a sprinkle of sugar (about ¼ to ½ teaspoon); toss the greens again and taste.

3   Drizzle with 2 to 3 teaspoons or so of red wine vinegar and toss. Taste for tanginess and seasoning. Adjust the salt, pepper, and vinegar to taste. Serve immediately.

manicotti with sheep's milk ricotta

This is my great-grandmother's recipe, transcribed by my mother. Manicotti has been served at every family gathering for as long as I can remember. Every time these manicotti, with their delicate pancake covering and ethereally light filling, are set down on the table there is but a second of silence just to gaze at them tucked into their tomato-swathed pans. Then the clamoring starts immediately over who gets the first one. This dish freezes very well and can be popped in the oven frozen, covered with foil, for reheating. I suggest making extra and freezing them for your next unexpected soiree.

You will never see a dried pasta manicotti tube at my house. The pancakes are so much easier to make and fill that the thought of buying premade never crosses my mind. The pancakes are made from the same ingredients as pasta dough albeit in very different proportions. It is in essence very loose pasta dough. The pancakes can be used to wrap a variety of fillings not just ricotta. Use them in the same way as you would a savory crepe.

Very few ingredients allow the delicate flavor of the fresh sheep's milk ricotta in the filling to shine through. The same is true of fresh cow's milk ricotta, which may be substituted if sheep's milk ricotta is unavailable. These fresh ricottas do not have any fillers, stabilizers, or thickeners and have a shelf life of about a week. Large-scale, commercial ricottas available at most supermarkets have a shelf life of 4 months or more because of additives and preservatives. They can be substituted for the fresh ricotta, sheep's or cow's milk, but may have to be gussied up a bit with a teaspoon of minced garlic and a ¼ cup of Parmesan cheese to boost their flavor.

SERVES 8

1   Prepare the pancakes: Mix the flour and salt together in a large bowl. Make a well in the center of the flour.

2   In a separate bowl, beat the eggs until smooth then mix in 2 cups water and the olive oil. Beat together lightly.

3   Slowly pour half the egg mixture into the well of the flour. Stir as you pour the eggs so that the flour is gradually incorporated with the eggs. Beat the paste until smooth, then gradually beat in the remaining eggs. Let the batter rest for 20 minutes, covered.

4   Brush a 7-inch nonstick frying pan lightly with olive oil. It is not necessary to brush the pan with olive oil for each pancake. Brush it again when the batter begins to stick.

5   Fill a ¼-cup measure three-quarters full to scoop the batter or, if you have it, a 2-ounce ladle. Pour the batter into the pan and roll around to thinly cover the bottom. If the batter is too thick add a little more water so that it rolls easily around the pan to coat.

6   Cook on one side over medium heat until the batter is set and the edges curl from the sides of the pan. Flip the pancake over and cook for a few seconds on the other side. Stack the pancakes on a plate with the paler side face up. Let cool. The pancakes can be stored at room temperature overnight, tightly wrapped after cooling.

7 Prepare the filling while the pancakes are cooling. In a large bowl, combine the ricotta, parsley, and nutmeg. Season to taste with salt and pepper. Beat the eggs lightly and fold in. Refrigerate until ready to use.

8 To assemble the manacotti: Preheat the oven to 350 degrees F.

9 Place 2 heaping tablespoons of filling on the edge of the pancake and roll it up. Ladle some tomato sauce in the bottom of a baking dish to coat and place the manicotti seam side down in the pan.

10 After the pan is full, ladle tomato sauce over the manicotti to cover. Bake in the preheated oven for 40 minutes, covered with foil, and uncover for the last 10 minutes of baking.

Pancake Batter (40 Pancakes)
(See Note Below)

2 cups all-purpose flour

2 teaspoons salt

6 large eggs

2 tablespoons extra virgin olive oil, plus more for brushing

Sheep's Milk Ricotta Filling

4 pounds fresh sheep's milk ricotta or substitute fresh cow's milk ricotta

2 tablespoons chopped Italian parsley

¼ teaspoon freshly ground nutmeg

Salt

Freshly ground black pepper

4 large eggs

Tomato Sauce (recipe follows)

NOTE: The pancakes may be made 1 day ahead and stored at room temperature overnight. The sauce can be made 2 to 3 days ahead and stored in the refrigerator. It is not necessary to reheat the sauce before assembling the manicotti, as they will be thoroughly heated in the oven. The filling can be prepared up to a day in advance. Mix well before using.

tomato sauce

Look for canned tomatoes that contain only tomatoes and juice. There should be no salt or citric acid. If your canned tomatoes have salt, adjust or omit the salt in this recipe until the final seasoning at the end of the cooking time. Canned San Marzano plum tomatoes from Italy are famous for their flavor. They frequently come packed with the addition of basil leaves, which are fine for use in this recipe. There are excellent brands of boxed Italian tomatoes that come chopped or pureed and have no other ingredients except the tomatoes. These tomatoes work very well in a sauce.

Tomato paste should have only tomatoes as an ingredient. It is far better to use good canned tomatoes than inferior fresh tomatoes. See Note opposite for using fresh in-season tomatoes.

MAKES 4½ QUARTS

1   Remove the core and as many seeds as possible from the canned tomatoes. Strain the juices. Chop the tomatoes and reserve them in their juice.

2   Heat a large pot over medium-high heat. Add ¼ cup of olive oil and then the minced garlic. Lightly toast the garlic and add the finely chopped onions. Cook until the onion is lightly browned, about 4 minutes.

7 pounds peeled canned or boxed tomatoes

¼ cup extra virgin olive oil

8 garlic cloves, peeled, trimmed, and finely minced

2 medium yellow onions, peeled, trimmed, and finely chopped

2 tablespoons tomato paste

1 tablespoon toasted whole fennel seed

¼ cup chopped fresh oregano or 1½ tablespoons dried

¼ cup chopped Italian parsley

1 bay leaf, fresh or dried

1 tablespoon sugar

2 teaspoons salt

Freshly ground black pepper

3   Add the tomatoes, paste, fennel seed, herbs, sugar, and 4 cups of water. Season the sauce with 2 teaspoons of salt and freshly ground black pepper.

4   Simmer over low heat for 1½ hours until the sauce has thickened and the flavors have married. Add more water if sauce gets too thick before the cooking time is up. Season to taste with salt. Remove the bay leaf before using the sauce. For a smoother sauce, puree half or all of the sauce in a blender or food processor. Remove the bay leaf before pureeing.

NOTE: During tomato season 8 pounds of ripe plum tomatoes may be substituted for the canned tomatoes. The tomatoes need to be peeled, seeded, and chopped. Proceed with the recipe the same way as for canned tomatoes, omitting the water. The sauce needs to be simmered longer for fresh tomatoes than for canned, about 2 hours to thicken and develop its full flavor.

caramelized rum-scented bananas with vanilla ice cream

This dessert took the place of a citrus salad on our dessert menu in a pinch one night at PlumpJack Café. The citrus was beginning to look tired and there weren't a lot of other great fruits around at the time. We took bananas from their lowly status on the back rack and crowned them king. Diners loved it so much we let bananas reign for a week. Serve the bananas with chocolate sauce and some toasted nuts and you will swear you are eating a banana split or a fancy version of Bananas Foster.

SERVES 8

1 Lightly butter a sheet pan and reserve in a handy place to receive the cooked bananas. Preheat the oven to 250 degrees F.

2 Peel and slice the bananas ½ inch thick on the diagonal. Heat 2 tablespoons of butter over high heat in a heavy-bottomed nonstick or regular pan until the butter bubbles and turns golden. Add one third of the bananas and cook until they are golden brown on the edges. Turn the bananas over and brown the other side. Sprinkle with ¼ cup of sugar and cook until the sugar is caramelized (see Note below) and dark gold in color.

3 Remove the pan from the heat or turn off the flame and add ¼ cup of the rum. Keep the pan away from your face and other flammable objects. Place it back on the heat and shake the bananas. *Be careful! The rum could flame at any time. Do not lean over the pan.* Simmer the bananas until the rum has reduced to a syrup,

8 large ripe but firm bananas

6 tablespoons unsalted butter

¾ cup sugar

¾ cup dark rum

Vanilla Ice Cream, homemade (recipe follows) or store-bought

Bittersweet Chocolate Sauce (page 241), optional

Toasted Almonds (page 319), optional

3 minutes. Pour the caramelized bananas onto the buttered sheet pan and place in the preheated oven to keep warm. Repeat with the remaining bananas.

4   Scoop the ice cream into bowls and top with the warm bananas and a drizzle of syrup. If desired, drizzle with chocolate sauce and top with a sprinkle of Toasted Almonds.

NOTE: Whenever I work with caramelized sugar I keep a big bowl of ice water near the stove. If some hot sugar happens to land on my hand I simply plunge my hand into the ice water and it cools it instantly and lessens the burn. Do not stick your finger with hot caramel into your mouth or you will also burn your mouth.

vanilla ice cream

A simple and deliciously pure Vanilla Ice Cream that is sure to please everyone.

MAKES 1 ½ QUARTS

1   Combine the milk and cream in a heavy-bottomed saucepan.

2   Split the vanilla beans lengthwise. Scrape the seeds out and add both the seeds and the pods to the milk and cream. Bring the pan to a boil, turn off the heat, and let the mixture steep for 20 minutes.

3   In a large bowl, whisk together the sugar and egg yolks to a thick ribbon.

4   Return the milk mixture to a boil and pour it slowly into the beaten egg mixture while whisking furiously. Cool and strain. Freeze the ice cream base according to the ice cream maker's instructions. The ice cream should have at least 4 hours in the freezer before serving.

3 cups whole milk

2 cups heavy cream

2 vanilla beans

¾ cup sugar

8 large egg yolks

summer

The scent of jasmine wafts through the air.

The sun burns bold and bright.

Sweet berries burst forth from their vine.

Melons, sweet swelling orbs of summer nectar,

Loll beneath the shade of their umbrella leaves.

All faces turn to the glistening sky

Until the cooling moon doth bid us good night.

—MARIA HELM SINSKEY, 1989

Life is simpler in summer. The days are longer. We wear fewer clothes. Less laundry, more time, time that can be devoted to the garden or to visiting the farmers' market. The hardest part about summer is choosing what to devour next. Meals can be planned around what is ready in the garden or finds from the farmers' market.

As if possessing a sixth sense, nature provides fruits and vegetables that can be eaten raw or with little cooking during the summer. A barely warm green bean salad, thickly sliced tomatoes sprinkled with sea salt and extra virgin olive oil, a round of fresh goat cheese and a grilled slice of crusty bread, followed by an eagerly eaten handful of cherries, can make the most satisfying meal.

Life moves outside. Corn is shucked on the kitchen stoop, the husks thrown into a wheelbarrow, destined for the compost heap. Meats are grilled on an outside hearth and ice cream and sorbet are turned on the back porch. Each day has a rhythm. Tend the garden or visit the farmers' market, go to work, prepare dinner and enjoy it as the sun hangs low and the night's cooling air envelopes us.

Gone are the short dreary days of winter and the heady green days of spring. Memories of mouth-staining blackberries, tomatoes warm from the vine, and juicy sweet corn have sustained us for many long months. We are rescued just in time, for to spend another moment without these fruits and vegetables would be unbearable.

Relish each long and languid day of summer. Run through the grass in the morning until your feet are wet with dew. Breathe in deeply the warm sultry air of the afternoon. Settle into a hammock with a good book. Fall asleep to the low buzz of a honeybee in lavender and dream of summer meals to come.

summer menus

Summer Menu I

sweet corn soup with rosemary 298

crispy skinned salmon with a shaved fennel
  and toy box tomato salad 300

strawberry-rhubarb crisp 303

WINES: The soup can be served without wine or with a German Riesling Spätlese with a hint of sweetness. The fish goes well with a crisp, juicy Spanish or French Grenache rosé. For the dessert try a Muscat de Beaumes-de-Venise or a German Riesling Beerenauslese.

sweet corn soup with rosemary

Sweet corn gives its all to create this wonderfully light soup. The scent of rosemary and the earthiness of the garlic complement the sweetness and intense flavor of the corn. Yellow or white corn can be interchanged. I test the sweetness of the corn by taking a bite off the cob while it is still raw. Ask the farmer or green grocer for a sample taste; they will be happy to oblige. The pureed corn provides enough body so neither a thickener nor a cream is necessary. Warm Buttermilk Biscuits (page 76) or freshly baked bread make wonderful accompaniments for the soup.

SERVES 8

1   Husk the corn. Remove as much of the silk from the kernels as you can. Place a small cutting board in the center of a sheet pan. Break the cobs in half and lean the end of the cob on the cutting board. Slice the kernels off the cob using a sharp knife. The sheet pan will catch the kernels and keep them from littering your kitchen floor. Reserve the kernels in a bowl and discard the cobs.

2   Peel, core, and dice the onion. Peel the garlic cloves, trim the ends, and leave the cloves whole.

3   Heat a large pot over medium heat. Add the olive oil to the hot pan. Add the onion and the garlic and sauté until they are golden, about 5 minutes. Drizzle the honey, if desired, over and cook until it bubbles, about 3 minutes. Add the rosemary sprig and corn kernels to the pot.

4   Sauté the vegetables over medium heat until the corn is heated thoroughly but not browned, about 5 minutes. Add enough water to the pot to cover the vegetables by 2 inches and bring the soup to a boil. Simmer for 40 to 50 minutes until the corn is very tender. Turn off the heat and let the soup cool in the pan for 30 minutes. Remove the rosemary sprig.

5   Puree in a blender in batches. Do not fill the blender more than two-thirds full or you risk having the contents of the blender explode. Allow the steam to escape by removing the center plug in the lid and covering the hole with a thick towel to protect your hand. Hold the lid securely down and lift the towel slightly to allow the pressurized air to escape as you blend.

6   Strain the pureed soup through a coarse strainer back into the pot and season with salt and pepper. Return the soup to a simmer before serving.

8 large ears sweet, white, or yellow corn, 8 cups kernels

1 medium yellow onion

5 garlic cloves

1 tablespoon extra virgin olive oil

1 teaspoon wildflower honey, optional if the corn is very sweet

One 2-inch fresh rosemary sprig

Salt

Freshly ground black pepper

NOTE: If you accompany the soup with biscuits, bake them 20 minutes before serving the soup so they are warm from the oven. The dough can be prepared up to a day in advance and the unbaked biscuits stored tightly wrapped in the refrigerator. Place them in the hot oven directly from the refrigerator to bake.

crispy-skinned salmon with a shaved fennel and toy box tomato salad

This salmon preparation is simple and beautiful. Colorful toy box tomatoes, which are a mix of different types of cherry tomatoes, are found in abundance mid- to late summer. It is a simple throw-together dish for a warm summer night.

Use wild salmon whenever possible. Good management of wild salmon is restoring old runs and increasing school numbers. Quality fish can be found in abundance during the salmon season mid-spring to mid-fall.

SERVES 8

1   Prepare the Sherry Vinaigrette according to the recipe below. This may be done a day in advance. Refrigerate and bring to room temperature before using.

2   Remove the pin bones from the salmon fillets with a pair of tweezers or kitchen pliers. Most salmon fillets come with their pin bones intact. These bones appear in the front two thirds of the fish and form a ridge above the center of the fillet in the thickest part of the flesh. Pull the bone out in the same plane and angle that it enters the fish to prevent the bone from tearing the flesh of the fish. If you have a hard time seeing the bones lay the fillet over the back of a small upside down bowl. Refrigerate the salmon until ready to sauté.

3   Remove the tops from the fennel bulbs and reserve some of the smaller sprigs for garnishing the finished plate. Trim off the bottom. Wash the fennel well. Halve the bulbs and remove the core. Slice the fennel thinly, with the grain, using a sharp knife or Japanese mandolin. Season the sliced fennel with salt and pepper to taste and moisten with a little Sherry Vinaigrette. Reserve at room temperature for up to 1 hour; otherwise refrigerate for longer storage. Bring to room temperature before serving.

4   Wash the tomatoes, remove the stems, and cut in half. Drizzle the tomato halves lightly with olive oil, season with salt and black pepper. Reserve at room temperature for up to 1 hour; refrigerate for longer storage. Bring to room temperature before serving.

5   Preheat the oven to 400 degrees F.

6   Heat a large nonstick ovenproof pan over medium-high heat. Season both sides of the salmon well with salt and black pepper. Pour a teaspoon of olive oil into the pan and place the fish flesh side down in the pan. Cook until a golden crust forms and the fish releases from the pan, about 4 minutes. Turn the fish over and continue searing with the skin side down until the skin is crisp and releases from the pan, about 4 minutes.

7   Place the pan in the preheated oven to finish cooking for approximately 7 to 10 minutes. Test for doneness by pressing your finger down firmly on the center of the fillet. If the flakes begin to slide it is done.

8   Combine the fennel and tomatoes in a bowl. Toss with more of the Sherry Vinaigrette, season with salt and pepper. Serve the fish on a platter garnished with the reserved fennel fronds. Serve the shaved fennel and toy box tomato salad on the side.

---

1 recipe Sherry Vinaigrette (recipe follows)

Eight 6-ounce salmon fillets with skin left on and scales removed

2 large fennel bulbs with some of their tops

Salt

Freshly ground black pepper

2 pints assorted toy box tomatoes

1 teaspoon extra virgin olive oil, plus more for drizzling

sherry vinaigrette

Macerating the shallots with vinegar, salt, and pepper before adding the olive oil gives the vinaigrette a stronger shallot flavor. If you do not dissolve the salt in the vinegar before adding the olive oil, the salt will be suspended in the olive oil rather than dissolved, making the vinaigrette taste flat.

MAKES I CUP

1   Combine the shallot, vinegar, and honey in a large bowl; season the mixture well with salt and pepper. Let it sit for 10 minutes.

2   Whisk in the olive oil until the desired tanginess is achieved.

1 medium shallot, peeled, trimmed, and minced

¼ cup sherry vinegar

1 teaspoon honey

Salt

Freshly ground black pepper

½ to ¾ cup extra virgin olive oil

strawberry-rhubarb crisp

This recipe captures the essence of sweet ripe strawberries and mouth-puckering rhubarb. The result is a vivid red crisp with the perfect balance of tang and sweetness. Don't mind that the juices are exuded when you serve this crisp; simply drizzle them over the top. If you like your crisp piled with topping, double the topping recipe and use as much as you like.

SERVES 8 TO 10

1   Prepare the Crisp Topping: Combine the flour, brown sugar, and salt in a mixing bowl. Use a standing mixer with a paddle attachment or mix by hand with a pastry cutter.

2   Add the butter to the bowl and mix until everything is evenly combined but still crumbly. Store at room temperature overnight for the next day. Crisp Topping can be stored tightly sealed in the refrigerator for up to 2 weeks or in the freezer for a month.

3   Preheat the oven to 350 degrees F. Butter an 11 by 7 by 3-inch rectangular pan or eight 8-ounce dishes (see Note on page 304).

4   Prepare the filling: Wash the strawberries in a large bowl of cold water. Lift them out of the water so that the dirt remains on the bottom of the bowl and drain in a colander. Hull and thickly slice the strawberries.

5   Wash the rhubarb and trim the ends and any bit of leaves off. The leaves are poisonous so you don't want to include any part of them in the crisp. Cut the rhubarb into ½-inch slices.

Crisp Topping (2 cups)

1 cup all-purpose flour

⅔ cup brown sugar

½ teaspoon salt

8 tablespoons (1 stick) cold unsalted butter, cut into chunks

Filling:

2 pints ripe strawberries

1½ pounds very red rhubarb stalks

3 tablespoons all-purpose flour

1 cup granulated sugar

1 tablespoon lemon juice

2 teaspoons pure vanilla extract

6 In a large bowl, toss all the ingredients together except for the Crisp Topping. Arrange the mixture evenly in the pan(s) and top with a good ½ to 1 inch of Crisp Topping. Bake for 1½ hours in the preheated oven or until the top is golden and the fruit is bubbling in the center. The smaller crisps should take about 45 minutes to bake. Fill the smaller dishes no more than two-thirds full to prevent the fruit juices from bubbling over the sides.

NOTE: The crisps can also be baked in oversize coffee cups or bowls. Make sure they are ovenproof to prevent them from breaking.

CRISP TOPPING VARIATIONS: Add ½ teaspoon ground cinnamon, 1 teaspoon finely grated lemon zest, or ½ cup lightly toasted chopped pecans. Keep your combinations simple to retain the purity of flavor in the topping.

Summer Menu II

shaved zucchini salad with toasted almonds,
    lemon, and parmesan

roasted pork tenderloin with bing cherries

white peaches poached in vin gris with raspberries

shortbread points

WINES: A citrusy American Sauvignon Blanc without oak or an Italian Pinot Grigio with crisp acidity will complement the zucchini salad nicely. Choose a fruity lightly chilled Italian Dolcetto or a concentrated Amarone di Valpolicella to drink with the roasted pork. Pair the peaches with a California Late Harvest Muscat.

shaved zucchini salad with toasted almonds, lemon, and parmesan

Never plant more than three zucchini plants unless you have a family of ten or more for you will become sick to death of zucchini before you have exhausted all your recipes. This recipe enlivens your taste buds with the sweetness of squash, the crunchiness of almonds, the fragrance of olive oil, and the tanginess of lemon. Not to mention the salty chewiness of the shaved Parmesan. Larger squash may be used in place of smaller ones—quarter them before slicing.

SERVES 8

1　Preheat the oven to 350 degrees F.

2　Spread the almonds on a sheet pan and toast them in the preheated oven until they are golden, about 8 minutes. Reserve.

3　Wash the zucchini and dry them. Trim off the ends. Cut the squash in half lengthwise. By hand or using a Japanese mandolin (see Resources, page 380), slice the zucchini on the bias as thinly as possible (see Note below). Reserve in a big bowl.

½ cup blanched slivered almonds (see page 345)

2 pounds small zucchini, 2-inch diameter (see Headnote)

1 lemon

Fleur de Sel (see Notes on page 49)

Freshly ground black pepper

½ cup picked Italian parsley leaves, fluffy not packed

½ cup shaved or coarsely grated Parmesan cheese, 2 ounces

¼ cup extra virgin olive oil

4　To assemble the salad, toss the zucchini with the juice of the lemon and season with Fleur de Sel and pepper. Add the toasted almonds, parsley leaves, Parmesan cheese, and olive oil. Adjust the seasoning to taste and serve immediately.

NOTE: Whatever you use to cut the zucchini should be very sharp, otherwise you will bruise the flesh and the squash will exude a lot of undesirable liquid.

roasted pork tenderloin with bing cherries

Pork's versatility with fruit is proven once again in this dish. Fresh from the tree cherries burst with juiciness and add a hint of sweetness to the roasted pork without becoming cloying. The cracked black peppercorns add their brooding heat to the mix to create a sweet spiciness. While the cherries provide enough richness for the pork to be served without further accompaniments, polenta, couscous, or good piece of bread can be used to sop up the juices. The pork should be marinated overnight for maximum flavor.

SERVES 8

1   Trim the pork tenderloins of any fat and remove the silvery-looking nerve that starts at the thick end of the tenderloin and runs toward the thin pointed end. You may leave the nerve on but removing it will keep the tenderloin from curling when it is cooked. To remove the nerve, start at its thickest point and slip the tip of your knife under it with the blade flat against the meat. Slide the blade along the underside of the nerve to its end. It will come off in long ribbons. Repeat the process until all of the nerve has been removed.

4 pounds Pork Tenderloin

12 fresh thyme sprigs

8 large whole garlic cloves, unpeeled and crushed

2 teaspoons cracked black peppercorns

¼ cup plus 2 tablespoons extra virgin olive oil

4 cups Bing cherries, 2 pounds (see Variation on page 308)

Salt

2 medium shallots, peeled, trimmed, and diced coarsely

¼ cup red wine vinegar

2 tablespoons unsalted butter

Freshly ground black pepper

¼ sugar

2 cups strong chicken stock

2 teaspoons chopped fresh thyme leaves

1 bay leaf, fresh or dried

2   Place the cleaned tenderloins in a nonreactive dish and add the thyme sprigs; crush them with your hands to release their perfume. Add the crushed garlic cloves, 2 teaspoons of cracked peppercorns, and ¼ cup olive oil. Marinate, covered, overnight in the refrigerator.

3   Cut the cherries in half, remove the pits, and reserve the halves in the refrigerator until ready to use. The cherries should be pitted the day they are used to prevent them from tasting bruised.

4   Preheat the oven to 400 degrees F.

5   Remove the tenderloins from the marinade. Leave as many cracked peppercorns intact as possible. Discard the crushed garlic and the thyme. Season the tenderloins well with salt on both sides; no further pepper is necessary to season the meat.

6   Heat two large ovenproof sauté pans over medium-high heat. Add 1 tablespoon of olive oil to each and then two tenderloins per pan. Sear until they are golden on all sides, about 10 to 15 minutes. Adjust the heat to keep the pan from smoking. Divide the cherries and shallots between the pans.

7   Place the seared tenderloins in the preheated oven and roast for 10 minutes for medium / medium-well. Remove the tenderloins from the pans immediately and let them rest on a plate for at least 10 minutes before slicing. Cover them with a piece of foil to keep them warm. Make your pan sauce while they are resting.

8   For the pan sauce: Consolidate the cherries and shallots in one pan. Pour the vinegar into the empty pan and bring it to a boil over medium-high heat. Use a wooden spoon to release any caramelized bits on the bottom of the pan. Turn off the heat and reserve.

9   Place the pan with the cherries and shallots over medium-high heat. Add the butter to the pan. Stir the cherries and sauté until the butter sizzles and browns, about 2 minutes; season with salt and black pepper. Sprinkle the cherries with the sugar and stir until the sugar melts and bubbles thickly, about 3 minutes. Pour the reserved vinegar over the cherries and bring the liquid to a boil. Boil until the vinegar has reduced to a thick syrup, about 3 minutes. Add the chicken stock, chopped thyme, and bay leaf and bring to a boil. Turn the heat down slightly and simmer for 10 to 15 minutes until the sauce has thickened. Remove the pan from the heat and check the seasoning, adjust if necessary.

10   Remove the bay leaf from the sauce. Slice the pork across the grain and arrange on a platter, spoon the sauce over the meat. Serve with sautéed spinach or couscous.

VARIATIONS: Try grilling the tenderloins for a wonderful smoky nuance. The cherries can be sautéed separately to make the quick and easy side sauce. Two cups of dried sweet cherries may be substituted for fresh. Reconstitute them in hot water before using.

white peaches poached in vin gris with raspberries

Aaaah! I dream about the fragrance of white peaches. Local white peaches are a precious commodity when they are in season. They tend to bruise very easily so cradle them carefully until you have time to consume them.

I love this recipe because of the pink brilliance the poaching syrup takes on from the skins of the peaches. After the skins have served their purpose, and the peaches are cool, they can be slipped off and discarded. These peaches keep well for a week in the refrigerator.

SERVES 8

1 Place the sugar, 2 cups water, and the wine in a large pot and bring it to a simmer. Split and scrape the vanilla bean and add it to the syrup along with the lemon peel. Simmer for 20 minutes until reduced and slightly thickened.

2 Halve the peaches and remove the pits. Add the peaches to the syrup and poach at a simmer for 30 minutes or until just tender. Ripe peaches will take less time than underripe ones. Cool in the syrup.

3 To serve: Place two peach halves in a bowl. Sprinkle each bowl with some of the raspberries. Spoon the syrup over. Serve alone or garnish with Shortbread Points (recipe opposite) and Vanilla Ice Cream (page 289).

3 cups sugar

One 750-ml bottle Vin Gris or other dry pink wine such as a Bandol Rosé from Provence

2 vanilla beans

Peel of 1 lemon

8 white peaches

2 pints raspberries

shortbread points

MAKES 1 DOZEN POINTS

1   Preheat the oven to 350 degrees F.

2   Cream the butter in a mixing bowl. Use a standing mixer
with the paddle attachment or an electric hand mixer.
Scrape down the sides of the bowl. Add the sugar, salt,
and vanilla extract. Beat until the butter is fluffy and
white. Scrape down the sides of the bowl.

3   Add the flour to the mixing bowl. Mix on low until the
flour is combined. Turn the dough out onto a lightly
floured board. Knead lightly to ensure that the dough is uniform.

8 tablespoons (1 stick)
    unsalted butter, at room
    temperature

⅓ cup sugar

½ teaspoon salt

½ teaspoon pure vanilla
    extract

1 cup all-purpose flour

4   Press the dough into an ungreased
10-inch pie plate. Prick well with a
fork. Bake for 30 to 35 minutes in the
preheated oven until the edges are
golden brown. Cool slightly and turn
out onto an odor-free cutting surface.
Cut into twelve points (thin wedges)
while the shortbread is still warm.
As the shortbread cools it will crisp,
which will make it difficult to cut.
If your shortbread cools before you
have time to cut it, slide it onto a
cookie sheet and rewarm it in the
oven for 5 minutes. Slide the warmed
shortbread back onto a cutting
surface and cut it into points
immediately. Prepare the shortbread
up to 2 days in advance and store in
a tightly sealed container.

Summer Menu III

bruschetta of garden tomatoes,
    fresh mozzarella, and basil   314

herb-marinated flank steak with a new potato salad   315

summer berry sorbet   318

anise-scented almond biscotti   319

WINES: Choose a crisp Pinot Grigio or Chianti for the bruschetta. The steak will pair well with a Rioja or an American Cabernet Franc or Cabernet Sauvignon. The sorbet is fun and light with a sparkling Muscato d'Asti.

bruschetta of garden tomatoes, fresh mozzarella, and basil

Bruschetta is a good way to use up day-old crusty artisanal baked breads. The juices of the sliced tomatoes soak into the warm toasted bread and mingle with the olive oil. Grilling the bread adds a smoky nuance. If fresh mozzarella is not available use fresh goat cheese or shaved Parmesan instead. For a lighter appetizer divide the recipe in half and serve one piece of bruschetta per person. A baguette sliced ¼ inch thick can be used for hors d'oeuvre–sized portions of this dish.

SERVES 8

1 Preheat the grill or the oven to 400 degrees F.

2 Slice the tomatoes ¼ inch thick and marinate them with the minced shallot, ¼ cup of olive oil, sea salt, freshly ground black pepper. Tear eight of the basil leaves into small pieces and sprinkle over the tomatoes.

3 Slice the mozzarella the same thickness as the tomatoes and marinate with a drizzle of olive oil, sea salt, and freshly ground black pepper; toss well to combine.

4 Marinate the tomatoes and cheese at room temperature for 30 minutes.

5 Rub the bread on both sides with the garlic clove. Rub the clove on the hard crust to get the juices flowing, then rub all over the bread. Drizzle or brush the bread well with olive oil. Grill or toast the bread until golden but still soft.

3 pounds ripe tomatoes, mixed varieties

1 medium shallot, peeled, trimmed, and minced

¼ cup extra virgin olive oil, plus more for drizzling

Sea salt

Freshly ground black pepper

8 large basil leaves, plus 8 more leaves for garnish

Four 8-ounce balls of fresh mozzarella

Sixteen 1-inch-thick slices of day-old bread, pugliese or Italian

1 large garlic clove, peeled and left whole

Fleur de Sel for finishing (see Notes on page 49)

6   To assemble the bruschetta: Alternate the tomato and mozzarella slices on top of toasted bread. Pour the juices from the marinated tomatoes over the tops of the bruschetta. Sprinkle lightly with the Fleur de Sel and a good grind of black pepper. Tear the 8 remaining basil leaves into small pieces. Drizzle the tops of the finished bruschetta with olive oil and garnish with the torn leaves.

herb-marinated flank steak with a new potato salad

Flank steak used to be considered a lesser (and cheaper) cut until restaurant chefs began turning diners on to it in an attempt to keep menu prices down and still deliver flavor.

The flank is a chameleon of tastiness, readily adapting to all types of marinades. Because this cut comes from the flank, the muscles work a lot, which creates a tougher cut of meat. Correct slicing renders it tender and delicious. The steak must not be overcooked and must be sliced thinly. For a more casual dinner serve the steak on a good crusty baguette with juicy sliced tomatoes, a drizzle of good olive oil, and freshly grated horseradish. The potato salad is the perfect accompaniment however the steak is served.

SERVES 8

1   Crush the herb sprigs to release their perfume and mix with the garlic, peppercorns, and ½ cup of olive oil. Rub both sides of the steak with the herb mixture and place in a nonreactive dish. Cover and marinate overnight in the refrigerator.

Eight 6-inch fresh rosemary sprigs

16 fresh thyme sprigs

10 large garlic cloves, unpeeled and smashed

1 tablespoon cracked black peppercorns

½ cup extra virgin olive oil

2 large flank steaks, 2½ to 3 pounds each

Salt

2   Preheat the grill. The steak may also be cooked on the stove top in a grill pan or a regular sauté pan.

3   Remove the steak from the refrigerator a half hour before cooking. Scrape the excess herbs from the steak and season with salt; it should already have enough pepper.

4   Grill or sear for 7 to 8 minutes on each side over medium-high heat for medium/medium-rare. Let the steak rest for 10 minutes before slicing. Slice thinly at a 45 degree angle across the grain of the meat.

new potato salad

Creamer-sized red potatoes have become synonymous with the label "new potatoes." In actuality, the term "new potato" applies to any freshly dug potato. I love potatoes right from the ground because the balance of their sugar and starch has not yet been disrupted by age or refrigeration. In this salad the potatoes are bound with a lemony Gribiche Sauce instead of mayonnaise. I always make extra potato salad because I love eating the leftovers the next day or two.

SERVES 8

1   Prepare the potato salad either the day before or on the day of serving: Bring a large pot of well-salted water to a boil. Cut the new potatoes in half and add to the pot. Return the pot to a boil and reduce the heat to a simmer. Simmer the potatoes for 12 minutes after the water returns to a boil. Check for tenderness and drain. Cool.

2   Prepare the Gribiche Sauce according to the recipe that follows while the potatoes are cooling.

3 pounds creamer-sized red or Yukon Gold new potatoes, scrubbed well

Gribiche Sauce (recipe follows)

3 celery stalks

Salt

Freshly ground black pepper

3　　Slice the celery thinly and place in the bottom of a large bowl. Add the potatoes and toss with the Gribiche Sauce; season with salt and pepper to taste. Refrigerate until ready to serve.

gribiche sauce

This sauce develops more flavor as it sits, so it can be made a day ahead of time.

MAKES 1 CUP

1　　Place the shallots and capers in a food processor fitted with the steel blade and chop finely. Add the eggs, mustard, lemon juice, and vinegar, puree until smooth, and season with salt and pepper.

2　　Drizzle the olive oil into the food processor while it is running to emulsify.

3　　Add the chopped parsley and adjust the seasoning to taste. Add more lemon juice if more tanginess is desired.

3 medium shallots, peeled, trimmed, and coarsely chopped

2 tablespoons capers

2 hard-boiled large eggs

2 tablespoons strong Dijon mustard

2 tablespoons lemon juice, plus more if desired

¼ cup red wine vinegar

Salt

Freshly ground black pepper

¾ cup extra virgin olive oil

2 tablespoons chopped Italian parsley

summer berry sorbet

This cooling sorbet tastes like you're eating fresh berries from your hand. The flavor bursts in your mouth. The sorbet can be served alone, garnished with fresh berries or with Anise-Scented Almond Biscotti (recipe follows).

SERVES 8; MAKES 1½ QUARTS

½ cup sugar

3 cups mixed ripe berries (raspberries, blackberries, strawberries, or blueberries)

1　Stir the sugar and 1 cup of water together in a small saucepan over medium heat until the sugar is dissolved, about 5 minutes. Bring to a boil, reduce the heat, and simmer for 5 minutes. Cool.

2　Clean and wash the berries. Puree them in a food processor or blender and strain the puree through a coarse strainer.

3　Stir the cooled syrup into the berry puree and chill. Turn according to the ice cream maker's instructions. Freeze for 2 hours before serving.

4　Serve the sorbet in a glass or glass dish with the accompaniment of your choice.

anise-scented almond biscotti

The biscotti can be made ahead and stored in an airtight container. The biscotti recipe yields a great deal of crisp crunchy cookies that keep very well. They are addictive and will be gone before you know it. Try them with a glass of Italian Vin Santo for a simple dessert.

MAKES 10 DOZEN SMALL BISCOTTI

1   Preheat the oven to 400 degrees F.

2   Spread the almonds on a sheet pan and toast in the preheated oven for 8 minutes; cool, chop coarsely, and reserve.

3   Place the fennel seed in a small ovenproof pan and toast in the oven for 6 minutes or until their perfume is released. Cool and chop coarsely. Cover the back of your knife with a dishcloth. Place your hand on top of the cloth to contain the bouncing seeds while chopping. Make sure that your fingers are out of the way of the blade on the hand that's holding the knife. You can also use a spice grinder to chop the seed; just be careful not to grind them too finely. Reserve.

4   Reduce the oven heat to 375 degrees F.

5   Beat the eggs and sugar to a thick ribbon in a standing mixer fitted with a paddle attachment or with an electric hand mixer. Add the vanilla and fennel seed.

6   Combine the flour, baking powder, and salt in a bowl. Add to the egg mixture. Mix until incorporated. Fold in the almonds.

2 cups whole almonds

1 tablespoon fennel seed

3 large eggs

1¼ cups sugar

1½ teaspoons pure vanilla extract

2 cups all-purpose flour

1½ teaspoons baking powder

¾ teaspoon salt

Egg wash: 1 large egg beaten with
    1 tablespoon cold water

7   Spoon the batter into a pastry bag fitted with a ½-inch tip or a sturdy plastic bag with the corner cut on the bias. Pipe into 1½-inch-thick logs, 2 inches apart on a parchment-lined baking sheet and brush the tops with the egg wash.

8   Bake the biscotti in the preheated oven until lightly golden, about 20 to 25 minutes. Remove from the oven. If you overbake the biscotti they will be difficult to cut and shatter when you attempt to slice them. They need to be sliced when they're warm and soft. If they cool and harden while you're slicing them, place them back in the oven for a few minutes to soften them again.

9   Reduce the oven heat to 325 degrees F.

10   While the biscotti are still very warm, remove them from the paper by peeling the paper away from the back of the biscotti. With a thin sharp serrated knife, slice the biscotti on the bias, ½ inch thick, one log at a time. Keep the whole logs on the sheet pan to stay warm.

11   Place the sliced biscotti on their sides on a parchment-lined sheet pan. Bake again in the preheated oven until lightly toasted, 25 to 30 minutes. Serve alongside the berry sorbet or with a good cup of coffee or tea.

Summer Menu IV

white corn, caramelized onion,
  and marjoram-scented strudel with spicy greens   322

grilled pork chops with a fresh apricot glaze   324

herbed couscous   326

lemon verbena crème brûlée   327

WINES: A Sancerre or New Zealand Sauvignon Blanc will pair nicely with the strudels. Look for a fruity California Viognier or semi-dry Vouvray to drink with the pork chops. For the brûlée choose a German Riesling Beerenauslese or a New Zealand Late Harvest Chenin Blanc.

white corn, caramelized onion, and marjoram-scented strudel with spicy greens

The scent of marjoram dances with the sweetness of the corn. The fontina adds the perfect amount of creaminess. This recipe is a play on the strudel name. It substitutes packaged filo dough for homemade strudel dough, which is torturous to make. Rolling the filo creates the flaky "strudel" layers. The slits across the tops give the strudels a strudel-like appearance. You can make the strudels as large or as small as you like. Adjust their size for larger appetites or smaller hors d'oeuvres.

MAKES 8 STRUDELS

1 Defrost the filo dough in the refrigerator overnight for best results.

2 Husk the corn. Remove as much of the silk from the kernels as you can. Place a small cutting board in the center of a sheet pan. Break the cobs in half and lean the end of the cob on the cutting board. Slice the kernels off the cob using a sharp knife. The sheet pan will catch the kernels, and keep them from littering your kitchen floor. Reserve the kernels in a small bowl and discard the cobs.

3 Peel, trim, and dice the onion so that the pieces are about the same size as the corn kernels.

4 Heat 1 tablespoon of olive oil in a sauté pan over medium-high heat. Add the diced onion and cook until golden and caramelized, about 5 minutes. Adjust the heat if the pan gets too hot and the onions start to burn. Add the corn and sauté until tender and beginning to caramelize, about 2 to 3 minutes. Drizzle with the honey and cook for a minute or two until it bubbles. Add the marjoram and season to taste with salt and black pepper. Cool. Mix in the grated fontina.

5 Preheat the oven to 400 degrees F.

6   Open the package of filo dough and unroll the sheets. Lay them flat on a clean cutting board so that the longest side is parallel to the edge of the counter. Cut them in half from top to bottom so that you have two equal pieces several sheets thick. Stack the two halves on top of each other and cover with a clean, barely damp dishcloth.

7   Remove one sheet from the pile and brush it with olive oil. Place another sheet on top and brush with olive oil again. Top with a third sheet. Do not brush the top sheet with olive oil. Line up the oiled sheets so that the short side is parallel to the counter.

8   Sprinkle 1 cup of the filling evenly over the sheets leaving the top 2 inches of the filo empty. Starting at the end closest to you, roll the strudel away from you. Halfway up the sheets, fold the edges over and continue rolling. Think of how a burrito is rolled. Place the rolled strudel seam side down on a parchment-lined sheet pan. Brush the top of the strudel with olive oil and repeat the same technique for the remaining strudels.

9   With a sharp knife, score the tops of the strudels with parallel lines about ¼ inch apart. Bake in the preheated oven until puffed and golden, about 30 to 40 minutes. Cool slightly before serving. Toss the arugula with 3 tablespoons to ¼ cup Sherry Vinaigrette and serve on the side.

NOTE: Marjoram can taste soapy if too much is added to a dish. The idea is to scent the strudels with marjoram, not soak, therefore only a small amount of marjoram is necessary.

1 pound box filo dough

6 large ears sweet white corn, about 6 cups kernels

1 medium yellow onion

1 tablespoon extra virgin olive oil, plus more for brushing

1 teaspoon honey

1½ teaspoons chopped marjoram (see Note below)

Salt

Freshly ground black pepper

2 cups shredded Fontina, ¾ pound

2 bunches of arugula, washed and dried

Sherry Vinaigrette (page 302)

grilled pork chops
with a fresh apricot glaze

Your friends will think you've been praying to the pork gods when they take their first bite of these succulent chops. The brine seasons the meat through and through and keeps even the leanest chops moist when grilling. Marinate them overnight to allow time for the brine to penetrate the meat. These chops touch on all the flavors we crave and love—salty, sweet, spicy, and tangy. The Apricot Glaze makes a great finish for barbecued ribs and chicken. For an exotic twist serve them with Herbed Couscous (recipe follows) or with your favorite potato salad.

SERVES 8

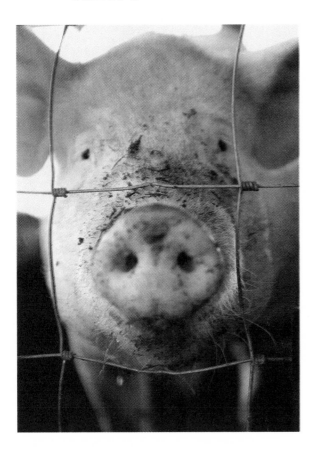

1   Prepare the brine: Peel and slice the garlic cloves in half. Place all ingredients in a medium pot with 5 cups of water. Bring to a boil, turn the heat down, and simmer for 5 minutes. Cool completely before using.

2   Place the pork chops in the cold brine and let them marinate overnight in the refrigerator.

3   Prepare the Apricot Glaze: Wash, halve, and pit the apricots. Chop coarsely. Combine all of the glaze ingredients with 2 cups of water in a pot and bring to a boil. Reduce the heat and simmer for 40 minutes or so until it has thickened. Cool and puree in a blender or a food processor fitted with the steel blade. The glaze can be made up to 4 days in advance and stored in the refrigerator.

4   Preheat the grill or the broiler.

5   Remove the chops from the refrigerator, drain well, and pat dry before grilling. Discard the brine.

6   Brush the chops lightly with olive oil. No additional seasoning is necessary. Grill or broil 10 minutes on one side and turn over and brush with the Apricot Glaze (see Note below). Grill or broil the second side for 10 minutes, turn over and brush with the glaze. Cook an additional 1 to 2 minutes on each side to lightly caramelize the glaze. To test for doneness, let the chops rest for 5 minutes, then cut into the meat at the bone; the meat should be a rosy pink and opaque. If it looks rare, continue to cook for 4 to 5 minutes more.

VARIATIONS: As the apricot season is fleeting, 1½ cups of apricot preserves can be substituted for the fresh. Omit the brown sugar and 1 cup of water. Add an additional tablespoon of vinegar. Fresh ripe plums may be substituted for the apricots.

Brine

4 large garlic cloves

2 tablespoons peeled, thinly sliced fresh ginger

½ cup kosher salt

¾ cup granulated sugar

½ teaspoon chile flakes

1 bay leaf, fresh or dried

8 double-cut pork chops, 1½ inches thick

Apricot Glaze

2 pounds very ripe apricots

1 cup brown sugar

3 tablespoons white wine vinegar

¼ teaspoon chile flakes

2 tablespoons minced ginger

2 teaspoons minced garlic

2 teaspoons salt

Extra virgin olive oil for brushing

NOTE: When broiling the chops, brush with the apricot glaze before turning the chops over.

herbed couscous

Couscous is oftentimes looked at as more of a curiosity than a food to be consumed. Perhaps it's because it's difficult to eat. As a bite is raised to the mouth it tends to crumble through the fork tines. People either give up trying to eat it or ask for a spoon instead. It's a shame because it is effortless to prepare and takes only a matter of minutes. Harking back to its Middle Eastern and Mediterranean roots, it makes the perfect accompaniment for grilled or roasted meats that have been prepared with fruit.

SERVES 8

1 Peel, trim, and finely dice the onion.

2 Heat a medium sauté pan over medium-high heat and add 2 tablespoons of olive oil. Add the diced onion and sauté until golden, about 5 minutes. Stir as necessary so that the onion cooks evenly. Season the onion with salt and pepper and turn out onto a plate to cool.

3 Mix the couscous, ¼ cup of olive oil, and the parsley in a big bowl.

1 medium yellow onion

2 tablespoons plus ¼ cup extra virgin olive oil

Salt

Freshly ground black pepper

2 cups couscous

2 tablespoons chopped parsley

2 tablespoons chopped cilantro

2 tablespoons chopped mint

4 Bring 2¼ cups of water to a boil and add 2 teaspoons of salt. Pour the water over the couscous making sure that all the couscous is moistened. Cover the bowl tightly with plastic wrap and let it sit for 10 minutes.

5 Add the remaining chopped herbs and the sautéed onion. Fluff the couscous with a fork and season to taste before serving. Cover with plastic to keep warm or serve at room temperature.

VARIATION: For an added taste sensation add ¼ cup of currants or chopped golden raisins. Fold them in at the end to retain their texture.

lemon verbena crème brûlée

I have had a love affair with lemon verbena most of my life. When I was first married, I would pick sprigs and place them on my pillow so I could fall asleep with their scent. One morning my husband leaped out of bed like something was attacking him. The lemon verbena, curled and dried, was stuck to his back. After that he forbade me to bring herbs of any kind into our bed. I still use large amounts for flavoring ice creams, teas, crème anglaise, and crème brûlée. I often keep a sprig in my pocket, which I crush in my hand to release its scent. Its perfume carries me through the day.

SERVES 8

1. Combine the milk and cream in a large saucepan and bring to a boil. Turn off the heat and add the lemon verbena. Steep for 10 minutes.

2. Place an oven rack on the lowest rung. Preheat the oven to 350 degrees F. Place eight 6-ounce ramekins or custard cups in a deep roasting pan.

1½ cups whole milk

3½ cups heavy cream

6 large lemon verbena sprigs

12 large egg yolks

¾ cup granulated sugar

8 tablespoons superfine or granulated sugar for caramelizing tops

3. Lightly whisk the egg yolks and sugar together in a large bowl.

4. Bring the cream back to a boil. Pour it in thirds over the egg yolks while whisking constantly. Strain the custard and discard the verbena leaves. Skim off any air bubbles that are on the surface of the custard.

5. Pour the custard into the ramekins. Fill them to ¼ inch below the top edge of the ramekins. Pour hot, not boiling, water into the roasting pan filling it three-quarters of the way up the sides of the ramekins. Bake, covered with a flat sheet of parchment paper or foil, on the bottom rack of the preheated oven for 30 minutes or until the custard is set and has a loose spot the size of a nickel at the center of the brûlée when the cup is gently jiggled.

6   Remove the brûlées from the hot water bath. Cool, uncovered, at room temperature for 1 hour and then chill overnight in the refrigerator. Do not wrap with plastic until chilled to prevent condensation from forming.

7   Sprinkle the top of each brûlee evenly with 1 tablespoon of sugar and caramelize with a blowtorch or under a hot broiler. Serve on doily- or napkin-lined plates.

SUBSTITUTION: If fresh lemon verbena is unavailable, use a pure lemon verbena tea bag or 2 teaspoons of the dried herb to scent the custard. Add it to the milk and cream after it has boiled and steep for 5 to 10 minutes depending on the strength of the dried verbena.

Summer Menu V

chilled garden tomato soup with spicy rock shrimp   330

grilled lamb and potato brochettes
  with basil-mint pesto   332

caramelized peach tart   334

caramel ice cream   336

WINES: The piquant soup will pair nicely with an Alsatian Pinot Blanc or a New Zealand Sauvignon Blanc. The fragrant lamb calls for an American Cabernet Franc or a Spanish Rioja. The peach tart is delicious with a Muscat de Beaumes-de-Venise or a California Late Harvest Muscat.

chilled garden tomato soup with spicy rock shrimp

I love this soup on a hot summer day. It captures the essence of a perfectly ripe, fresh tomato from the garden. Marinating the ingredients overnight draws out and marries the wonderful flavors. This soup does not have to be cooked if you can tolerate raw onions and garlic and plan on eating all of it within a day of preparation. Kept longer than a day or two the vegetables will start to ferment. Add an English cucumber if you prefer a more gazpacho-like soup. The cooking time is not long, only enough to smooth the sharp flavors of the garlic and onions. The sweetness, texture, and flavor of the shrimp make a wonderful garnish.

SERVES 8

1   Core and cut the tomatoes into large pieces. Peel and cut the onion into large pieces. Wash, trim, and cut the celery into large pieces. Cut the garlic cloves in half.

2   Mix together the soup ingredients from the tomatoes through the coarse sea salt and marinate in the refrigerator overnight. The following day, pour the marinated ingredients into a large pot and sauté for 5 minutes over medium-high heat. Add enough water to barely cover the vegetables and bring to a boil. Reduce the heat and simmer for 15 to 20 minutes.

3   Cool the soup to warm and puree in a blender until smooth. Strain the soup through a coarse strainer and chill.

4   Prepare the rock shrimp: Rinse the shrimp with cold water and drain well. Remove any visible black veins with your fingers. Season the shrimp with salt and cayenne. Heat a large sauté pan over medium-high heat and add 2 tablespoons of olive oil. Add the shrimp and cook until they are pink and curled, about 4 minutes. Squeeze the ½ lime over the shrimp; spread out on a plate and chill (see Note below). Keep the shrimp refrigerated until ready to serve.

5   Add the sherry vinegar to the cold soup and season to taste with salt. Pour the soup into flat bowls. Divide the rock shrimp among the bowls and garnish with a drizzle of extra virgin olive oil and basil sprigs.

SUBSTITUTION: If rock shrimp are not available small shrimp such as bay shrimp or larger shrimp cut into small pieces may be substituted.

NOTE: The rock shrimp can be cooked up to 1 day in advance. Refrigerate, well wrapped, until ready to serve.

Soup

4 pounds ripe tomatoes

1 medium red onion

1½ celery stalks

3 garlic cloves, peeled and trimmed

¼ teaspoon chile flakes

6 basil sprigs, leaves only, plus more for garnish

2 cups cubed day-old peasant bread

½ cup extra virgin olive oil, plus more for garnish

2 tablespoons coarse sea salt

¼ cup sherry vinegar

Salt to taste

Spicy Rock Shrimp

1 pound rock shrimp (see Substitution)

Salt

¼ teaspoon cayenne pepper

2 tablespoons extra virgin olive oil

½ lime

grilled lamb and potato brochettes with basil-mint pesto

Lamb sirloins come from the top of the leg of lamb. They are flavorful, tender, and the perfect size. They pack more flavor than rack of lamb and are not as pretentious, making them superb for the grill. The lamb skewered with the potatoes makes a complete meal on a stick, which is always fun and festive in the summer.

Marinating the cubed lamb sirloins for 1 to 2 days with fresh herbs intensifies the flavor. The rosemary and thyme sprigs can be left whole but crush them with your hands to release their perfume. The garlic can be left in its paper and smashed with the flat side of a knife. By leaving the herbs and garlic whole they can be removed easily before grilling or roasting. Cook the potatoes and allow them to chill overnight to set their starch. This will prevent them from falling apart when they are grilled.

SERVES 8

1   Cut the lamb sirloins into 1½-inch cubes. In a large bowl, combine the cut lamb with the ½ cup of olive oil, crushed herb sprigs, and garlic cloves. Place the lamb in a nonreactive dish and marinate covered overnight or for up to 2 days.

2   Scrub the skins of the potatoes well to remove any dirt. Place them in a pot of cold water and bring it to a boil. Add 3 tablespoons of salt, reduce the heat to a simmer, and cook for 12 to 15 minutes until the potatoes are tender. Drain the potatoes and chill overnight in the refrigerator.

Eight 5- to 6-ounce lamb sirloins, cleaned and trimmed of excess fat and sinew

½ cup extra virgin olive oil

8 thyme sprigs

8 rosemary sprigs

12 garlic cloves, unpeeled and smashed

16 creamer-sized Yukon Gold potatoes

3 tablespoons salt

Freshly ground black pepper

Basil-Mint Pesto (recipe follows)

3   Preheat the grill or broiler.

4   Remove the lamb from the marinade and brush off the herbs and garlic. Divide the lamb among eight metal skewers or wooden skewers that have been soaked in water for 30 minutes. Place two potatoes on each skewer spaced equally with the cubed lamb. Season the lamb with salt and pepper.

5   Grill over medium heat or broil for 7 minutes on each side for medium/medium-rare. Let the lamb rest for 10 minutes before serving. Serve with the Basil-Mint Pesto and the accompaniments of your choice. Try cradling the lamb in a Flat Bread, homemade (page 254) or store-bought.

basil-mint pesto

The minty twist on this pesto suits lamb perfectly. It's best to use this pesto the day it is made as the mint has a tendency to oxidize and turn black. It should always be stored with a piece of plastic wrap smoothed directly on its surface.

MAKES I CUP

1   Blanch the basil leaves for 1 minute in heavily salted boiling water. Drain and cool immediately under cold running water or in an ice bath. Squeeze the leaves dry with your hands.

2   Place the blanched basil, mint, pine nuts, garlic clove, and honey in a blender or food processor fitted with the steel blade. Chop coarsely then drizzle in the olive oil gradually while blending to a thick puree; season with salt and black pepper to taste. Place the pesto in a small container and cover with plastic wrap (see Headnote). Store in the refrigerator until ready to use. Remove the pesto from the refrigerator ½ hour before serving; stir well to incorporate the ingredients.

2 cups packed basil leaves

½ cup packed mint leaves

3 tablespoons pine nuts, lightly toasted

1 medium garlic clove, peeled and trimmed

1 teaspoon honey

¾ cup extra virgin olive oil

Salt

Freshly ground black pepper

caramelized peach tart

This simple tart delivers a burst of ripe peach flavor. The rustic look comes from the skin of the unpeeled peach. The Caramel Ice Cream is luxurious and tempting enough to be gobbled up before the peach tart has finished baking.

There is a difference between peaches that look exactly the same from the outside. There are two types, cling and freestone. This means simply that the flesh of the peach either clings to the pit or it does not. Cling peaches are agonizing to work with; you have to cut the flesh of the peach away from the pit. It's doable, just not very pleasant. With freestone peaches you just cut the peach along the line nature has provided through to the pit and then twist the halves apart. If you get stuck with a cling peach by accident, use its naturally occurring vertical line as a guide for cutting. Measure half an inch from the line on either side and cut straight down. You will be left with a pit surrounded by an inch of flesh and two almost halves. Cut the remainder of the flesh from the pit and proceed with the recipe the same way. You will have a few extra bits of peach; just toss them in along with the halves. Make your own Caramel Ice Cream (recipe follows) to serve with the tart or use the store-bought flavor of your choice.

SERVES 8 TO 10

1   Roll out the brisée ⅛ inch thick to fit a 12-inch removable bottom tart pan. Chill in the refrigerator for 20 minutes or overnight.

2   Cut the peaches in half along their natural lines. Remove the stone from the peach and slice the peaches ⅛ inch thick crosswise. Keep the shape of the peach half intact; don't let the slices come apart.

3   Place an oven rack on the bottom rung and one on the top rung. Preheat the oven to 400 degrees F.

4   Remove the tart shell from the refrigerator. Place the peach halves closely together skin side up, in the tart shell. You'll have about ten halves lining the outer edge of the tart and four halves filling the center. The exact number of halves depends on the size of your peaches. If you have extra halves, eat them. Press lightly on each sliced half to fan and flatten them slightly to one side. Sprinkle them evenly with the sugar and dot with the butter.

½ recipe Pâte Brisée (page 55)

7 ripe medium freestone peaches

½ cup sugar

1 tablespoon unsalted butter, cut into small chunks

5   Bake the tart on the bottom rack of the preheated oven for 1 hour and on the top rack for 25 minutes until the tart dough is golden and the peaches are bubbling and caramelized. Cool to room temperature before serving alone or with Caramel Ice Cream.

caramel ice cream

Who doesn't love caramel? This ice cream is sensual. The extra sugar makes it a little softer than other ice creams. It is essential that you caramelize the sugar until it is dark brown, otherwise the ice cream will be too sweet and cloying. The caramelized sugar gives the ice cream an extra layer of bittersweet flavor.

MAKES 1 ½ QUARTS

3 cups whole milk

2 cups heavy cream

1 cup plus ½ cup sugar

8 large egg yolks

1   In a small saucepan, bring the milk and cream to a boil. Turn off the heat and cover to retain the heat.

2   Place 1 cup of sugar in a large saucepan to caramelize. Heat the sugar over medium heat while stirring constantly with a wooden spoon. The sugar will become lumpy before it melts and turns golden. Break up any large lumps with the spoon. Continue stirring until the sugar is a rich, dark golden brown.

3   *Slowly* pour the hot milk and cream into the caramelized sugar, stirring constantly to avoid hardening the sugar. *Be careful of the steam when the liquid hits the sugar;* it can cause a serious burn. Stir until the caramelized sugar is completely incorporated into the milk and cream. Bring to a boil and remove from the heat.

4   In a large bowl, whisk the egg yolks to a ribbon with the remaining ½ cup of sugar. Add the hot cream while whisking briskly. Cool and strain. Turn according to the ice cream maker's instructions. Chill in the freezer at least 4 hours before serving.

Summer Menu VI

WINES: An Alsatian Pinot Gris with a hint of sweetness or a Grenache rosé from Spain or France will carry you through the figs and the squab. A California Late Harvest Muscat or Malmsey Madeira will go nicely with the apricots.

pancetta-wrapped grilled figs with baby arugula

Flavors and rusticity abound in this dish. The idea is to get the salty pancetta slightly crisp and the sweet fig warmed to almost bursting. The arugula lends spiciness and the balsamic mellow tanginess to the dish. I like to use a young 8-year-old balsamic with its light acidity and sweetness to marinate the figs and then a fine aged 20-year or more balsamic to provide a burst of rich sweet-tart flavor at the end (see Headnote, page 12). Make a few extra figs to satisfy your cravings so you won't be caught short when dinnertime comes.

Cruise your deli counter and watch the employees using the meat slicers. Select the person who slices with confidence to slice your pancetta thinly. I've had some people behind the counter say it can't be done and others who just smile and slice it exactly the way I want it. I always remember their name and face for the next time that I need their slicing skill.

SERVES 8

1   Wash the baby arugula and drain well and dry. Reserve.

2   In a large bowl, whisk together the thyme, 2 tablespoons of 8-year-old balsamic vinegar, and honey. Season the mixture with salt and pepper and let it rest for 10 minutes. Whisk in 2 tablespoons of olive oil.

3   Cut the very tip off the stem of the figs. Starting at the top, cut the figs in half partway, stopping at their midpoint. Toss them in the bowl with the marinade. Spoon the marinade over the cut to make sure it penetrates the figs. Season the figs with salt and pepper and let them sit for 20 minutes.

4   Preheat the grill or the broiler.

5   To wrap the figs with pancetta, start at the stem end of the fig and wrap with the pancetta until you finish at the bottom of the fig.

6   Start the figs bottom side down on a preheated medium-hot grill or place on a broiler pan under the broiler. When the pancetta has crisped, roll the figs around as they brown and grill or broil on all sides. Grill or broil until the pancetta is crisp and the figs are still holding their shape. Brush the figs with the marinade as they cook. Brush them again as they come off the grill or out of the broiler.

½ pound baby arugula

1 teaspoon chopped thyme leaves

2 tablespoons 8-year-old balsamic vinegar

2 tablespoons honey

Salt

Freshly ground black pepper

Extra virgin olive oil

24 figs, plus a few extra

24 thin slices of pancetta, plus a few extra

Very fine aged (20 years or more) balsamic vinegar for drizzling or substitute good quality 10- to 12-year-old

7   To serve: Place the figs on a platter. Drizzle a drop or two of the aged balsamic on each of the figs. Toss the arugula with a little extra virgin olive oil to moisten, add salt and freshly ground black pepper to taste and a drop or two of aged balsamic vinegar. Place the dressed leaves on top of the figs.

wildflower honey and lavender–roasted squab

I prefer the name squab to pigeon. If you pronounce pigeon the way the French do it sounds much better, but we are not in France. Looking at the pigeons in the park and envisioning them as a tasty treat is just too much of a stretch. Rest assured the birds that are raised for eating are white of feather with nary a scraggly feather, broken beak, nor peg leg. The roasted birds are very elegant. Their crisp skin and plump and juicy breasts are perfumed with lavender. Serve the squab with a Warm Summer Bean Salad (recipe follows), roasted potatoes, or the accompaniment of your choice.

SERVES 8

1   Mix together the 4 sprigs of lavender, honey, 2 tablespoons of water, and 1 teaspoon of salt in a medium saucepan and heat gently until the mixture simmers. Turn off the heat and let the lavender steep until ready to use.

2   Cut off the neck, wing tips at the second joint from the tip, and the tail of the squab.

3   Season the cavity of the birds with salt and pepper and tie the birds (page 96). This can be done up to a day in advance; cover and refrigerate the birds.

4   Preheat the oven to 400 degrees F.

5   Rub the birds with olive oil and season with salt and pepper. Heat a large sauté pan over medium-high heat and add 2 tablespoons of olive oil and 1 tablespoon of butter to coat the bottom of the pan. Let the butter brown lightly, then add the birds to the pan breast side down. Do not crowd them in the pan. Sear them in two batches if necessary. Sear until all sides of the birds are golden brown, about 10 minutes. Adjust the heat as needed if the pan gets too hot and starts to smoke. Turn the birds as necessary with a pair of tongs. Be careful not to break the skin. Remove them from the sauté pan and place them in a large roasting pan. Drain the excess grease from the sauté pan.

6 Add the wine to the sauté pan and bring to a boil. Scrape the pan to remove any caramelized juices and bits of meat. Reduce the heat and simmer until the wine is reduced by half, about 5 minutes.

7 Pour the wine over the birds. Brush the birds liberally with the reserved honey mixture. Roast in the preheated oven for 30 minutes. Baste the birds with the pan juices and brush with more honey. Roast another 20 minutes. Remove from the oven and brush one last time with honey. Let the birds rest for 10 minutes before serving.

8 Serve the birds on a platter with the accompaniments of your choice. Garnish with the lavender sprigs.

4 sprigs lavender with flower plus eight for garnish

¼ cup wildflower honey

Salt

8 squab

Freshly ground black pepper

2 tablespoons extra virgin olive oil, plus more for rubbing the birds

1 tablespoon unsalted butter

1 cup dry white wine

warm summer bean salad

This bean salad is wonderful whether it's served warm or at room temperature. It's a beautiful mix of colors and size and the flavor of the beans is sublime. I don't have the heart to call it a three-bean salad.

SERVES 8

1 Clean the stem end from the beans. Cut the beans on the diagonal into 2-inch pieces. Refrigerate in a sealed container or bag until ready to use. The beans may be cleaned a day in advance.

2 To serve the salad warm, cook the beans while the birds are resting. Bring a large pot of well-salted water to a boil and add the beans. Cook them for 5 to 7 minutes after the water returns to a boil. When they are cooked, the beans should be tender and sweet. (See Note below.)

1 pound yellow wax beans

½ pound Blue Lake green beans

½ pound flat Romano beans

1 medium shallot, peeled, trimmed, and minced

1 tablespoon chopped Italian parsley

3 tablespoons extra virgin olive oil

½ lemon

Salt

Freshly ground black pepper

3 Drain the beans well and toss them with the minced shallot, parsley, olive oil, and a good squeeze of lemon; season with salt and pepper. Serve warm or at room temperature.

NOTE: The beans may also be cooked ahead and cooled in an ice bath. Store at room temperature for several hours or in the refrigerator overnight. Bring to room temperature before serving. Beans that have been cooked ahead of time should be tossed with the shallots, parsley, etc., at the last moment before serving.

brown-sugar baked apricots

Organic apricot season is fleeting. They are picked perfectly ripe and do not travel well. If you see them at the farmers' market scoop them up, take them home, and make this dessert to achieve apricot nirvana.

The intense perfume of Tahitian vanilla complements the perfectly ripe apricots. Use Madagascar beans if Tahitian is not available. Accompany the warm apricots with Vanilla Ice Cream, homemade (page 289) or store-bought. The Pine Nut Macaroons (recipe follows) are wonderful with the apricots and can be served on the side, or use a cookie of your choice.

SERVES 8

1 Tahitian vanilla bean, split and scraped

4 tablespoons unsalted butter

1 cup brown sugar

1 cup Beaumes-de-Venise or other sweet Muscat wine

12 large ripe apricots

1 Place the vanilla bean in a small saucepan with the butter. Heat slowly over medium heat until the butter foams and the solids start to brown.

2 Stir in the brown sugar and the wine and bring to a simmer until the sugar has dissolved and the syrup has slightly thickened, about 5 to 10 minutes.

3 Preheat the oven to 350 degrees F.

4 Slice the apricots in half; remove the pits and place the halves cut side up in a buttered baking dish or divide the halves equally among individual gratin dishes. If you are using one large dish the vanilla bean may be left in the syrup, otherwise remove it. Pour the hot syrup over the apricots and bake in the preheated oven until they are soft and the syrup is bubbling, about 45 minutes.

5 Cool to warm and serve alone or with a big scoop of Vanilla Ice Cream.

VARIATION: The apricots can also be topped with Cobbler Biscuit Dough (page 379) and baked for the same amount of time for a variation on a theme.

pine nut macaroons

These rustic, chewy pine nut–studded cookies are like an Italian dream. The flavor of the almonds and pine nuts intensifies a day or two after baking. I recommend using European pine nuts versus Chinese pine nuts. European pine nuts are long, slender, and uniform in size. Chinese pine nuts are short and squat and have a great deal of size variation.

Chinese pine nuts are less expensive but they can have a really intense smoky flavor that will make the cookies taste as if they had bacon bits in them. If you must buy Chinese make sure that you can taste them before buying to avoid smoky-tasting cookies. Store cookies in an airtight container and they will keep for a week if they last.

MAKES 3 DOZEN 3-INCH COOKIES

1 Preheat the oven to 400 degrees F.

2 Spread 1 cup of pine nuts in a single layer on a sheet pan and toast for 5 minutes. Cool and coarsely chop.

3 Increase the oven heat to 425 degrees F.

4 Place the almonds and sugar in a food processor fitted with the steel blade. Grind until they are very fine. Add the egg whites and pulse until thoroughly mixed. Pulse in the flour and salt. Turn out onto a board and knead in the coarsely chopped pine nuts until well incorporated.

5 Place the 2 cups of pine nuts for garnish in a bowl. Roll the dough into 1½-inch balls. The dough will be sticky. Place 2-inches apart on a parchment-lined sheet pan. Brush the tops of the balls with the beaten egg white, then pick up each cookie and press it into the bowl of pine nuts. Place the cookie pine-nut side up on the sheet pan and press down lightly to flatten the ball and set the pine nuts.

6   Bake in the preheated oven until shiny and golden, about 16 minutes. Turn the sheet pan around halfway through baking.

7   Cool the cookies on the parchment paper and then peel the parchment away from the backs of the cookies. If you try to remove the cookies from the parchment when they are hot they will crumble. Cool completely before storing.

1 cup pine nuts plus 2 cups for garnish

2 cups whole almonds, blanched (see Note below)

2½ cups sugar

4 large egg whites, ½ cup

¼ cup all-purpose flour

1 teaspoon salt

1 egg white, beaten, for brushing the cookies

NOTE: Blanching almonds at home is very simple. It's easy to do by yourself or have several people peeling the almonds at once to speed the process. Bring a large pot of water to a boil. Add the almonds and blanch for 30 seconds. The skins will pucker. Drain the almonds and peel the skin off quickly before the almonds have a chance to cool down. The skins will adhere to the almond meat as they start to cool so it is important to work rapidly. Dry the almonds in a 350 degree F oven for 7 to 10 minutes and cool before using.

Summer Menu VII

prosciutto with summer melons and shaved parmesan   348

pan-roasted ling cod with sweet red peppers,
    capers, and lemon   350

golden potato coins   352

sour cherry and almond clafoutis   353

WINES: Sparkling Muscato d'Asti is a festive pairing with the prosciutto and melon. You could also start and end the meal with a Muscat de Beaumes-de-Venise but that might send some over the top. The fish calls for Sancerre or American or New Zealand Sauvignon Blanc. Accompany the clafoutis with a California Late Harvest Muscat or Muscat de Beaumes-de-Venise.

prosciutto with summer melons and shaved parmesan

This dish is a twisted French-Italian classic combining small intensely flavored orange-fleshed Cavaillon melons with sheets of thinly sliced, delicately salty prosciutto. The small and succulent Cavaillon melons, native to the Provence region of France and named after the town of Cavaillon, are perhaps most famous for being served as a refreshingly simple dessert, half a chilled melon filled with a few sips of the sweet dessert wine Muscat de Beaumes-de-Venise. For many years French Cavaillon were imported for those who wanted to experience in America the same amazing melon they had eaten in France. Not only did the melons lack a sense of place, they didn't transport well and lacked flavor, the result of being picked under-ripe.

Local farmers are now growing some pretty fine Cavaillons and have saved us from mediocre imports. If you grow them, they should be picked fully ripened at their height of flavor. You can substitute locally grown cantaloupes. The smaller ones are intensely flavored and are the perfect size for this dish. I usually end up eating some of the prosciutto or the melon, not to mention the cheese, before I assemble the plates so I always have extra on hand. This dish can also be prepared with ripe white figs when they are available.

SERVES 8

1   Wash the arugula and spin it dry.

2   Slice each melon into four wedges. Remove the seeds and rind. Cut each wedge in half lengthwise. On each serving plate, place 2 of the wedges so they form a circle when placed end to end on their sides.

3   Drape 3 slices of prosciutto in a ruffle across the center of each melon circle so it hits the plate on both sides.

¼ pound baby arugula

2 small ripe Cavaillon or cantaloupe melons, 4-inch diameter

24 slices of prosciutto, thinly sliced

Extra virgin olive oil

Fleur de Sel (see Note, page 49)

Freshly ground black pepper

A good-sized chunk of Parmesan cheese for shaving

4   Toss the arugula with a little extra virgin olive oil, Fleur de Sel, and pepper. Sprinkle the leaves over the sliced prosciutto.

5   Shave curls of Parmesan cheese over the arugula with a vegetable peeler. Drizzle around the plate with extra virgin olive oil. Grind a small amount of black pepper over all.

pan-roasted ling cod with sweet red peppers, capers, and lemon

Fishermen used to throw ling cod back into the water. It was not considered a commercially viable fish. When other species became scarce, ling cod (see Substitution below) came into fashion. It is an excellent eating fish despite its unglamorous name. It's tender and succulent with large flakes. It is a flavor chameleon, readily taking to all the flavors with which it is prepared. The sweet peppers, salty capers, and zesty lemon make your taste buds dance. The Golden Potato Coins (recipe follows) absorb the juices and provide a grounding earthiness to this dish. The fish can also be served with simple steamed rice, couscous, or the accompaniment of your choice.

SERVES 8

1   To prepare the peppers: Roast the peppers over an open flame until the skin is charred or roast in the oven (see Note below). Place them in a paper bag, close the bag, and cool. Remove the skin by rubbing it off with a clean kitchen towel. Cut the peppers in half and remove the core and seeds. Dice into ½-inch squares, place in a small bowl, and squeeze the ½ lemon over. Season the pepper with salt and freshly ground black pepper. Reserve.

2   In a medium sauté pan heat ½ cup of olive oil over medium heat. Add the sliced garlic and cook until it is toasted and golden. Remove the pan from the heat and let the oil cool for 10 minutes.

3   Add the capers and peppers to the oil. Heat the peppers gently over medium heat until the capers sizzle, about 2 minutes. Turn off the heat and add the chopped parsley. Season to taste with salt and pepper. Cover to keep warm.

4   Preheat the oven to 400 degrees F.

5   Season the fish on both sides with salt and pepper.

6   Heat a large sauté pan over medium-high heat. Add 2 tablespoons of olive oil to the pan. Add the fish to the pan and sear until golden on one side, about 5 minutes. Turn the fish over and roast in the preheated oven for 5 to 10 minutes, depending on the thickness of the fish, until the fish flakes when gently pressed in the middle. Remove the pan from the oven and squeeze the lemons over the fish.

7   Spoon the sweet red peppers over the fish and serve from the pan. Serve the Golden Potato Coins or the accompaniment of your choice on the side.

NOTE: The peppers may also be roasted in the oven. Cut them in half and remove all the seeds. Place the cut side down on a sheet pan and drizzle with olive oil. Roast in a 500 degree F oven until the skin puffs and blackens. Place in a paper bag and proceed according to the recipe.

Sweet Red Peppers and Capers

4 medium red bell peppers or eight small gypsy peppers

½ medium lemon

Salt

Freshly ground black pepper

½ cup extra virgin olive oil

2 medium garlic cloves, peeled, trimmed, and sliced

3 tablespoons capers

2 tablespoons chopped Italian parsley

Eight 6-ounce ling cod, halibut, or Pacific cod

Sea salt

Freshly ground black pepper

2 tablespoons extra virgin olive oil

2 lemons, cut in half, pips removed

SUBSTITUTION: Unfortunately at this writing, ling cod is now scarce. Substitute line-caught Atlantic cod, Pacific cod, or Alaskan halibut.

VARIATION: Serve the sweet red peppers and capers with grilled skewers of big fat prawns or chicken. Use as a topping for pizza or toasted slices of bread. Spoon them over grilled calamari or seared sea scallops for an appetizer or light entrée.

golden potato coins

We should appreciate the Yukon Gold potato. Its golden color, subtle sweet nutty flavor, and creamy texture when cooked make it seem that nature has already added the butter. The potato coins expose the maximum amount of potato surface to the heat, making them crunchy and golden. Season the potatoes well with salt to bring out their sweetness.

SERVES 8

3 pounds creamer-sized Yukon Gold potatoes

¼ cup extra virgin olive oil

8 thyme sprigs

Salt

Freshly ground black pepper

1   Wash the potatoes well. Scrub off any stubborn dirt spots. Drain the potatoes well or rub lightly with a towel.

2   Preheat the oven to 400 degrees F.

3   Cut the potatoes into ¼-inch-thick coins and put them in a large bowl. Toss them with the olive oil and thyme sprigs, season with salt and pepper.

4   Turn them out onto a sheet pan and spread in one layer. If one sheet pan is not large enough, use two. Roast in the preheated oven for 40 to 50 minutes until golden.

NOTE: To serve the potatoes with the fish, start roasting them 40 minutes before cooking the fish.

sour cherry and almond clafoutis

The first time I was served a clafoutis in France I suddenly realized with a loud crack that the cherries still had their stones. I highly recommend not giving your guests the same surprise. Sour cherry season is fleeting so you have to be diligent about checking the market. Baked cherries, especially the sour varieties, have a hint of almond flavor. The toasted almonds play upon this subtlety. Bing cherries will work very well but they will not have the same tart contrast as the sour cherries. The clafoutis can be served in their mold(s) dusted with confectioners' sugar and topped with the ice cream flavor of your choice.

SERVES 8

1 Preheat the oven to 350 degrees F. Butter eight 1-cup gratin dishes or one 9 by 12-inch baking dish.

2 Spread the almonds out on a sheet pan and toast in the preheated oven for 6 minutes. Cool.

3 In a large bowl, whisk together the eggs, egg yolks, and sugar until very smooth. Whisk in the flour and salt. Whisk in the Crème Fraîche a little at a time and then the heavy cream. Stir in the vanilla. Whisk until smooth.

4 Divide the cherries equally among the prepared dish(es). Pour the batter over the cherries. Sprinkle the sliced almonds evenly on top. Place in the oven and bake until the custard has set and is puffed and golden, about 50 minutes for a large clafoutis. Smaller clafoutis will take 30 minutes or so. Serve warm, lightly dusted with confectioners' sugar or with Vanilla Ice Cream (page 289).

VARIATION: Substitute chunks of ripe apricots for the cherries.

1 cup sliced almonds

2 large whole eggs

4 large egg yolks

¾ cup granulated sugar (½ cup for Bing cherries)

¼ cup all-purpose flour

¼ teaspoon salt

1 cup Crème Fraîche (page 39)

1 cup heavy cream

¼ teaspoon pure vanilla extract

3 cups pitted sour cherries, 1½ pounds

Confectioners' sugar for dusting

Summer Menu VIII

provençal tart with herbed goat cheese 356

herb-marinated grilled leg of lamb
    with olive-tomato relish 358

mexican hot chocolate ice cream with
    toasted almonds and bittersweet chocolate sauce 360

WINES: For the tart a crisp Italian Pinot Grigio, Sancerre, or New Zealand Sauvignon Blanc. The grilled lamb calls for a Rioja, California Zinfandel, or Cabernet Sauvignon. The dessert has enough going with all of its components, but if you insist on a sweet wine try a Banyuls.

provençal tart with herbed goat cheese

This recipe is a great way to use up summer vegetables when you realize you've planted way too many. It makes a great luncheon dish with a side of mixed greens. The tart can be made any size, just increase the amount of vegetables and roll the Pâte Brisée to suit a larger pan. The tart can also be made free form like a galette (see Variation opposite).

Fresh goat cheese is a mild-tasting unripened cheese. In this instance fresh is not an indicator of quality but an indicator of age. The cheese is often no more than a few days old when it is packaged. Its soft texture makes it ideal for a spread or filling. It ranges from barely salted to quite salty so it is important to taste it before making the decision on how much salt to add. The herbed cheese makes an excellent spread for juicy tomato or grilled vegetable sandwiches.

SERVES 8 TO 10

1   Prepare the Herbed Goat Cheese: Bring the goat cheese to room temperature and mix in 1 tablespoon of thyme leaves using a fork or wooden spoon; season to taste with salt and black pepper. Mix until well combined. Reserve at room temperature if you will be using it within the hour, otherwise refrigerate. Bring to room temperature to soften before using.

2   Roll the Pâte Brisée ⅛ inch thick and cut into a circle to fit a 12-inch tart pan. Press the dough well into the corners and trim the edges. Refrigerate while you prepare the vegetables. The tart pan may be lined a day in advance and refrigerated overnight well wrapped.

3   Vegetable preparation: Wash and trim the ends of the eggplants and zucchini. Slice into even ⅛-inch-thick rounds. Reserve separately.

4   To peel the tomatoes: Remove the core, make an "X" in the bottom, dip in boiling water for 20 seconds, then shock in ice water. The skin should peel off easily. Slice into ¼-inch rounds. Reserve.

5   Place an oven rack on the bottom rung. Preheat the oven to 400 degrees F.

6   To assemble the tart: Spread the goat cheese ¼ inch thick over the brisée dough. Make tightly packed concentric rows of vegetables starting at the outside edge of the brisée with the eggplants, then the tomatoes, and then the zucchini. Repeat the pattern until the tart is full.

7   Season the tart well with salt and pepper. Drizzle with olive oil. Bake on the bottom rack of the oven for 50 minutes to an hour. The crust and goat cheese should be golden and the vegetables slightly puckered. Drizzle or brush lightly with olive oil upon removal from the oven. Cut the tart into wedges to serve.

Herbed Goat Cheese (1½ cups)

12 ounces fresh white goat cheese

1 tablespoon lightly chopped fresh thyme leaves

Salt

Freshly ground black pepper

½ recipe Pâte Brisée (page 55)

1 pound Japanese eggplants

1 pound extra fancy zucchini

6 small tomatoes, Roma or plum

Salt

Freshly ground black pepper

Extra virgin olive oil for drizzling

VARIATION: To make a galette, cut the brisée dough into a circle or a rectangle. Layer the vegetables in the same way as above, leaving a two-inch edge all the way around. Fold the dough over the vegetables and crimp. Seal with water and bake until the crust is golden and the vegetables are tender.

herb-marinated grilled leg of lamb with olive-tomato relish

Lamb on the grill is one of the finer, simpler things in life. The relish pairs beautifully with the smoky flavor of the grilled lamb. The Provençal tart from the first course can be served as a vegetable alongside the lamb. It's not necessary to serve them separately. Small creamer-sized red potatoes roasted with a little extra virgin olive oil, sea salt, and pepper also go well.

SERVES 8

1. Ask your butcher to debone and butterfly the leg of lamb or, if you want a challenge, you can do it yourself. Trim off excess exterior and all the interior fat, glands, and sinew. Score the fat on the outside of the leg in a crisscross pattern to prevent the leg from curling as it grills. Open the leg as much as possible so that it lies almost flat. You might have to split a couple of muscles with a knife to open them up. Place the leg between two pieces of plastic wrap and pound with a mallet or a small sauté pan to flatten as much as possible. Remove the plastic wrap.

2. Crush and tear the rosemary and thyme sprigs in your hand and mix them with the crushed garlic and ½ cup of extra virgin olive oil in a small bowl. Coarsely grind some black pepper, about 1 teaspoon, and add it to the mixture. Mix together well and rub it on the inside and the outside of the lamb leg. Allow the lamb to marinate for 1 to 2 days well wrapped in the refrigerator.

3. Prepare the Olive-Tomato Relish: Slice the olives into quarters. Core and slice the tomatoes ¼ inch thick. Dice the slices into ¼-inch cubes.

4. Place the olives and the diced tomatoes in a large bowl; add the minced shallot to the bowl. Season the mixture with salt and pepper to taste.

5   Add ¼ cup of olive oil, the sherry vinegar, and chopped Italian parsley to the relish. If the tomatoes are very sweet with low acid and the relish needs more acid, add another tablespoon of sherry vinegar. Season to taste with salt and pepper. The relish may be prepared up to a day in advance and refrigerated.

6   Remove the lamb from the marinade, brush off the excess herbs, and allow it to rest at room temperature for 30 minutes.

7   Preheat the grill.

8   Season the lamb well with salt and grill over medium heat, 15 to 20 minutes on each side, until the temperature reads 125 degrees for medium-rare to medium lamb. Let the lamb rest for 10 to 15 minutes before slicing.

9   Slice the lamb and arrange on a platter top with the Olive-Tomato Relish or serve the relish on the side.

One 5-pound leg of lamb (about 4 pounds boneless)

8 fresh rosemary sprigs

12 fresh thyme sprigs

12 cloves garlic, unpeeled and crushed

½ cup extra virgin olive oil

Freshly ground black pepper

Salt

Olive-Tomato Relish (5 cups)

1½ cups pitted Niçoise or Kalamata olives

6 medium red tomatoes

1 medium shallot, peeled, trimmed, and minced

Salt

Freshly ground black pepper

¼ cup extra virgin olive oil

1 tablespoon sherry vinegar

2 tablespoons chopped Italian parsley

mexican hot chocolate ice cream with toasted almonds and bittersweet chocolate sauce

All summer long I crave the taste of a big steaming mug of cinnamon-spiked Mexican hot chocolate without the steam and without the heat. I figured why not the same flavors in an ice cream? On a humid 90 degree day it's the best of both worlds. I like to use the traditional Ibarra chocolate from Mexico. If this is unavailable you can substitute bittersweet chocolate and a cinnamon stick; this is noted in the recipe. The salt in the almonds provides a nice contrast to the Bittersweet Chocolate Sauce. It is definitely necessary for the yin-yang.

A fun way to serve this dessert is in a hot chocolate mug with the chocolate sauce and toasted almonds over the top, and a cinnamon stick for garnish. (My two-year-old uses it as a straw.)

MAKES 1½ QUARTS

1   Prepare the toasted almonds: Preheat the oven to 400 degrees F.

2   Toss all of the ingredients together and spread on a sheet pan. Toast in the preheated oven for 10 minutes. Cool and coarsely chop. Reserve at room temperature tightly sealed.

3   To make the ice cream: Chop the chocolate finely. Heat the milk and cream to boiling and remove from the heat. Add the chopped Ibarra chocolate or the cinnamon stick if you are using bittersweet chocolate. Stir well until dissolved. Let the mixture steep for 10 minutes.

4   Whisk the egg yolks (with the sugar if you are using bittersweet chocolate) to a thick ribbon. Return the cream-Ibarra chocolate mixture to barely a simmer and pour over the egg yolks while whisking constantly. Add the finely chopped bittersweet chocolate to the custard if you are using it. Strain the custard and cool.

5   Turn according to the ice cream maker's instructions. Chill in the freezer for 4 hours before serving.

6   To serve: Scoop the ice cream into a mug. Pour the chocolate sauce over and top with the chopped almonds and a cinnamon stick.

Toasted Almonds (1½ cups)

1½ cups whole almonds

2 teaspoons vegetable oil, expeller pressed (see Note, page 16)

1 teaspoon salt

Mexican Hot Chocolate Ice Cream

3 rounds of Ibarra chocolate or 8 ounces bittersweet chocolate and 1 cinnamon stick (If you are using bittersweet chocolate you will also need ½ cup sugar)

3 cups whole milk

2 cups heavy cream

8 large egg yolks

Bittersweet Chocolate Sauce (Page 241)

Cinnamon sticks for garnish

Summer Menu IX

summer vegetable salad with pecorino cheese
and extra virgin olive oil   364

roasted halibut with sweet corn and chanterelles   366

italian prune galette with sweet vanilla cream   368

WINES: For the summer salad serve a crisp Italian Pinot Grigio, Tocai Friulano, or New Zealand or American Sauvignon Blanc. Continue on with one of these wines or move on to a young Puligny Montrachet or crisp fruity American Chardonnay. Try a Banyuls or a Riesling Beerenauslese for the galette.

summer vegetable salad with pecorino cheese and extra virgin olive oil

The vibrant colors of this salad remind me of a still life study of summer vegetables. Present the vegetables on a large white platter so that they are not piled too deeply, thereby allowing each vegetable to flaunt its color and shape. Use the ingredients below as a guideline but feel free to substitute your favorite vegetables or those special finds at the farmers' market.

SERVES 8

1   Reserve all the vegetables separately after they are cleaned and trimmed. Trim the stem of the carrots to ¼ inch and cut the tips off. Peel the trimmed carrots and cut them in half.

2   Trim and peel the beets and turnips. Cut them in halves or quarters depending on their size. Trim the beans and cut into 2-inch lengths on the bias.

3   Trim the green tops of the pearl onions to 1 inch. Barely trim the root end so that the onion layers stay intact when they are blanched. Peel the onions and leave whole.

4   Remove the stems of the tomatoes. If the tomatoes are large, cut them in half, otherwise leave them whole. The tomatoes will not be blanched.

5   Bring a large pot of heavily salted water to a boil. Blanch the vegetables, except for the tomatoes, separately until tender (about 3 to 5 minutes depending on the vegetable). Bite the vegetables to test if they are done. They should be tender with a little bite. When they are done remove the vegetables with a slotted spoon and chill in ice water. Drain well in a colander and then on a clean thick towel.

6   Cut the pearl onions in half after they are blanched.

7   In a large bowl, toss all of the vegetables together with 3 tablespoons of extra virgin olive oil. Season them with Fleur de Sel and freshly ground black pepper to taste. Squeeze the lemon over and lightly toss.

8   Transfer the vegetables to a large white platter. Use a vegetable peeler to shave the Pecorino cheese over the top of the vegetables. Drizzle liberally with olive oil and sprinkle with snipped chives.

NOTE: The vegetables may be cleaned the day before serving. Store the root vegetables in cold water to keep them crisp.

20 baby carrots

12 baby yellow or Chioggia beets

12 baby turnips

¼ pound haricots verts

¼ pound wax beans

12 red pearl onions, with tops if possible

1 pint mixed toy box tomatoes

Salt

3 tablespoons extra virgin olive oil, plus more for drizzling

Fleur de Sel (see Note, page 49)

Freshly ground black pepper

½ lemon

½ pound chunk of Pecorino-Romano cheese

3 tablespoons snipped chives

roasted halibut with sweet corn and chanterelles

What would late summer be without chanterelles? The color of the summer sun, they are found in abundance in the wilds of northern California. They have a sweet meaty earthiness unlike any other mushroom and smell of freshly pressed carrot juice. I always choose small mushrooms that are more compact. That way you can enjoy their shape without slicing them. Pairing chanterelles with corn and halibut has become a new American classic and it is heavenly!

SERVES 8

1   Husk the corn. Remove as much of the silk from the kernels as you can. Place a small cutting board in the center of a sheet pan. Break the cobs in half and lean the end of the cob on the cutting board. Slice the kernels off the cob using a sharp knife. The sheet pan will catch the kernels, and keep them from spreading afar and littering your kitchen floor. Reserve the kernels in a small bowl and discard the cobs. Reserve.

2   Clean the chanterelles by cutting off the very bottom of the stem. Brush off the dirt with a small soft brush. If they are really dirty, clean them by filling a large bowl with water and quickly dipping the mushrooms in and swishing them around. Drain them well before sautéing.

3   Heat 2 tablespoons of the butter in a large sauté pan over medium-high heat until it bubbles and begins to brown. Add the cleaned mushrooms and sauté until all of their liquid has evaporated and the mushrooms are lightly browned, about 10 minutes, longer if the mushrooms are very wet. Season with salt and pepper and add the thyme, shallot, and garlic. Sauté 3 minutes more to cook the shallot and garlic. Add the white wine to the pan and simmer for 5 minutes. Reserve.

4   Preheat the oven to 400 degrees F.

5   In a separate pan, heat 2 tablespoons of the butter over medium-high heat until it is lightly browned. Add the corn to the pan. Sauté the corn until it is tender, about 5 minutes. Taste for seasoning; add the stock or water and 2 tablespoons of the butter. Bring to a boil and check the seasoning. Cover to keep warm while cooking the fish.

6   Season both sides of the halibut fillet well with salt and pepper. Place the remaining 2 tablespoons of butter in a large nonstick ovenproof sauté pan and brown lightly over medium-high heat. Add the fish and sauté until golden, about 5 minutes; turn over and place in the preheated oven for 7 to 10 minutes, depending on the thickness of the fish. The fish will flake when gently pressed in the center. Remove the fish to a plate to stop the cooking.

6 large ears sweet corn, about 6 cups of kernels

2 pounds chanterelles

8 tablespoons unsalted butter

Salt

Freshly ground pepper

1 teaspoon chopped fresh thyme

1 medium shallot, peeled, trimmed, and minced

1 garlic clove, peeled, trimmed, and minced

1 cup dry white wine

1 cup vegetable stock or water

Eight 6-ounce halibut fillets without skin

1 bunch of chives, chopped for garnish

7   Fold the corn and chanterelles together in one pan and bring to a simmer. Season to taste with salt and pepper. Spoon the mixture into a large flat bowl or plate. Place the halibut on top. Garnish with chopped chives.

VARIATION: Substitute seared scallops or roasted split lobster for the halibut. For those of you who are landlocked, herb-roasted chicken or a pork roast also works very well.

italian prune galette with sweet vanilla cream

The word prune commonly conjures up the thoughts of a high-fiber brown wrinkled orb. How far this is from the reality of a fresh Italian prune. The flesh to pit ratio is small but what flesh there is, is oh so succulent. Prunes are usually available in late summer. Santa Rosa plums, which ripen midsummer, may be substituted if you can't wait for prunes. I like this galette on the tart side; if you like it sweeter, add more sugar. The Sweet Vanilla Cream adds a wonderful creamy contrast to the galette.

The cream cheese dough is my mother's famous recipe. The cream cheese makes the dough so rich that you don't need any other filling beside the fruit. It's pure magic. Use natural cream cheese without additives or fillers for the best results.

SERVES 8 TO 10

1   Prepare the Cream Cheese Tart Dough: Combine the flour, salt, and sugar in a mixing bowl. Add the cream cheese and butter and mix in a standing mixer fitted with the paddle attachment or by hand with a pastry cutter until the butter and cream cheese chunks are the size of small peas.

2   Add just enough ice water to bring the dough together. Turn the dough out onto a floured board and knead it lightly. Pat the dough into a flat round about 1 inch thick and wrap well in plastic or wax paper. Chill for at least 1 hour before rolling out. The dough may be prepared up to 2 days in advance, tightly wrapped, and refrigerated or frozen for 3 months

3   To make the filling: Cut the prunes in half lengthwise at their seam. Remove and discard the pit.

4   Roll the chilled cream cheese dough into a 16-inch circle ⅛ inch thick. Place the circle on a parchment-lined sheet pan. The dough will hang over the edges. Wrap the sheet pan with plastic and chill for 30 minutes before filling with prunes to allow the dough to relax.

5   Place an oven rack on the bottom rung. Preheat the oven to 400 degrees F.

6   Remove the chilled dough from the refrigerator. Starting 2 inches from the outside edge of the dough, place the prunes cut side down slightly overlapping, one halfway on top of the other like fallen dominoes. Continue in concentric circles until you reach the center of the tart. Mark the center with half a prune like a bull's-eye. Sprinkle the tart evenly with half the sugar.

7   Pick up the outside edges of the dough and make darts every couple of inches so that the dough fits snugly around the prunes. Moisten the darts with cold water and seal.

Cream Cheese Tart Dough

2½ cups all-purpose flour

1½ teaspoons salt

1 tablespoon sugar

4 ounces natural cream cheese, cut into cubes and chilled

½ pound (2 sticks) unsalted butter, cut into cubes and chilled

5 to 6 tablespoons ice water

Filling

30 ripe Italian prunes or small Santa Rosa plums

1 cup sugar

Sweet Vanilla Cream

2 ounces natural cream cheese, softened

1 tablespoon sugar

1 vanilla bean

1 cup heavy cream

8   Bake on the bottom rack of the preheated oven for 30 minutes and then sprinkle the remaining sugar over the tart. Bake another 30 to 40 minutes until the prunes are soft and their juices bubble. Don't worry if the juices leak out and burn on the pan, drain some off if it becomes excessive.

9   Prepare the Sweet Vanilla Cream while the tart is baking. In a mixing bowl, combine the cream cheese and sugar and mix thoroughly.

10   Split the vanilla bean lengthwise and scrape the seeds into the cream cheese mixture. Save the pod for vanilla sugar. Slowly whisk in the cream until the mixture is thick and uniform and there are no more lumps. Beat until fluffy and soft peaks form. Use immediately or store in the refrigerator for 1 day. Gently mix before serving.

11   Loosen the galette from the parchment with a metal spatula when you take it out of the oven and continue to do so every 10 minutes until the tart has cooled to warm, otherwise the hot sugar will glue the crust to the pan. If this happens place the galette back in the oven until the sugar is soft enough to allow you to remove the galette from the parchment. Cool to warm before serving. If the juices run when you cut the galette simply spoon them over the top. Serve wedges of the galette with Sweet Vanilla Cream on the side.

NOTE: The Sweet Vanilla Cream makes a wonderful topping for strawberries and a filling for berry shortcakes.

Summer Menu X

hearts of romaine and sweet 100 tomatoes with
    a lemon-pepper vinaigrette and garlic chapons   372

grilled t-bone steak   375

sea salt and herb–roasted potato packets
    with herbed sour cream   376

black- and blueberry buttermilk cobbler   378

WINES: The strong flavors of this salad will take away anything a wine has to offer. So skip a wine for the salad and go for a rich fruity American Cabernet Sauvignon, Zinfandel, or Spanish Rioja for the steak. As always the berries will pair wonderfully with a California Late Harvest Muscat or Muscat de Beaumes-de-Venise.

hearts of romaine and sweet 100 tomatoes with a lemon-pepper vinaigrette and garlic chapons

All the elements you hope for in a salad are contained in this one: crunchy romaine, tiny sweet tomatoes, creamy dressing with a kick of pepper and the tang of lemon, and crisp, chewy garlic chapons. Traditionally chapons are fresh chewy bread cubes or crusts that have been rubbed with garlic and tossed with the salad for added garlic flavor. For my version of chapons, I trim the crust from an artisanal bread loaf, leaving a little of the insides attached to the crust. They are toasted in the oven until they are crisp on the edges but still slightly chewy at the center. When they're still warm from the oven I toss them into my salad.

SERVES 8

1 Wash the tomatoes with their stem end intact; drain and remove the stems. This prevents the tiny tomatoes from splitting. Reserve. Refrigerate to store overnight.

2 Trim any brown off the root end and trim the very top of the lettuce leaves if they are torn or brown. Cut the lettuce hearts in half and then lengthwise. Then cut them crosswise into 1-inch ribbons. If you are using baby romaine leaves, wash, dry well, and use them whole. Cover with a damp towel and refrigerate. Seal with plastic to store overnight.

3 Preheat the oven to 400 degrees F.

2 pints sweet 100 tomatoes

8 small hearts of romaine or 1½ pounds baby romaine leaves

16 pieces of trimmed crust from an artisanal loaf with ¼ inch of bread attached

2 large garlic cloves, peeled

¼ cup extra virgin olive oil

Salt

Freshly ground black pepper

¾ to 1 cup Lemon Pepper Vinaigrette (recipe follows)

Shaved Parmesan cheese for garnish

4 Rub the crusts all over with garlic cloves and tear into 1½-inch pieces. Toss the torn bread with ¼ cup olive oil to moisten and season with salt and pepper. Bake on a sheet pan in the preheated oven until lightly toasted, 10 to 15 minutes. Cool to warm before using.

5 Toss the tomatoes with the garlic chapons and half of the vinaigrette in the bottom of a large bowl. Add the romaine and toss again. Add more vinaigrette until you reach your desired saturation. Salt and pepper to taste. Garnish with shaved Parmesan cheese.

lemon-pepper vinaigrette

MAKES 2 ¼ CUPS

1 Place the egg yolk, Dijon, lemon juice, vinegar, shallot, garlic, and black pepper in a blender. Blend until smooth. Add the Parmesan cheese and blend until smooth; season with salt to taste.

2 Turn the blender to low and drizzle in the olive oil through the hole in the lid until the dressing is creamy and emulsified. Adjust the seasoning according to taste. If the dressing is too thick, thin with a few drops of water.

NOTE: Raw eggs should not be served to pregnant women, children, elderly people, or those with compromised immune systems.

1 large egg yolk

1 teaspoon Dijon mustard

¼ cup lemon juice, 1 to 2 medium lemons

1 tablespoon red wine vinegar

1 medium shallot, peeled, trimmed, and chopped

1 large garlic clove, peeled, trimmed, and minced

¾ teaspoon coarsely ground black pepper

½ cup finely grated Parmesan cheese

Salt

1 to 1¼ cups extra virgin olive oil

grilled t-bone steak

Marinating the steak in crushed herbs and garlic provides loads of flavor. I rarely grill any piece of meat without marinating it with one herb or another. You can experiment with different herbs and different aromatic vegetables. Find the flavors you like and use them.

I ask the butcher to cut the steaks 2 inches thick so that they can be split between two people. Call ahead to special order your steaks. You can have them cut thinner and serve one per person but it's more fun to share. The Herb Roasted Potato Packets with Herbed Sour Cream (recipe follows) are an easy accompaniment. Instead of preparing a vegetable, serve the salad alongside rather than as a first course.

SERVES 8

8 garlic cloves, unpeeled and crushed

20 fresh thyme sprigs

1 teaspoon coarsely ground black pepper

¼ cup extra virgin olive oil

Four T-bone steaks cut 2 inches thick or eight 1¼-inch-thick steaks

Salt

1   In a large bowl, combine the garlic, thyme, black pepper, and olive oil. Add the steaks and coat well. Layer the steaks with the marinade in a nonreactive dish; cover and marinate overnight or up to 2 days in the refrigerator.

2   Preheat the grill or broiler.

3   Remove the steaks from the refrigerator 30 minutes before cooking. Scrape off the marinade and season the steaks with salt.

4   Grill the steaks over medium-high heat for 12 to 15 minutes on each side for medium-rare or for the same amount of time under the broiler. Thinner steaks will take about 7 to 8 minutes per side.

5   Serve thin-cut steaks whole, one per person. To serve thick-cut steaks, cut the meat away from each side of the bone. Cut the pieces in half. If you know your guests well, pile the bones on a plate and let them choose. Serve with the Herb Roasted Potato Packets and Herbed Sour Cream or a simple baked potato.

sea salt and herb–roasted potato packets with herbed sour cream

SERVES 8

1   Prepare the Herbed Sour Cream: Place the sour cream in a small bowl and mix in the chopped herbs. Season to taste with salt and freshly ground black pepper. Prepare up to a day in advance and store in the refrigerator until ready to use.

2   Prepare the Herb Roasted Potato Packets: Wash the potatoes well, leave them whole, and place them in a large pot. Add cold water to cover the potatoes by 1 inch. Bring the potatoes to a boil and add 2 tablespoons of salt to the pot. Reduce the heat and simmer for 10 minutes. Drain and cool the potatoes.

3   Place the potatoes in a large bowl. Toss them with some olive oil to moisten, the thyme sprigs, 2 tablespoons of coarse sea salt, and a few grinds of black pepper. Cut four large squares of heavy duty foil.

Herbed Sour Cream

1 cup sour cream

1 tablespoon chopped Italian parsley

1 tablespoon chopped chives

1 tablespoon chopped tarragon

Salt

Freshly ground black pepper

Potato Packets

3 pounds creamer-sized Yukon Gold or Red Bliss potatoes, about 1½ inches in diameter

2 tablespoons salt

Extra virgin olive oil

12 bushy fresh thyme sprigs

2 tablespoons coarse sea salt

Freshly ground black pepper

4   Divide the potatoes equally among the four sheets of foil. Fold the foil over and seal the edges well. Reserve to finish cooking with the steaks. The Potato Packets should be prepared the day they are going to be served.

5   After the coals in the grill have turned gray, place the Potato Packets directly on top of the coals, just before grilling the steaks. Cook for 5 minutes. Turn over and cook for another 5 minutes.

6   Remove the Potato Packets from the fire and shake off the ashes. Reserve them tightly sealed in the foil while you cook the steaks. Serve the packets alongside the steak with the Herbed Sour Cream on the side.

black- and blueberry buttermilk cobbler

The only really good blackberries I ever eat are the small juicy intense ones that grow wild just about everywhere. It seems that cultivation kills their wild blackberry spirit. If you can't pick your own, or convince someone else to, there are some organic growers that grow them in an almost wild state and some foragers that will pick wild ones and sell them commercially. If you find these, jump on them. Otherwise taste a lot of berries before you settle for your pints.

This cobbler is simple to make and captures the essence of the blackberry. The blueberries are added to the cobbler to provide relief from the intense seeds of the blackberries. If you enjoy the seeds the blueberries may be omitted altogether.

Don't wash your blackberries before using them or you will dilute their flavor. Gently pick through them and remove under-ripe berries, leaves, and other debris before using. Blueberries may be rinsed but they should be well drained before using.

SERVES 8 TO 12

1   Butter a 13 by 9 by 2-inch rectangular baking dish.

2   Prepare the Cobbler Biscuit Dough: Combine the dry ingredients in a large bowl. Add the butter and mix until the dough resembles coarse cornmeal. It will still have small chunks of butter.

3   Add the buttermilk and mix until just combined. Turn out onto a floured board and knead lightly to incorporate all the ingredients. Press into a 1-inch-thick patty. Wrap well in plastic and store in the refrigerator if you will not be using the dough immediately.

4   Prepare the filling: Clean the berries (see Headnote). Remove the stems and other debris. In a large bowl, combine all of the filling ingredients and place them in the baking dish.

5   Preheat the oven to 400 degrees F.

6   Roll the Cobbler Biscuit Dough into a large rectangle to fit inside the edge of the baking dish. Using a fork, prick the dough to demarcate squares for serving. Brush the dough with the heavy cream.

7   Bake the cobbler in the preheated oven for 45 to 50 minutes until the Cobbler Biscuit Dough is golden and the fruit is bubbling. Cool to warm and serve in bowls.

VARIATIONS: Other fruits such as peaches and apricots can be added instead of blueberries. Rinse them, chop them, measure them in a cup, and add them in the same proportion as the blueberries. The blackberries can also be mixed with strawberries and raspberries for a mixed berry cobbler.

Cobbler Biscuit Dough

1¾ cups all-purpose flour

¼ cup finely ground semolina

2 tablespoons sugar

½ teaspoon salt

1 tablespoon baking powder

1 teaspoon baking soda

12 tablespoons (1½ sticks) cold unsalted butter, cut into chunks

1 cup buttermilk

Filling

2 pints blackberries

2 pints blueberries

3 tablespoons all-purpose flour

1 cup sugar

2 tablespoons lemon juice

½ teaspoon pure vanilla extract

2 tablespoons heavy cream for brushing tops of biscuits

index

aioli, lemon, poached artichokes with, 224–26

almond(s):

    biscotti, anise-scented, 319–20

    candied, Fuyu persimmon and goat cheese salad, 18–19

    madeleines, 210–11

    and sour cherry clafoutis, 353

    toasted, Mexican hot chocolate ice cream with bittersweet chocolate sauce and, 360–61

    toasted, shaved zucchini salad with lemon, and Parmesan, 306

almond paste, 211

anchovy lemon dressing, escarole and Belgian endive salad with, 84–85

anise-scented almond biscotti, 319–20

apple(s):

    galette, caramelized, 80–81

    goose with roasted turnips and, 160–62

    pie, heirloom, 54–55

    spice cake, 98–99

apricot(s):

    in black and blueberry buttermilk cobbler variation, 379

    brown-sugar baked, 343

    glaze, fresh, grilled pork chops with a, 324–25

    in sour cherry and almond clafoutis variation, 353

artichokes, poached, with lemon aioli, 224–26

artichokes, roasted baby:

    Rock Cornish game hens with lemon and, 268–69

    and Teleme cheese bruschetta, 214–16

arugula:

    baby, pancetta-wrapped grilled figs with, 338–39

    grilled hanger steak with lemon and, 125–26

    prosciutto with figs and, 26–27

asparagus:

    grilled, with prosciutto and a Meyer lemon vinaigrette, 234–35

    and lemon risotto with shaved Reggiano, 246–47

bacon, smoked, and caramelized onion tart, 108–9

bananas, caramelized rum-scented, with vanilla ice cream, 288–89

basil:

    bruschetta of garden tomatoes, fresh mozzarella and, 314–15

    opal, grapefruit sorbet with a citrus salad and, 248

basil-mint pesto, 333

    grilled lamb and potato brochettes with, 332–33

bean(s):

    basic recipe, 94–95

    salad, warm summer, 342

    shelling, minestrone with, 92–94

    see also white bean(s)

beef:

    prime rib, salt and herb–crusted, with horseradish cream, 188–90

    shanks, braised, with rough-cut pasta, 86–89

    short ribs, red wine–braised, with roasted root vegetables, 152–53

    see also steak

beet, roasted, and blood orange salad with spicy greens, 142–43

beignets, herbed cheese, 132–33

Belgian endive and escarole salad with lemon anchovy dressing, 84–85

berry sorbet, summer, 318

    see also specific berries

biscotti, almond, anise-scented, 319–20

biscuits, buttermilk, 76

bittersweet chocolate, grated, sweet ricotta pie with, 183–84

bittersweet chocolate sauce, 241

    Mexican hot chocolate ice cream with toasted almonds and, 360–61

    strawberry ice cream profiteroles with, 238–39

black- and blueberry buttermilk cobbler, 378–79

blood orange and roasted beet salad with spicy
  greens, 142–43

blueberry and blackberry buttermilk cobbler,
  378–79

blue cheese, watercress and endive salad with
  toasted walnuts, and walnut vinaigrette,
  186–87

bouillabaisse with a spicy red pepper rouille,
  180–82

brandied pears, 33–34

brochettes, grilled lamb and potato, with basil-mint
  pesto, 332–33

brown butter:
  lemon-caper, soft-shell crab with, 262–63
  sage, pumpkin tortellini with, 51–53

brown-sugar baked apricots, 343

bruschetta:
  of garden tomatoes, fresh mozzarella and basil,
    314–15
  Teleme cheese and roasted baby artichoke,
    214–16

buckwheat crepes, orange-laced, 63–64

butter(ed):
  brown, *see* brown butter
  cake, chocolate-glazed, 256–57
  peas, 219

buttermilk:
  biscuits, 76
  cobbler, black and blueberry, 378–79
  lemon pound cake with lemon glaze, 147–48

butternut squash soup, 74–75

butterscotch crème brûlée, 127–28

cabbage, savoy, sautéed, with golden raisins, 78–79

cakes:
  almond madeleines, 210–11
  apple spice, 98–99
  butter, chocolate-glazed, 256–57
  fig spice, with maple cream cheese frosting,
    154–55

honey walnut, 23–24

orange-scented fallen chocolate soufflé, 220–21

pound, *see* pound cake

caper(s):
  -lemon brown butter, soft shell crab with, 262–63
  pan-roasted ling cod with sweet red peppers,
    lemon and, 350–51

caviar, celery root galettes with crème fraîche and,
  178–79

celery root galettes with crème fraîche and caviar,
  178–79

chanterelles, roasted halibut with sweet corn and,
  366–67

chard, Swiss, egg drop soup with pastini and, 124

cheese:
  beignets, herbed, 132–33
  see also specific cheeses

cherry(ies):
  Bing, roasted pork tenderloin with, 307–9
  sour, and almond clafoutis, 353

chicken:
  coq au vin, 134–36
  livers, peppered, with two endives and a sherry-
    mustard vinaigrette, 266–67
  Rock Cornish game hens with lemon and
    roasted baby artichokes, 268–69
  sage-roasted, with sweet potatoes and cipollini
    onions, 96–97

chocolate:
  crust, for sweet ricotta pie, 183
  -glazed butter cake, 256–57
  ice cream, Mexican hot, with toasted almonds
    and bitter sweet chocolate sauce, 360–61
  shortbread with vanilla cream filling, 121–22
  soufflé cake, fallen, orange-scented, 220–21
  soufflés with vanilla bean crème anglaise, 174–75
  see also bittersweet chocolate; bittersweet
    chocolate sauce

citrus salad, grapefruit sorbet with opal basil and,
  248

clafoutis, sour cherry and almond, 353

clams, cherrystone, in bouillabaisse, 180–82

mint(ed):

-basil pesto, grilled lamb and potato brochettes with, 332–33

and fava crostini with spring greens, 244–45

sweet pea soup, 260–61

monkfish, in bouillabaisse with a spicy red pepper rouille, 180–82

morels, pan-fried halibut with a ragout of sweet peas and, 276–78

mozzarella, fresh:

bruschetta of garden tomatoes, and basil, 314–15

rapini with hot peppers and, 150–51

mushroom(s):

papardelle with, 118–20

wild, risotto, 20–22

see also chanterelles; morels; porcini mushrooms

mussels:

in bouillabaisse with a spicy red pepper rouille, 180–82

steamed, in red wine and shallots, 110–11

new potato salad, herb-marinated flank steak with, 315–17

nutmeg custard, 112–13

nuts:

brittle, 35–36

caramel tart, 71–72

see also specific nuts

olive(s):

roasted tomatoes with Pecorino Toscano and, 58–59

slow-roasted pork with fennel, tomatoes and, with flat bread, 253–54

-tomato relish, herb-marinated grilled leg of lamb with, 358–59

olive oil, extra virgin:

grilled porcini with shaved Parmesan and, 66–67

summer vegetable salad with Pecorino cheese and, 364–65

onion(s):

caramelized, and smoked bacon tart, 108–9

caramelized, white corn, and marjoram-scented strudel with spicy greens, 322–23

cipollini, sage-roasted chicken with sweet potatoes and, 96–97

spring, and green garlic tart, 274–75

sweet Vidalia, and Gruyère soufflé, 204–6

orange(s):

blood, see blood orange

-laced buckwheat crepes, 63–64

-scented fallen chocolate soufflé cake, 220–21

pancetta:

salad of two endives with tiny croutons and, 116–17

-wrapped grilled figs with baby arugula, 338–39

papardelle with mushrooms, 118–20

Parmesan:

asparagus and lemon risotto with shaved Reggiano, 24–47

shaved, grilled porcini with extra virgin olive oil and, 66–67

shaved, prosciutto with summer melons and, 348–49

shaved zucchini salad with toasted almonds, lemon and, 306

parsnip soup with crispy parsnip chips, 168–69

pasta, rough-cut, braised beef shanks with, 86–88

see also specific pastas

pastini, egg drop soup with Swiss chard and, 124

peach(es):

in black and blueberry buttermilk cobbler variation, 379

tart, caramelized, 334–35

white, poached in Vin Gris with raspberries, 310

pear(s):

brandied, 33–34

fritters, 15–16

peas, sweet, *see* sweet pea(s)

pecan shortbread fingers, 129

Pecorino cheese, summer vegetable salad with extra virgin olive oil and, 364–65

Pecorino Toscano, roasted tomatoes with olives and, 58–59

pepper(ed):

    chicken livers with two endives and a sherry-mustard vinaigrette, 266–67

    -crusted, black, new York steak, 68–69

    see also lemon-pepper vinaigrette

peppers:

    hot, rapini with fresh mozzarella and, 150–51

    sweet red, capers and lemon with pan-roasted ling cod, 350–51

    see also rouille, spicy red pepper

persimmon, Fuyu, candied almond, and goat cheese salad, 18–19

pesto, basil-mint, *see* basil-mint pesto

pie:

    apple, heirloom, 54–55

    sweet ricotta, with grated bittersweet chocolate, 183–84

pine nut:

    breast of veal with golden raisin, and spinach stuffing, 226–28

    macaroons, 344–45

    toasted, couscous, 14

polenta, simple soft, 229

porcini mushrooms, grilled, with extra virgin olive oil and shaved Parmesan, 66–67

pork:

    chops, grilled, with a fresh apricot glaze, 324–25

    loin, roasted, with figs, 12–13

    slow-roasted, with fennel, tomatoes, and olives with flat bread, 253–54

    tenderloin, roasted, with Bing cherries, 307–9

port, figs poached in, 90

potato(es):

    coins, golden, 352

    crust, for spinach and sheep's milk ricotta "pie," 10–11

fingerling, roasted garlic, herb-marinated rack of lamb with, 236–37

gnocchi, Nana's tomato sauce with, 28–32

gratin, 191–92

and lamb brochettes, grilled, with basil-mint pesto, 332–33

new, salad, see new potato salad

packets, sea salt and herb-roasted, with herbed sour cream, 376–77

and shallots, oven-roasted, 70

pound cake:

    lemon buttermilk, with lemon glaze, 147–48

    marble, 264

prawns, in bouillabaisse, 180–82

profiteroles, strawberry ice cream, with bittersweet chocolate sauce, 238–39

prosciutto:

    with figs and arugula, 26–27

    grilled asparagus with, and a Meyer lemon vinaigrette, 234–35

    with summer melons and shaved Parmesan, 348–49

Provençal tart with herbed goat cheese, 356–57

prune galette, Italian, with sweet vanilla cream, 368–70

pudding, tapioca, with Tahitian vanilla, 270–71

pumpkin:

    custard, spiced, 44–45

    puree, fresh, 45

    tortellini with sage brown butter, 51–53

puree, fresh pumpkin, 45

quince compote, 42–43

    roasted duck breast with, 40–41

raisin(s), golden:

    breast of veal with pine nut, spinach stuffing and, 226–28

    sautéed savoy cabbage with, 78–79

rapini with fresh mozzarella and hot peppers, 150–51

raspberry(ies):

jam tart, crisscross, 137–39

with white peaches poached in Vin Gris, 310

red snapper, in bouillabaisse with a spicy red pepper rouille, 180–82

Reggiano:

shaved, asparagus and lemon risotto with, 246–47

see also Parmesan

relish, olive-tomato, herb-marinated grilled leg of lamb with, 358–59

rhubarb-strawberry crisp, 303–4

ricotta, sheep's milk:

manicotti with, 283–85

"pie," spinach and, 8–11

ricotta pie, sweet, with grated bittersweet chocolate, 183–84

rillettes, duck, 173

risotto:

lemon, *see* lemon risotto

wild mushroom, 20–22

Rock Cornish game hens with lemon and roasted baby artichokes, 268–69

rock shrimp, spicy, chilled garden tomato soup with, 330–31

romaine, hearts of, and sweet 100 tomatoes with lemon-pepper vinaigrette and garlic chapons, 372–73

rouille, spicy red pepper, 182

spicy red pepper bouillabaisse with, 180–82

rum-scented caramelized bananas with vanilla ice cream, 288–89

rutabagas, in red wine–braised short ribs with roasted root vegetables, 152–53

sage:

brown butter, pumpkin tortellini with, 51–53

-roasted chicken with sweet potatoes and cipollini onions, 96–97

salads:

bean, warm summer, 342

citrus, grapefruit sorbet with opal basil and, 248

escarole and Belgian endive, with lemon anchovy dressing, 84–85

frisée, with a poached egg, lardons and Dijon vinaigrette, 48–49

Fuyu persimmon, candied almond, and goat cheese, 18–19

gathered greens with red wine vinaigrette, 282

hearts of romaine and sweet 100 tomatoes with lemon-pepper vinaigrette and garlic chapons, 372–73

new potato, see new potato salad

peppered chicken livers with two endives and a sherry-mustard vinaigrette, 266–67

roasted beet and blood orange, with spicy greens, 142–43

shaved fennel and toy box tomato, crispy-skinned salmon with, 300–301

shaved zucchini, with toasted almonds, lemon, and Parmesan, 306

summer vegetable, with Pecorino cheese and extra virgin olive oil, 364–65

of two endives with pancetta and tiny croutons, 116–17

watercress and endive, with blue cheese, toasted walnuts, and walnut vinaigrette, 186–87

salmon, crispy-skinned, with a shaved fennel and toy box tomato salad, 300–301

sauces:

caramel, 46

gribiche, for new potato salad, 317

sauces (*cont.*)

mushroom, in papardelle with mushrooms, 118–20

see also bittersweet chocolate sauce; tomato sauce

savoy cabbage, sautéed, with golden raisins, 78–79

sea salt and herb–roasted potato packets with herbed sour cream, 376–77